A Practical Approach to Teaching Physical Education

David L. Kizer, Ed.D.
Donna L. Piper, M.S.
Waldo E. Sauter, P.E.D.
Central Michigan University

MOUVEMENT PUBLICATIONS INC.
109 East State Street
Ithaca, New York 14850

Woodstock
19 Oaks Way, Gayton
Heswall, Wirral
L60 3SP England

Woorkarrim
Lot #7 Strathmore Drive
Torquay 3228
Australia

A Practical Approach to Teaching Physical Education

David L. Kizer, Ed.D.
Donna L. Piper, M.S.
Waldo E. Sauter, P.E.D.
Central Michigan University

DEDICATED
To Sharon, Danielle and Darren.
To Deanna, Ross and Richard.
To Judy, Robin and Michele.

TABLE OF CONTENTS

SOME BASIC THOUGHTS CONCERNING PHYSICAL EDUCATION

The treatment of any topic must begin with a definition. If we are to discuss the proper way to teach the subject of physical education within the schools, we must define it. Some definitions are very brief. The shortest definition of physical education we have encountered is: "Physical education is the art and science of human movement" (Seidel and Resick, 1972, p. 4). This is an accurate definition, but it leaves certain questions in the reader's mind. For example, what part of the subject is an art and what part is a science? Also, what activities are included in those categorized as human movement? More information is needed. The most complete, and longest, definition of physical education comes from a publication of the American Alliance of Health, Physical Education, Recreation and Dance. It is as follows:

1

"Physical Education is that integral part of total education which contributes to the development of the individual through the natural medium of physical activity which is human movement. It is a carefully planned sequence of learning experiences designed to fulfill the growth, development, and behavior needs of each student. It encourages and assists each student to develop the skills of movement, the knowledge of how and why one moves, and the ways in which movement may be organized; to learn to move skillfully and effectively through exercise, games, sport activities, dance, and aquatics; to enrich the understanding of the concepts of space, time and force related to movement; to express culturally approved patterns of personal behavior and interpersonal relationships in and through games, sport and dance; to condition the heart, lungs, muscles, and other organic systems of the body to meet daily and emergency demands; to acquire an appreciation of and a respect for good physical condition (fitness), a functional posture and a sense of personal well-being; and to develop an interest and a desire to participate in lifetime recreational sport activities" (AAHPERD, 1970).

The trouble with this definition is that it is too long to be usable in our daily thought. We believe physical education should be defined as follows: *Physical education is that phase of general education that deals with the physical, mental, emotional, and social development of the individual through human movement.*

THE AIM OF PHYSICAL EDUCATION

The next point that needs to be addressed is "What is the purpose of the subject in the broad area of general education?" It is true that the youth of our country encounter human movement experiences in environments other than at school, such as recreation programs, their own unstructured play, and in other institutional and organizational settings. However, as educators, we are concerned with the general education that students get within the school environment. Specifically, we are concerned with what human movement experiences students encounter within the school setting. So, to repeat our question, "What is the aim of physical education as it is taught in our schools?"

At first this might seem a simple question to answer. But years of observation of physical education, as presently taught in school settings, have convinced us that it is quite often misunderstood. Therefore, we need to state the aim and analyze how it is developed.

To arrive at the aim of our subject, it is necessary to "backtrack" in one's thinking in order to get at the roots of what is going to be our aim. For example, it is often stated that the aim is a posture that is arrived at philosophically. Where does this philosophy stem from? What is its origin? To answer the above we must ask a series of sub-questions: What is our philosophy of life? What things does our society hold primary? What values do we rank highly? and, What are the most meaningful values we should strive to live by and encourage in our young people? Once these questions are answered, we can begin to translate this into a philosophy of education. When we have developed a philosophy of education, we can turn our attention to single subjects within general education — in this case physical education — and devise a philosophy for that subject. The philosophy of each subject in the total curriculum must be compatible with the philosophy of education in general.

The *aim* of physical education is a single statement, arrived at philosophically, that explains in general terms what we are trying to accomplish with our subject in the school setting. Many years of experience, and many hours of debate and thought, have finally given form to the following: *The aim of physical education is to develop every individual to their full potential physically, mentally, socially, and emotionally, through human movement, so that they might become efficient citizens in a democratic society.*

In analyzing this aim, considerable thought must be given to several key words. In the beginning, we see that the aim is to develop every individual to his or her full potential. We are not to develop just the talented motor performer or the athlete — but every individual. Also, students come to us with many different physiques, interests, abilities, and needs. Correct application of the aim mandates that we take this fact into consideration in each class.

According to our aim we are using human movement to develop four aspects of each student, specifically the physical, mental, social, and emotional. Unfortunately, often only one or two of these aspects are emphasized. Correct application of our aim directs us to work diligently in all four.

The next concept to be identified in our aim is that of human movement. This, of course, is the real reason our subject exists. We supply movement experiences so the students can interact with their environment and mankind. Movement experiences are designed to build fitness, provide participation in sport, experience cross-cultural activities with other ethnic groups, and allow students to feel the joy associated with learning to move as they move to learn.

The final concept to be examined in our aim points out what all this development is for, why we have this subject and why it is so important.

3

We have this subject, with its attendant development of students in four dimensions, to build citizens that can function efficiently in our society, which is identified as a democratic society. Students graduate from school and become citizens. The entire process of education is responsible for developing citizens who are economically self-sufficient, conduct themselves in a socially acceptable manner, and are healthy and physically fit individuals. In a democratic society this education is for all individuals, not a select few. We do not have as our aim just to build strong bodies fit for military service, or to conduct programs of physical fitness and sport to promote one political ideology. The final thought in our aim is to produce efficient citizens for a democratic society, as exemplified by the type of government we have in the United States.

The aim is the ultimate of what we hope to accomplish in our subject. It gives us something for which to strive. It is attainable only in degrees with any one student or any one class, but we need to keep it in our mind constantly.

The next obvious question is "How do you reach the aim?" The answer lies in our Developmental Objectives. Each time teachers organize an experience that helps a student to develop organically, neuromuscularly, intellectually, socially, or emotionally, they are making a significant contribution toward reaching the aim. It would then follow that only experiences and methods that help students develop in one of these ways should be included in the program. The developmental objectives are sometimes referred to as the vehicle that the students use to aid them in reaching the aim.

DEVELOPMENTAL OBJECTIVES

Developmental objectives or general objectives, as they have traditionally been known, are grouped into categories numbering from four to six by various authors. We would like to present five objectives which can be affected by physical education.

Organic Development

The organic objective pertains to the proper functioning of the body systems so that individuals can meet their normal daily functions and not be unduly fatigued. The specific components of organic development include:
1. Muscular strength. The maximum amount of force that can be exerted by a muscle or muscle group.
2. Muscular endurance. The ability of a muscle or muscle group to sustain a contraction over a period of time.

4

3. Cardiovascular endurance. The capability of an individual, due to the efficiency of the heart, blood vessels, and lungs, to continue total body activities for a sustained period of time.
4. Flexibility. The development and maintenance of a range of motion in joints to benefit health and produce efficient movement.
5. Body composition. The maintenance of the desired percentage of body weight that is fat compared to other body tissues such as bone and muscle.

Neuromuscular Development

This objective refers to the harmonious functioning of the nervous system and the muscular system to produce efficient and desired movement. The various skills included under fundamental and sport skills are:
1. Locomotor skills. Walking, running, hopping, skipping, leaping, jumping, galloping, dodging, and rolling are common examples.
2. Nonlocomotor skills. Bending, twisting, stretching, hanging, and swaying are representatives of this category.
3. Manipulative skills. Catching, throwing, striking, kicking, bouncing, trapping, volleying and similar eye-hand and eye-foot movements.
4. Sport skills. Badminton, tennis, archery, golf, football, basketball, track and field, volleyball, swimming, boating, wrestling, soccer, and softball are representative of sports in which specific skills may be taught.

Perceptual-Motor Development

The perceptual-motor objective involves the act of receiving information from stimuli of the various senses, processing the information, and responding to its meaning through movement. Included in this category are:
1. Improved awareness and movement capabilities in spatial relationships.
2. Visual-motor coordination.
3. Hand and foot dominance.
4. Laterality.

Intellectual Development

The intellectual objective relates to the acquiring and ordering of knowledge, understanding relationships, and making cognitive judgments. Included in this area are:
1. Knowledge of game rules, etiquette, scoring, and safety measures.

2. Application of strategies and techniques to the performance of sport activities.
3. Understanding the structure, functions, and biomechanical principles of the body and how they relate to movement and sport skills.

Social-Emotional Development

The social-emotional objective expresses the desire for individuals to interact, through movement and sport, in both a cooperative and competitive manner which is supportive to society. The individual should attain:
1. The ability to participate in a group in a cooperating manner.
2. A feeling of acceptance and belonging with others.
3. Desirable attitudes and values relevant to participation as a member of society.
4. An appreciation for the aesthetic values of sport and movement.
5. An ability to react positively and in a sportsmanlike manner to both success and failure.
6. An appreciation for sport and movement as a viable leisure time pursuit.

PERFORMANCE OBJECTIVES

Many educators feel that developmental objectives are not sufficient in themselves. They believe developmental objectives are too remote and undefined to guide instruction and learning. They also feel they will not stand the test of accountability. *Accountability* is the concept that the effectiveness of schools should be judged by results achieved, which are measured in terms of student accomplishment. If teachers are to be held accountable for what is learned in their classes, there must be ways to observe and measure students against some stated standards. Therefore, the need arises for writing performance objectives. It is commonplace in the literature to use the terms "performance" and "behavioral" objectives inter-changeably.

The Three Domains of Performance Objectives

Performance objectives are written in three domains, or dimensions of learning. They are classified as the psychomotor domain, the cognitive domain, and the affective domain. They may be distinguished from each other in the following manner:
1. Psychomotor Domain. Movements, or learning involving muscular action, that require little mental activity, constitute the psychomotor

domain. An example of performance in this domain would be shooting a jump shot in basketball.

2. Cognitive Domain. This domain includes all the mental processes with which the student becomes involved while learning. An example of performance in the cognitive domain would be learning the rules of basketball.

3. Affective Domain. Student attitudes, feelings, and values make up the affective domain. An example of performance in this domain would be exhibiting the correct reactions to defeat, and to victory.

Writing Performance Objectives

Performance Objectives are specific statements of observable and measurable behaviors that the teacher expects the students to accomplish. The instructor should write a number of performance objectives in each of the three domains for each activity or unit covered in the curriculum. The number of objectives in each domain would depend upon the complexity of the unit. Hence, there would be a set of performance objectives in the psychomotor, cognitive, and affective domains for the softball unit, another set in each of the three domains for the tumbling unit, and so on for each activity taught.

The three generally accepted criteria that must be included in a properly stated performance objective are: (1) the performance to be accomplished by the student, (2) the conditions under which the performance will be accomplished, and (3) the level or standard at which the performance must be accomplished.

An example of a performance objective written for cardiovascular endurance in the psychomotor domain might be: Each student will perform the 12 minute run around the quarter mile track while dressed in proper attire, and the distance covered will be _____ miles for boys and _____ miles for girls. In this example the performance to be met is "perform the 12 minute run," the conditions are "around the quarter mile track dressed in proper attire," and the acceptable level of performance is "_____ miles for boys and _____ miles for girls."

An example of a performance objective written in the cognitive domain is: Each student will demonstrate his or her knowledge of the rules of tennis by achieving at least 80% on a 100 question written test. In this objective the peformance is "demonstrate his or her knowledge of the rules of tennis," the conditions are "100 questions and a written test," and the acceptable level is "80% accuracy."

An example of a performance objective written in the effective domain might be: The student will, while playing volleyball under the observation of the teacher, accept the decisions of the student official

7

without complaint for three games. In this example the performance to be met is "accept the decisions of the student official without complaint," the conditions are "while playing volleyball and under the observation of the teacher," and the acceptable level is "three games."

In the writing of performance objectives, the verb is the key word, regardless of which domain is being considered. Without specificity of what the student is required to do, or perform, the objective remains incomplete. A list of action verbs acceptable for use in writing performance objectives would include the following: demonstrate, shoot, swim, kick, hit, identify, order, name, construct, describe, state, apply, interpret, and distinguish. For further guidance in writing performance objectives the reader is referred to Safrit's (1981) evaluation text which contains an excellent chapter on performance objectives.

Criticisms of Performance Objectives

It should be noted that not everyone shares enthusiasm for performance objectives. Some of the more prominent criticisms of performance objectives are: (1) they are inappropriate for certain behaviors, (2) they restrict teacher creativity, (3) they lead to only minimal level performance by students, (4) they are destructive to opportunities for teaching which cannot be identified in advance, and (5) they cannot account for individual differences. Although there may be some validity to these objections, the value of the performance objective in establishing accountability, the way they assist the teacher in planning, and the direction they give to each individual in the class, seem to outweigh the suggested disadvantages.

Outcomes

As discussed above, performance objectives define the level of skill, fitness, knowledge, or behaviors toward which the teacher is working during each unit. However, because of individual differences among various members of the class, and because of teaching failures and successes, the end result for each class member is not the same. While the majority of the class may exhibit successful performance of the objective, a few students will not meet it, and a few students will be able to exceed it. These conditions we identify as the outcomes. They follow whatever evaluation techniques the teacher uses and are of utmost importance in planning succeeding lessons.

A graphic portrayal of the relationsip of the aim, developmental objectives, performance objectives, and outcomes experienced by students in physical education class may be seen in Figure 1.1.

8

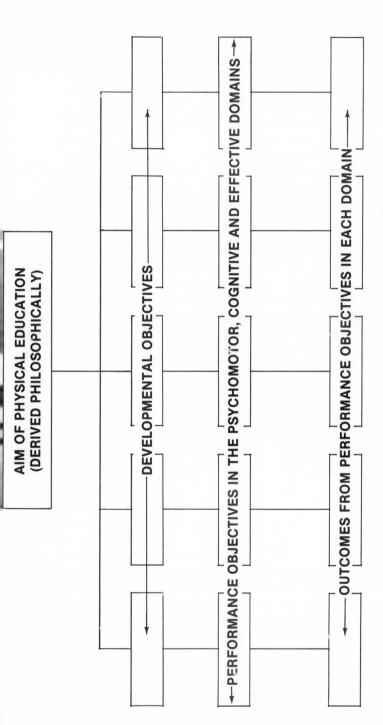

Figure 1.1 Hierarchy of guidelines in physical education.

9

THE DEVELOPMENT OF SELF—CONCEPT

The previous paragraphs have dealt with the theoretical constructs underlying the definition, aim, and objectives of physical education. Without an understanding of these, no physical educator is prepared to initiate the teacher-learning process. Yet, this process is doomed to failure if the individual teacher is not aware of the role played by the feelings students have of themselves.

Self-concept is also referred to as self-esteem or self-worth. Regardless of the name given, the important aspect is that it is a feeling that people have about themselves. Self-worth is largely calculated based upon one's own perception of how they are viewed by others.

Teachers can have a great impact upon the self-concept of their students. The teacher is an authority figure and therefore one to be listened to and believed. This important relationship between students and teachers makes it imperative that teachers use care with their communication. Dr. James Dobson, noted child psychologist, speaks well to this point when he states "self-esteem is the most fragile attribute in human nature; it can be damaged by a very minor incident and its reconstruction is often difficult to engineer" (Dobson, 1970, p. 19).

In general, acceptance and success enhance the self-concept, whereas, rejection and failure undermine the self-concept. Every effort should be made by the teacher to insure that each student experiences success in some form or manner each day.

The physical education teacher may be in the unique position to enable students to meet with a sense of accomplishment in or through some movement endeavor. Without getting into teaching technique at this point, it may be wise to point out the importance of using a good progression of movement skills so each student is successful. In addition to experiencing success, students need to feel acceptance for who and what they are, whether tall or short, bright or dull, wealthy or poor. Sometimes in their exuberance to make everyone well educated, teachers fail to recognize individual differences. Some students will never be able to reach stated norms in some areas. Let us be careful to strive for improvement, but also encourage an acceptance for limitations within our students.

Teachers of physical education often are guilty of some abominable practices which are destructive to the self-concept of various students. The practice of lining up by height to count off for squads serves no useful purpose and is harmful to certain individuals in the class. Consider the girl in the seventh grade class who is taller than all the rest of the students, or the boy who is the shortest one in the entire class. It is simply a fact of child growth that girls mature physically more rapidly than boys.

Lining up by height tends to spotlight this fact and makes some individuals feel self-conscious or different. A better method may be selected to accomplish the same pupose, thus preserving someone's positive self-concept.

Another practice that can be harmful to the self-concept of students is allowing students to choose individuals for squads or teams. This practice simply enhances an already healthy self-concept for the first chosen, and further decays an already poor self-concept for the last chosen. The practice of students choosing sides should not be used in any of its forms.

Teachers do not intend to make students feel inadequate and worthless. However, many practices used have dire consequences for the self-concept of specific individuals in their classes. Each activity that is planned, and every word spoken, should be examined for its effect upon the feelings of those being taught. A few suggestions for enhancing the self-concept of students are:

1 . The teacher should learn and use the name of each individual. One's name is a valuable possession and should be used with respect. Refrain from using or allowing students to use derogatory nicknames. The teacher may need to use name tags on the students' shirts to help learn their names.
2. The teacher should speak in a respectful manner at all times. For some students this may be the only respect they receive.
3. The teacher should attempt to speak to each class member on a "personal" basis at least one time each week. Set this as a goal and keep records to see that it is accomplished. Locker room time, or before and after class, are excellent times for these personal conversations.
4. The teacher should give personal instructional time to every student in class. Don't allow yourself to gravitate only toward the student who is well-skilled, beautiful, or the one with the pleasing personality.
5. The teacher should teach in such a manner that all students may experience success. Success may be defined as doing something better than previously. In some instances success may simply be making an attempt.
6. The teacher should praise individuals for what they accomplish. Don't confuse "praise" with "flattery." Flattery is unearned and occurs by giving compliments for something the student did not achieve. Praise, on the other hand, is positive reinforcement for some specific, constructive behavior.
7. The teacher should spread responsibilities and rewards, such as being squad captain, equipment manager, locker room attendant, and student assistant around the class. Everyone needs to feel they can handle responsibility.

Figure 1.2 depicts how a positive self-concept can have a protective effect upon the student. Success, pride, and encouragement contribute to the student developing a strong positive self-concept. This positive self-concept acts as an umbrella to shield the student from too many negative experiences such as doubt and small doses of failure. The teacher is in the position to provide experiences which will allow the student to develop a positive self-concept.

Figure 1-2   The umbrella of self-concept.

SELECTED READINGS AND REFERENCES

AAHPERD. *Guidelines for Secondary School Physical Education: A Position Paper.* Washington, D.C., 1970.

Dobson, James. *Dare to Discipline.* Bantam Book, Toronto, 1970.

Safrit, Margaret J. *Evaluation in Physical Education.* Prentice-Hall, Inc., Englewood Cliffs, 1981.

Siedel, Beverly L. and Mathew C. Resick, *Physical Education: An Overview.* Addison-Wesley Publishing Company, Reading, Mass., 1972.

14

THE EFFECTIVE TEACHER

2

Without question, the single most important factor in the classroom, next to the student, is the teacher. Changing times, changing students, and changing methodologies never seem to diminish the need for and the importance of an effective teacher.

A description of the ideal teacher would be impossible to construct. Two individuals, as different as night from day, may both prove to be effective in the classroom. Although there is no single description of the ideal teacher, there certainly are some commonalities to be found in those who are effective and successful in the classroom.

THE TEACHER AS ROLE MODEL

The role of the teacher is a many-faceted one. In addition to instruction, the teacher is called upon to be substitute parent, nurse, and counsellor. The dominant and overall function of the teacher is to be the director of learning within the classroom. The teacher is the one who orchestrates the many experiences and procedures that occur through which students grow, develop, and learn.

These authors believe that one of the most important functions of the teacher is that of being a role model. The teacher should be the type of individual that students respect. The model provided can certainly influence what the student learns to respect and value. The life lived by the teacher will influence the students much more than what is said about living. The way in which a teacher relates to students will outweigh what is taught about relating to others. The model represented by the teacher includes, among other things, appearance, mannerisms, manner of speaking, and personal relationships.

Students look to their teachers as a source of leadership and counsel. Teachers must always be aware that students have many peers in the class but only one teacher. They do not need a teacher who wants to be "one of the gang," so to speak. Instructors who try to become too close with students on a personal basis are not only asking for difficulty, but they are also jeopardizing their ability to lead and counsel students when the need arises. This problem is most prevalent with the beginning teacher in a high school where there may be only a few years difference in age between the teacher and the students. A helpful guideline might be always to seve as a "friend" but be careful of becoming a "buddy."

QUALITIES THAT CONTRIBUTE TO BEING A GOOD TEACHER

Early efforts at identifying the effective teacher involved the identification of qualities which principals, researchers, and educators felt contributed to being a good teacher. The lists compiled were not based upon sound research findings. Therefore, information of this kind is not given much attention today. Although we agree that this information should be treated with care, we believe there are some important thoughts for the teacher contained therein. Being a role model is a significant responsibility, and these qualities can be good reminders for guiding one into being that model.

One writer has identified the "good" teacher as one who: (1) is excellent in his or her own field of teaching and, in addition, is appreciative of other fields of endeavor, (2) is a student and is constantly desiring to learn more, (3) has the teaching spirit and is inspirational and challenging to all, (4) arouses curiosity in students, and (5) is fair to all students and at the same time recognizes differences in students (Lohse, 1974).

Another author, speaking in general terms, says that to be effective teachers must: (1) take stock of themselves and determine their strengths and weaknesses, following which they will attempt to improve the weaknesses through clinics, professional meetings and reading the professional literature, (2) set realistic goals and vigorously move to accomplish them, and (3) excel at being themselves by learning from their mistakes and continually attempting to correct what can be corrected (Miller, 1978).

16

There could be an unending list of qualities desirable in a teacher. Some of the more important qualities are:

A. Personal qualities
1. The teacher should have a heart-felt desire to serve students in the role of teacher.
2. The teacher should be of high moral and ethical character.
3. The teacher should be well groomed and dress appropriately for the teaching situation.
4. The teacher should have a sense of humor and be able to laugh at himself and with the students when appropriate.

B. Teaching qualities
5. The teacher should have good knowledge of the subject matter to be taught.
6. The teacher should possess the ability to motivate students to their maximum learning capabilities.
7. The teacher should have the ability to be flexible when warranted.
8. The teacher should avoid practices which are harmful to students in terms of physical and emotional growth and in the development of a healthy self-concept.

C. Professional qualities
9. The teacher should show responsibility in meeting classes and carrying out all duties associated with teaching in general, and one's own job in particular.
10. The teacher should be enthusiastic toward students, teaching, and the specific subject being taught.
11. The teacher should be growing as a professional educator by attending conferences, clinics, and other pertinent activities.
12. The teacher should treat the students, other staff members, and school property with respect.

STUDENT PERCEPTIONS OF EFFECTIVE TEACHERS

In recent years it has become popular to have students rate their teachers on various qualities associated with teaching. Being the product of education, the students are considered to have worthwhile opinions as to what qualities about teachers contributed the most toward their ability to learn. Considerable research has been conducted to determine what qualities are considered most important by students. Some representative studies of this type are presented in this section.

Samuels and Griffore (1980) investigated the characteristics perceived by third and fourth grade students to be most and least typical of effective teachers. Third grade students rated the four most important

17

characteristics of a teacher to be:
1. The teacher helps the students understand assignments.
2. The teacher is interested in how the students do.
3. The teacher knows what he or she is teaching.
4. The teacher is self-confident.

The fourth grade students rated the four most important characteristics as:
1. The teacher knows what he or she is teaching.
2. The teacher helps the students understand assignments.
3. The teacher gives examples of what is to be done.
4. The teacher is interested in how the students do.

It would seem that all of these young students were most of all desirous of a teacher who had a personal interest in their performance in the classroom. Both third and fourth grade students agreed that the least important characteristics of a good teacher were that "the teacher makes jokes and kids around" and "the teacher gives hard but fair tests."

In a study involving 566 students in grades seven through twelve, the students were asked, "What do you like about the ways teachers help you learn?" Their responses in descending order of occurrence were:
1. The teacher gives clear, complete explanations and concrete examples. Questions are answered and the teacher reviews materials and concepts.
2. The teacher creates a positive, relaxed learning environment. The teacher expects students to learn, but also makes learning fun.
3. The teacher treats each student as an individual. The teacher knows that students are different and constantly checks the progress of students and informs them of their progress.
4. The teacher gives students adequate academic learning time. The students are expected to use their time wisely and the teacher helps them to keep working so they will learn.
5. The teacher has the ability to keep the students interested and motivated. The teacher is excited about the subject and makes the students want to learn (Mosley and Smith, 1982).

Samuels and Griffore (1980) also gathered data on what characteristics were considered most and least typical of effective teachers as perceived by undergraduate and graduate university students. The ratings by the two university groups were almost identical. The five most important characteristics in a good teacher as perceived by the undergraduate students were:
1. The professor should know the field extensively.
2. The professor should always be fair.
3. The professor should be enthusiastic.

4. The class should be told in advance what material will be covered.
5. All assignments should be explained carefully.
The graduate students named the same first three items and reversed numbers four and five in their ratings. Listed as the least important characteristics of a good teacher by both the undergraduate and graduate students were that the "professor stays close to the text" and that the "professor gives hard but fair tests."

An interesting, and perhaps surprising, result of this study was the close agreement between the university students and the elementary students in what impressed them as characteristics of a good teacher. After making a few adjustments so the scales were comparable, the researchers found the ratings of the fourth grade students and the undergraduate students to be in very strong agreement.

SYSTEMATIC OBSERVATION OF TEACHERS

The most recent research on teacher effectiveness has emphasized the systematic observation of teachers actually teaching. This type of research has commonly been referred to as process-product research. The process is the actual teaching, which is measured by direct observation, and the product is the student learning that occurs. The student learning is usually measured by standardized achievement tests.

The typical method of process-product research is one in which a rather large number of classrooms are selected for study over an extended period of time. During this time many observations are made of the teacher's behavior, students' behavior, and classroom procedures. At the end of the observation period, achievement of the students is measured. Based upon the achievement measures, the classes are divided into high-achieving and low-achieving classrooms. The data that was collected from the high and low-achieving classrooms is studied to determine the behaviors that may have contributed to the achievement levels of the students. As teacher patterns and behaviors are found that are common to those classes in which high-achievement was experienced, they are classified as characteristics of more effective teachers. The teacher patterns and behaviors which regularly showed up in low-achievement classrooms are associated with less effective teachers.

One important finding from this type of teacher effectiveness research is that the amount of time students actually spend on the learning materials correlates positively with student learning. The time students are actively involved with the learning materials and subject matter may be referred to as *engaged learning time*. The degree to which teachers can maintain a high percentage of engaged learning time in their classrooms has become associated with effective teaching.

Direct Instruction

The behaviors and processes used by teachers who maintain a high percentage of engaged learning time have become known as *direct instruction*. Rosenshine describes direct instruction as follows:

> Direct instruction refers to academically focused, teacher-directed classrooms using sequenced and structured materials. It refers to teaching activities where goals are clear to students, time allocated for instruction is sufficient and continuous, coverage of content is intensive, the performance of students is monitored, questions are at a low cognitive level so that students can produce many correct responses, and feedback to students is immediate and academically oriented. In direct instruction the teacher controls instructional goals, chooses materials appropriate for the student's ability, and paces the instructional episode. Interaction is characterized as structured, but not authoritarian. Learning takes place in a convivial academic atmosphere. The goal is to move the students through a sequenced set of materials or tasks (Rosenshine, 1979, p. 38).

Let it be stressed that direct instruction is not a "method" of teaching but rather a set of behaviors that accomplish a high degree of active learning by the students. Writing in *Quest*, Graham and Heimerer (1981) reviewed the literature and identified ten variables which comprised the direct instruction concept. Each of the variables is presented here, including how the more effective and less effective teachers behave with regard to each variable. As will be discussed later in this chapter, very little of this type of research had been conducted in physical education. For this reason we will make an application to physical education after each variable. In addition, the ten variables and the accompanying behaviors of more effective and less effective teachers are summarized in Figure 2-1.

Variable 1 — Teacher warmth. Teacher warmth is thought of as the classroom environment which is created by the mannerisms and verbalizations by the teacher. More effective teachers create warm classroom environments by interacting with students in sincere ways and by letting them know help is available when needed.

Less effective teachers, on the other hand, tend to shame, criticize, belittle, and ridicule students. These characteristics of less effective teachers do not serve as encouragement for students.

Application to physical education: The important elements of exuding teacher warmth through sincere interaction and letting students know help is available is no different for the physical education teacher than any other teacher. With large numbers of students in many physical

20

education classes, however, the teacher may have to work harder at accomplishing it. The teacher must speak to students as individuals regularly and communicate that "I am interested in you and how well you learn movement skills in my class." The teacher must use care not to concentrate on the better skilled student to the exclusion of the less skilled. Rather than shame or criticize a student for poor motor performance, the more effective teacher will show the student how improvement may be accomplished.

Variable 2 — Teacher expectancy. The quantity and quality of work that is expected from the students by the teacher is referred to as teacher expectancy. The teacher who shows high expectancy is one who communicates to the students that they are capable of doing good quality work and that is what is expected from them.

More effective teachers tend to rate higher than less effective teachers on expectancy. This expectation by the more effective teachers is communicated to the students by moving through the course content at a faster pace and with the assignment of more homework and practice. The less effective teacher, conversely, covers the subject matter at a much slower pace and demands less homework and practice.

Application to physical education: Teacher expectancy in the physical education class will be shown most often by the number of skills students are asked to learn and the quality of performance expected by the teacher. The teacher will present movement skills in some detail and will expect students to practice the skills diligently and thereby perform them well.

Out-of-class assignments are just as realistic for the physical education class as for other subject areas. The assignments could be to do exercises at home or practice sport skills at an appropriate facility. Properly planned reading and writing assignments on pertinent physical education topics would also be very appropriate.

Variable 3 — Task-oriented behavior of teachers. More effective teachers rate higher on the variable of creating a task-oriented climate than do less effective teachers. This task-oriented climate is created by an insistence upon promptness, beginning and stopping activities on time, and quickly changing from one activity to another. The more effective teachers also contribute to the task-oriented climate by placing an emphasis on meeting objectives and covering the content.

Application to physical education: A task-oriented climate may be created in the physical education class by establishing good management techniques. The more effective physical education teacher will insist upon students being out of the locker room on time, roll will be taken efficiently, and each demonstration, drill, and practice event will begin with a minimum of wasted time and movement. This saving in time will

Variable	More Effective Teachers	Less Effective Teachers
Teacher warmth	Interacts with students in sincere ways. Lets students know help is available.	Little sincere interaction with students. Shames, criticizes, belittles, and ridicules students.
Teacher expectancy	Expects a lot from students. Moves through curriculum at a fast pace. Assigns a lot of homework and practice.	Moves through course content slowly. Does not assign much homework or practice.
Task-oriented behavior of teacher	Insists upon promptness by students. Begins and stops activities on time. Quickly changes from one activity to another. Places emphasis upon covering the content and meeting the stated objectives.	Less demand for promptness and efficiency in starting, changing, and stopping activities. Not as concerned with covering the content and meeting the course objectives.
Allowing student choices	Gives few choices to students concerning assignments and learning activities.	Gives more choices to students concerning assignments and learning activities.
Structuring the lesson	Gives clear information of what students are to do. States objectives clearly. Presents lesson content clearly and reviews and	More vague in presenting instructions and organization procedures to students.

	More effective	Less effective
	...summarizes important lesson elements.	
Use of questioning	Asks more lower order questions. Waits less time for answers.	Asks more higher order questions. Waits longer for answers.
Use of praise	Uses less praise. Praises more for work than for behavior.	Uses more praise. Praises behavior and seeks out the students to offer praise.
Feedback to students	Uses immediate, non-evaluative, and task-oriented feedback. Compliments correct responses.	Tends to give more neutral feedback cues without telling what was correct or incorrect about the response.
Grouping for instruction	Uses more whole class and large group instruction than small group and individual. Supervises all grouping plans carefully.	Uses more small group and individual patterns of grouping. Does not supervise groups carefully.
Maintaining on-task behavior	Establishes class rules. Monitors students carefully. Redirects students who stray off-task rather than administer punishment.	Have less set procedures for class. Spends a lot of time dealing with off-task behavior. Issues a lot of warnings and criticism.

Figure 2.1 Summary of behaviors of more effective and less effective teachers. (From Graham and Heimerer, 1981, pp. 18-22)

result in more skills being covered in the class.

Variable 4 — Allowing student choices. Student choices may include the assignments to be done, the materials to be read, and the practices to be accomplished. Choices of this type are given more frequently by less effective teachers than by more effective teachers who tend to structure the learning environment and give students fewer choices. The more the teacher is learning oriented, the fewer choices are given.

Application to physical education: The physical education teacher will tell the students what skill they should practice and perhaps how many repetitions should be accomplished or how long they should practice the skill. The choices given to students will be within rather strict parameters established by the teacher.

The choices referred to in this context are not to be confused with giving students choices as a motivational device. Elective classes to be taken in physical education and "student choice" time that may be earned by students or classes are considered appropriate motivation techniques.

Variable 5 — Structuring the lesson. The idea of structuring may be described as providing a framework around which a lesson can be built. More effective teachers are seen to provide more structure for their students in the form of very clear information concerning what is to be learned and how they are to go about learning it. Specifically, they provide structure by stating objectives, clearly presenting lesson content, reviewing, and summarizing important elements of the lesson. Less effective teachers are more vague in their instructions and organization so that the students are less aware of what is to be learned and how they should learn it.

Application to physical education: The more effective physical education teacher will plan each lesson well, including clearly stated lesson objectives which will guide the selection and organization of student experiences. The teacher will structure presentations, demonstrations, and drills for maximum learning and participation. The teacher will review the skills learned the previous day and will progress into new skills in the present day's lesson.

Variable 6 — The use of questioning. As it relates to teaching effectiveness, questioning is normally categorized into higher order and lower order questions. Lower order questions are those that require simple recall or factual answers. Higher order questions are more complex and require students to compare, contrast, interpret, and evaluate in order to give acceptable answers.

More effective teachers tend to ask more lower order questions and less effective teachers ask more higher order questions. Another interesting observation regards the amount of time teachers wait for an answer. More effective teachers wait less time after asking a question before calling on another student for the answer.

Application to physical education: Although questions are asked in physical education, the greater amount of emphasis is placed upon performing motor skills and movements. Therefore, the use of questioning has the least application of the ten variables to the typical physical education setting. The application would be found in studying the history, rules, and strategy of a sport or the cognitive aspects of health-related fitness which may require a portion of the time to be spent in teacher-student discussion. Also, the less formal styles of teaching, such as guided discovery, utilize questioning to a great extent.

Variable 7 — The use of praise. More effective teachers are more sparing with their praise of students than are less effective teachers, and they generally withhold praise until the student comes to them. In addition, they tend to praise students more for their work than for their behavior. Less effective teachers, however, are more apt to lavish more praise upon the students, and they tend to seek out the student to offer the praise.

Application to physical education: Praise in the physical education class will be given largely for students' performance of movement skills. The more effective teacher will reserve praise for work that is deserving of praise and for good effort at performing the skill by the student. The less effective teacher will tend to over use praise.

Variable 8 — Feedback to students. Feedback has the specific meaning of the teacher's response to students' questions when used in process-product research. More effective teachers provide immediate, non-evaluative, and task-oriented feedback which includes the correct answer and how it is derived. They also tend to compliment students for correct answers. Less effective teachers tend to respond to the process rather than provide the correct answer, and they also give a lot of neutral feedback cues without telling the students what was right or wrong with the answer.

Application to physical education: The physical education teacher will also give feedback to questions from students. More feedback, however, will be given to students' attempts at movement. Applying the thoughts derived from the research would mean the more effective teacher would give immediate feedback of a task-oriented nature to performance attempts. That is, they would focus upon what the student needs to do to improve upon the performance, and they would compliment good performances by the students. Less effective teachers would respond to students' performance attempts with comments such as "pretty good" or "nice try" without being specific about what needs to be done to improve the performance.

Variable 9 — Grouping for instruction. Grouping for instruction refers to whether teachers work with the entire class, small groups, individuals, or various combinations of these groups. Although there are several factors involved here, it is observed that more effective teachers work with the whole class and large groups more than with small groups and individuals. More effective teachers do spend time with small groups and individuals where it is appropriate, and in these instances they supervise the students carefully. Conversely, less effective teachers work more with small groups than large groups in their classes, and they do not supervise the students as closely as do the more effective teachers.

Application to physical education: The physical education teacher would use a variety of grouping techniques including whole class, large groups, and small groups. Physical education instruction often involves small groups and even individual learning due to the nature of the subject, equipment, and facilities. The more effective teacher would use more large group instruction than small group or individual instruction. However, no matter what grouping technique is used, the more effective teacher would move around to help and supervise the students carefully.

Variable 10 — Maintaining on-task behavior. Maintaining on-task behavior is clearly a class management function. More effective teachers seem to establish a set of operating rules designed to keep order in the classroom but which can be altered if necessary. They closely monitor students, and if the students stray off-task, the teacher directs them back on-task rather than using punishment. Less effective teachers seem to spend an inordinate amount of time dealing with off-task behavior. These teachers issue a lot of warnings and criticism and use more punitive techniques.

Application to physical education: The large number of students, wide variety of equipment, and varying amounts of space involved in the physical education class presents many opportunities for students to wander off-task. The teacher will supervise and monitor the students' behavior closely for signs of negative behavior or failure to stay on-task. If students are observed moving away from assigned tasks, the teacher will refocus their attention on the drill or activity that is being conducted at the time. Such comments as "Do you need help Bill?" or "Keep working, Sally, until I get to you" will be used by the more effective teacher to re-establish the concentration of students upon the task at hand. Most importantly, the more efective teacher will be consantly observing the class so that he or she will be in tune with the mood and effort being put forth by the students.

26

Direct Instruction and Affective Behaviors

Direct instruction has been presented as a series of behaviors designed to bring about maximum engaged learning time. It is, therefore, a concept which places its emphasis upon student achievement. There may be a concern among educators that placing such great emphasis upon learning achievement may have a detrimental effect upon affective student behaviors such as attitude toward school or self-concept.

Although the research is somewhat sketchy on this point, the available information would lead one to believe that there is no conflict between achievement-focused learning and affective outcomes. Medley (1979) conducted an extensive review of the research on teacher effectiveness and was able to draw some relationships between achievement variables and affective variables. He looked for pairs of relationships where one teacher process would be measured by two different teacher effectiveness measures. One of the teacher effectiveness measures had to be achievement-oriented and the other affective. If the achievement and affective measures were both high or low on the same process measure, the pairs were said to agree. That is, they indicated that the same pattern of behavior was effective in producing both achievement and affective outcomes.

Ninety pairs of outcomes were found in which one was achievement-oriented and the other affective. In 73 percent of the pairs studied, the same pattern of teacher behavior that maximizes students' achievement gains was also found to have a positive effect upon affective outcomes. Conversely, the patterns of teacher behaviors that produced the least achievement gains in students were also accompanied by the least gains in affective outcomes.

The teacher must be careful not to assume that the affective outcomes that are strived for in physical education automatically occur as a result of teaching for achievement gains. The social-emotional developmental objective includes many outcomes that must be taught. Therefore, the teacher must plan specifically for teaching sportsmanship and acceptance just as one would plan to teach physical fitness or neuromuscular skills.

Limitations of Process-Product Research

Teacher effectiveness research to date has shed light upon some very important dimensions of teaching. Direct instruction seems to be an excellent model toward which teacher preparation may aspire. There are, however, certain limitations with process-product research that should cause us to move with cautious optimism.

The first limitation is that process-product research has largely been confined to the teaching of mathematics and reading. Only a very few studies have been done in physical education. This should not stop us from using what has been learned in process-product research, but it does suggest that we ponder the thought of how effective it will be in physical education. Siedentop suggests that we should not worry too much about this limitation when he states "the amount of confirming evidence from different studies has grown sufficiently to begin to warrant the generalization of this pattern of effective teaching to different subject matters and different kinds of settings than the ones in which the results were originally determined" (Siedentop, 1983, p. 41).

A second limitation on process-product research is that most of the research has been conducted with elementary age students. The question arises, might students of high school age respond differently than elementary age students to some of the direct instruction components?

The possibility certainly exists that continued growth of teacher effectiveness research in physical education and other subject matter areas, as well as with secondary school students, may show conflicting results to what is presently known. However, the evidence available at this time would seem to indicate that direct instruction has definite potential with elementary, junior high, and senior high school physical education students.

PERSONAL CHARACTERISTICS OF TEACHERS

Discussing personal characteristics of teachers may be treading upon dangerous grounds. There are many pesonal characteristics about each individual that cannot be altered even if the desire for change is present. Those are not at issue in this text. There are, however, many characteristics which can be changed or improved upon to make one a more effective teacher. A few selected items which are believed to be important for good teaching are enthusiasm, proper use of language, and manner of dress and appearance. These qualities are characteristic of the "professional" physical educator.

Enthusiasm

There is a commonly used phrase that goes "enthusiasm is contagious." This statement is true. Enthusiasm is contagious, but so is the lack of it. The teacher desirous of having good attitudes toward learning among his or her students must be willing and able to put forth an enthusiastic effort at teaching. As is true of many qualities regarding human behaviors, there is no one set of behaviors to be classified as being enthu-

28

siastic. The enthusiastic teacher may range from the "cheerleader" to the "low profile" individual. Caruso (1982) states "teacher enthusiasm is more than rapid body movements, smiling, or hand gestures. The behaviors characterizing teacher enthusiasm are a combination of interpersonal communication and competent pedagogical skills." She identifies the three most important behaviors representative of enthusiasm as described by secondary school students as participation, encouragement, and praise.

Participation means the teacher physically engages in the learning activity with the students. The participation should be as a true player and not as a means of showing off by the teacher. Care must be taken that the teacher's participation does not take away from proper instruction and supervision, or constitute a safety problem for the students.

Encouragement can be thought of as those teaching behaviors which stimulate the students toward improved performance. Any encouragement given by the teacher should be sincere and appropriate. It should also be distributed to all students in the class, regardless of skill level. The teacher must use caution not to express signs of encouragement only toward the highly skilled students.

Praise, the third representative of enthusiasm, may be defined as teacher approval of student achievement. This approval may be expressed either verbally or nonverbally. Generally, teachers will praise a performance which equals or exceeds expectations. In addition to praising students for meeting goals, there are instances in which an attempt may be worthy of praise. In no instances, however, should it be given for a poor performance.

Proper Use of Language

Children are bombarded with improper language ranging from cursing in the home and on the streets to advertising tricks on television and in the print media. There is sometimes a temptation for adults, including teachers, to attempt to "relate" to students by using questionable forms of the English language. Some of the areas where teachers may fail their students in the use of language are:
1. Speaking the slang of the students. Students do not need, nor do they want, their teachers to become one of them by talking or acting in the same way as the students.
2. Using swear words. Teachers are sometimes tempted to use curse words to drive home a point or to show that they are "with it." This is a mistake. Teachers should be role models in language as well as in other facets of their teaching. Many students are not accustomed to

29

foul language and should not be exposed to it by their teacher.

3. Speaking with improper grammar. Physical Education is but one part of the total education program. All aspects of education should work together to educate students. Not only does poor grammar by the teacher hurt the education of the student, but it also diminishes the credibility of the teacher in other areas.

4. Using improper phrases. Rampant among physical educators is a tendency to use phrases that may be acceptable in the athletic atmosphere but not necessarily in the classroom. Although these may be understood by the student, their use is a hazard to the development of good communication skills. The following are a few selected phrases along with their interpretations in meaning:

Phrase — Bring it in.
    Student's reaction — Bring what in?
        Interpretation — Come over here please.
Phrase — Grab a partner.
    Student's reaction — Physically grab another student.
        Interpretation — Select and stand beside another student.
Phrase — Grab a seat.
    Student's reaction — Look for a chair to grasp.
        Interpretation — Sit down please.
Phrase — Hit the showers.
    Student's reaction — Why?
        Interpretation — It is time to shower.

5. Sprinkling the verbal presentation with "filler" words. An otherwise good presentation can be destroyed by teachers who constantly interrupt their message with such words as "okay," "ah," "all right," and "you know."

Not only should teachers be careful to use proper language personally, but the students should also be encouraged to use acceptable language. Language becomes a habit and bad habits may develop if they are not guarded against. Teachers should consciously listen to themselves periodically to determine if improper patterns are being used.

Appearance and Manner of Dress

Although there are an increasing number of classes in physical education that emphasize the cognitive, or intellectual aspect, and therefore are held in the traditional classroom, the fact remains that the majority of physical education classes are still an "activity" or "participation" learning situation, with some sort of human movement as the main focus. In the context of such a class, it is as important for the teacher to be appropriately dressed as it is for the student. The question then arises,

30

"What is the appropriate dress for a teacher of physical education?"

A teacher does not need to buy one of the expensive warm-up suits now available, although they are appropriate if so desired. What is recommended is an attire that suits the activity of the day and is clean and well-tailored. Occasionally an activity dictates a specific type of dress. Two of these are gymnastics and swimming. The gymnastics teacher should wear apparel that stretches easily yet is not baggy enough to present a safety hazard. No rings, jewelry, watches, tight belts or shorts should be worn. In the swimming class, of course, the instructor should be dressed in swimming attire in case he or she needs to enter the water, either for instructional or recovery purposes.

If the reader is inclined to think too much emphasis is put on appearance, think of the following:

1. We want students to participate in activity the rest of their lives. In doing so, they should be dressed appropriately as far as the movement of their activity is concerned, and in a manner socially acceptable for the environment in which they move.
2. How people look affects how they perceive themselves, how they teach, and their self pride.
3. The very act of "dressing" for activity is a concept we need to emphasize to our students, both for safety and for maximum performance.
4. There are certain stereotypes the modern physical education teacher needs to help overturn. Appearance is one of those.

THE FITNESS FACTOR

Previous to this paragraph we have discussed appearance in relation to the physical education teacher's dress. There is an additional area that is very important when it comes to discussing appearance. This, of course, is the individual picture of fitness, health, or state of physical conditioning that the teacher presents to the class. Especially at the secondary school level, the teacher will be dealing with concepts of speed, agility, daily workout periods, conditioning, avoiding obesity, weight training, jogging, posture improvement, endurance, nutrition, training regimens, and many others. Teachers who present any of these concepts as desirable for the students, and assigns goals in these areas, are not professionals if they do not exemplify the concepts themselves.

What teachers do and how they look will speak much louder than what they say. If we, as teachers, do not practice what we preach, our personal appearance will show it, and the students we hope to "teach" will notice it all too quickly.

There is an added dimension to the personal appearance of the physical educator that extends beyond the class and teaching. The entire credibility of the discipline is enhanced in faculty meetings, in community relations, and in the entire education melieu if the teacher's personal appearance reflects physical fitness.

IMPROVING TEACHING EFFECTIVENESS THROUGH EVALUATION

If teachers are to be effective, they must be aware of their strengths and weaknesses. Administrators, parents, community groups, and teachers themselves, have been concerned with ways and means of evaluating teachers so that teaching effectiveness might be measured. Sometimes these evaluations are made to help arrive at decisions for retention, salary increments, and promotions. However, in the long run the most valuable contribution that can come from teacher evaluation is to improve personal ability as a teacher. It is that aspect that we are concerned with in this discussion.

Although evaluation by administrators is often used as the first step, it is suggested here that the two most valuable evaluations to improve teaching effectiveness are those from the two parties most intimately involved in the teaching-learning process — the *teacher* and the *student.* Various techniques have been employed to measure teacher effectiveness. A survey of the literature reveals numerous and complicated rating systems, scales, scorecards, and checklists. The items included on these evaluation tools range widely in characteristics evaluated. The reason for this is obvious. Not only do those who construct these instruments have different philosophies, but the factors that make a teacher effective vary from teaching situation to situation. Yet, there seems to be a core of agreed-upon characteristics possessed by effective teachers. They may be summed up in the following categories: (1) Personal characteristics (appearance, voice, work habits, cooperation, grammar), (2) Professional characteristics (knowledge of subject, instructional techniques, facilities and class management), and (3) Student-Teacher relationships (encouragement, treating all fairly, making oneself available, understanding the student, patience).

SUMMARY

The teacher is a very important factor in the classroom. One function of the teacher is to serve as a role-model. The way the teacher acts and speaks will have a big impact upon the students.

There are certain qualities that administrators and other education specialists have identified as important to being an effective teacher.

They are categorized as personal qualities, teaching qualities, and professional qualities. Students have also expressed themselves in terms of what makes an effective teacher. There is an amazing similarity between students of all ages as to their perception of what makes a teacher effective. Two characteristics that seem consistent among the various ages are that the teacher should be interested in the performance of students and make expectations and assignments clear.

Process-product research, although relatively new in the literature, is beginning to formulate a sketch of the effective teacher when the focus is upon student achievement. This type of research is based upon extensive observations of teachers in their classroom and recording all of their teaching behaviors. Behaviors which are observed from teachers whose students achieve at a high level are classified as "more effective" teacher behaviors. Those behaviors which are observed from teachers whose students do not achieve at a high level are classified as "less effective." Research has identified several behaviors which have consistently been observed in those teachers who bring about high achievement in students. There are also behaviors which have been consistently observed in those teachers who do not enjoy high achievement from their students. Although only a small number of studies of this type have been done in physical education, the few results available show promise that the same behaviors noted in effective teachers in other academic areas will also be observed in physical education teachers.

These authors propose that there are personal characteristics of teachers which contribute to their being effective in the classroom and contribute to their "professionalism." These personal characteristics are: exuding genuine enthusiasm, using proper language, and dressing appropriately for the subject being taught. In addition, physical education teachers should be aware of their fitness level. Not only will they perform better if they maintain a level of fitness, but they will also show students, by example, that physical fitness is important.

To become and remain effective as a teacher requires constant evaluation. Teachers would do well to constantly monitor themselves concerning their personal characteristics, professional characteristics, and student-teacher relationships.

SELECTED READINGS AND REFERENCES

Caruso, Virginia M., "Enthusiastic Teaching," *JOPERD*, March, 1982, pp. 47-48.

Graham, G., and E. Heimerer, "Research on Teacher Effectiveness: A Summary with Implications for Teaching," *Quest*, 1981, pp. 14-25.

Lohse, Lola L., "What Makes a Good Teacher?", *The Physical Educator*, October, 1974, p. 156.

Medley, D., "The Effectiveness of Teachers," in P. Peterson and H. Walberg (eds.), *Research on Teaching: Concepts, Findings, and Implications*, McCutchan, Berkeley, Calif., 1979.

Miller, David K., "The Effective Teacher." *The Physical Educator*, October, 1978, 147-148.

Mosley, Mary and Paul Smith, "What Works in Learning? Students Provide the Answers.", *Phi Delta Kappan*, December, 1982, p. 273.

Rosenshine, B., "Content, Time and Direct Instruction," in P. Peterson and H. Walberg, (eds.), *Research on Teaching: Concepts, Findings, and Implications.* McCutchan, Berkeley, Calif., 1979.

Samuels, Douglas D. and Robert J. Griffore, "Students' Perceptions of the Characteristics of Good Teachers," *Journal of Instructional Psychology*, Winter, 1980, pp. 28-34.

Siedentop, Daryl, *Developing Teaching Skills in Physical Education*, Mayfield Publishing Company, Palo Alto, 1983.

THE USE OF PROGRESSION IN THE TEACHING PROCESS

3

To be an effective teacher requires a great deal of planning. An integral part of this planning must deal with the concept of progression. Each teacher must plan practice opportunities so that the objectives and goals of physical education may be accomplished. These practice sessions need to be organized to create a series of tasks that are progressively ordered and developmentally sound. The complete progression should contain a level low enough for the least skilled student to achieve success and a level high enough to be a challenge for the highest skilled student. The primary purpose of teaching skills in physical education is to advance students to a better performance level in movement skills. Therefore, it would seem appropriate that considerable attention be devoted to the development of good teaching progressions.

OUTCOMES OF GOOD TEACHING PROGRESSIONS

It should be the goal of teachers that their teaching results in the best learning possible for their students. This would involve their looking at the skill in terms of how it should be taught, their own understanding of the skill, and the students' ability to learn the skill. Teaching with a good progression contributes to several desirable outcomes.

The Teacher Presents the Subject Matter Clearly

Thinking through the proper progression that should be used in

37

teaching a skill may enable the teacher to better understand the relevant components of the skill. This prepares the teacher to present the skill in a clear, understandable manner. In addition, it gives the teacher a better understanding for helping and correcting students as they perform the skill. Many details of the performance will become visible to the teacher only as the details necessary in developing the progression are considered. How one part of the skill flows into the next part will be better understood as a result of the development of a teaching progression for a specific skill, complete sport, or activity.

The Students Enjoy a Successful Experience

Enjoyment is enhanced when performance in any endeavor is accompanied by success. The possibility of success is greatly increased when students are taught by means of a good teaching progression. The progression will insure that the first attempts by students are at a level where success is probable. Early success in the progression will give students the necessary confidence to attempt the task at a higher level. Each time they experience success at a higher level of the skill, they become more prepared to attempt the next level.

Safety for the Students is Increased

Insuring the safety of students as they perform movement skills is of importance to the teacher. Safety is important for the health and welfare of students, and it is important to teachers from a liability standpoint. Another important consideration for safety in performance is its effect upon the willingness of students to attempt the skill repeatedly. Once a student experiences injury while attempting a skill, he or she may be less willing to attempt the same skill or related skills again. If the teacher develops a proper progression there would be little chance of injury occurring. As students perform one step in the progression successfully, they are adequately prepared to attempt the next step. This step-by-step learning eliminates the danger of attempting a task too difficult for the individual.

FACTORS IN DEVELOPING PROGRESSIONS

There are many factors that should be examined when developing a progression for a skill or concept in physical education. Movement experiences are dynamic and are therefore affected by many internal and external forces. Some of the factors that must be examined are the type of skill to be learned, the requirements of the task to be learned, and the prerequisite abilities of the learner to have a successful experience. Each factor should be studied in relation to developing a lesson progression that will result in the best learning possible for the students.

Type of Skill to be Learned

Before a good progression can be developed, the skill must be analyzed as to its type. One of the most important considerations is whether the skill is an open or closed skill. *Open skills* are those in which the environment is constantly changing and, therefore, requires constant adaptation by the performer. Examples of open skills are most of those contained in basketball, volleyball, badminton, and field hockey. In these examples the environment is constantly changing. The performer must be aware of other players on the field or court, changing positions during the game, different positions of the ball or other equipment, and changing speeds and flow of the movements in the game. Therefore, the progression for these activities must not only focus on the specific skill, but must also consider the skill under changing conditions. What may be true in one environmental condition may not be true in another.

Closed skills are those skills that are performed in a relatively stable environment. That is, the conditions remain constant and are not changing factors in the performance of the skill. Some examples of closed skills are those involved in archery, swimming, and gymnastics routines. In these examples such factors as opposition and equipment remain constant. When shooting archery the shooter is in a stable position with no moving or distracting opponents, the target is stable and unchanging, and the bow and arrow remain unchanged in their form or position. Since the environmental conditions are stable, the entire focus of the progression may be placed upon the precise performance of the skill itself, unhindered by external influences.

Requirements of the Skill to be Learned

All skills have specific requirements that must be mastered for the performance to be successful. The teacher must first identify these specific requirements. Once the requirements have been identified, they should be placed in a hierarchical order. This is done because learning is based upon the supposition that lower level skills must be learned prior to learning higher level skills. For example, the teacher may want to teach the students to dribble a basketball to the right side of the basket and shoot a jump shot. There are several skill requirements inherent in this rather simple-sounding act. The student must be able to dribble the basketball, dribble the ball while moving, stop and get in position to jump, jump while holding the ball, and shoot the basketball while suspended in the air. These necessary skills must be placed in a learning hierarchy. This hierarchy should consider which of these components of the task could be learned most easily, and which skills must be learned before the student can have success in attempting the next component of the task.

Prerequisite Abilities of the Learner

There are certain prerequisite learner capabilities necessary for the completion of each skill. These prerequisites may be psychological or physical. The psychological prerequisites are primarily those that allow students to comprehend the skill as achievable. They must not be overly intimidated by the requirements of the skill.

The physical prerequisites of the learner are viewed in terms of muscular strength and endurance, flexibility, cardio-respiratory endurance and body composition. The achievement levels of students in these physical fitness qualities must be compared to the requirements for the successful completion of the skill. For example, students must have the necessary arm and shoulder strength to support their own body weight before they can learn to do a handstand. The motor skill development involved in the handstand is secondary to the necessary level of strength. In this specific situation the progression is dependent upon the development of the necessary level of arm and shoulder strength before the rest of the progression can be successful.

STAGES OF SKILL ACQUISITION

Adler (1981) has identified three stages people go through in acquiring a skill. The three are the concept, adaptation, and automation stages. Though the stages appear highly recognizable, there does not seem to be a precise point at which the learner passes from one to the next. There is often overlap between stages, and learners often waver back and forth between them.

The *concept stage* is the time when the learner becomes aware of the whole task to be accomplished. This stage is especially important when an unfamiliar activity is to be learned. The student must conceptualize the important ingredients of the activity. The concept stage relies heavily upon students receiving visual information and actually performing the activity. Providing visual information may be accomplished through the use of films or live demonstrations. Verbal information in this stage has value but should be limited. It is suggested that the more practice possible at this point the better the result. The concept stage is complete, and

40

the next stage begins, when the student can perform the entire skill without much concern for form, and while their attention is focused upon one specific aspect of the skill. That is, the learner can complete the entire tennis serve while focusing attention upon the toss.

The *adaptation stage* is an adjustment period during which the performance is improved in efficiency. It is a time when the student focuses upon performing the skill close to proper form. In the adaptation stage there is greater value placed upon verbal cues than in the concept stage.

Practice during this stage should be specific for closed and open skills. Closed skills should be practiced with attention focused upon aspects of the skill that need correction. This practice should be repeated many times in situations which are as game-like as possible. To accomplish this the teacher should develop a vocabulary of teaching cues that replace several separate instructions. For example, "the single instruction 'put your rear elbow in your pocket' for the golf downswing could replace these separate instructions: 'point your elbow down at the top of

Teaching Cue	Replaced Instructions
1. Golf downswing — "Put your rear elbow in your pocket.	A. Point your elbow down at the top of the swing. B. Start the club down to the inside. C. Tilt the shoulders, don't rotate them. D. Keep the rear elbow bent at the start of the downswing.
2. Basketball behind the back dribble — "Swing the ball behind you and slap your opposite rear pocket."	A. Place your hand on the top front part of the ball. B. Push the ball toward the back of your body and then toward the opposite side. C. Continue to push the ball and continue to turn your hand so the ball will go forward.
3. Swimming front crawl arm recovery — "Touch your elbow to the ceiling."	A. When you have reached the end of your pull, rotate your forearm so it is vertical in the water. B. Lift your entire arm upward until the hand comes out of the water.
4. Can you think of one?	
5. How about one more?	

Figure 3.1   Examples of teaching cues.

the swing,' 'start the club down to the inside,' 'tilt the shoulders, don't rotate them,' and 'keep the rear elbow bent at the start of the down-swing''' (Adler, 1981, p. 78). Several other suggested teaching cues are presented in Figure 3.1.

Open skills should be practiced so students will develop proficiency in a skill under a variety of conditions. For example, students need to practice the soccer kick when the ball is stationary, moving at different speeds, coming from different directions, and when located at different levels. In addition, the skill should be practiced with and without opposition.

When the student can perform a skill without conscious effort the *automation stage* has been reached. At this point the student's attention should be focused away from the specific movement. This seems to enhance the performance, and it may be accomplished by having the student focus upon the result of the movement rather than the movement itself. Continued practice, once students have reached the automation stage, is referred to as overlearning. This concept is discussed further in Chapter 11.

TYPES OF PROGESSION

There are many ways that one may approach the concept of progression. It is simply a building process which enables students to learn quickly, efficiently, and with a high degree of safety. Whatever approach is taken it should provide for skill development in a progressive, or additive manner. These behaviors may proceed from simple to complex experiences. The learning of skills may proceed from a stationary performance to a performance while moving. The progression may be one that progresses from being self-paced to one that is externally paced. Self-paced activities are those that are unaffected by any environmental factors, whereas externally paced are those performances which are influenced by others within the environment. These forms of progressions, as well as others, may be included within the types of progression presented in this section. The three types of progressions are not exclusively independent. That is, they should be used concurrently by the teacher. They simply represent a method of thinking through the way various physical education experiences should be taught.

Intra Skill Progression

A single skill has within it a number of elements or components. If these are not presented in the proper sequence, the correct learning of that skill is made more difficult. The key to the correct progression

Progression Designed to Facilitate
Learning to Kick a Ball

General Learning Progression	Sample Practice Opportunities
1. Patterning	1. Student practices the kicking pattern by copying the teacher's demonstration; no ball involved.
2. Stationary	2. Student practices kicking a stationary ball placed within easy reach of the child's stationary position.
3. Stationary Player — Moving Object	3. Ball is rolled within reach of the student who practices kicking the moving ball.
4. Stationary Object — Moving Player	4. Ball is positioned a short distance from the student who must run toward the ball and kick it.
5. Moving Player and Object	5. Ball is rolled toward student who is encouraged to run toward the ball and kick it before it reaches a predetermined location.
6. Add an Opponent	6. Assign a student to be the defensive player.
a. Stationary	a. Position a stationary defensive player, then require the student to kick the ball toward a designated location or teammate.
b. Reaching	b. Allow the defensive player to reach (with legs) toward the ball that is being kicked to a teammate.
c. Pursuing	c. Design a practice so that the defensive player attempts to take the ball away from the student who must kick it to a teammate or designated position.
7. Lead-up Game or Relays	7. Play a modified game which requires the student to use the kicking skills practiced above.

Figure 3.2   Sample intra skill progression.

Figure 3.3 Progression for a performance objective.

Objective: In a game situation, the student will be able to move to meet the ball, catch it, and throw to a designated spot.

Progression and fundamental	Individual and partner activities	Group activities
The student is taught to run in an all-out sprint.	Taught to all individuals through the large-group pattern.	
The student is taught the overarm throw.	Students practice throwing against a wall. Students throw to a partner using the partner pattern.	
The student is taught the correct catching technique.	Students practice throwing and catching using the partner pattern.	
The student is taught to start sprints with a quick start.	Taught to all individuals through the large-group pattern.	
The student is taught to execute the overarm throw with a variety of velocities.	Students practice throwing and catching with a partner in the partner pattern.	
The student is taught to catch balls coming at various speeds.	Students practice throwing and catching with a partner.	
The student is taught to move quickly to a designated spot.	Taught to all individuals through the large-group pattern.	

44

The student is taught to catch throws of different levels and various degrees of accuracy.

The student is taught to throw accurately with a variety of velocities.

The student is taught to catch and continue into a throw.

The student is taught to catch and continue into throws of different velocities.

The student is taught to move in various directions and make the appropriate catch.

The student is taught to move in various directions to get to the ball, catch it, and in continued motion, throw accurately to a designated spot with the needed velocity.

Students practice throwing and catching using the partner pattern.

Students practice throws of various velocities with a partner at various infield positions.

Practicing with a partner the students catch and continue into a smooth and accurate throw.

The student plays different infield and outfield positions and makes various throws.

The student takes different defensive positions and fields a variety of batted balls.

The student participates in team infield and outfield drills.

In a game situation, the student moves to the ball, catches it, and throws accurately to a designated spot.

within a skill is to provide the student with a sequence of moves, usually from the simple to the complex. Therefore the instructor must identify the various stages of a skill through which students progress. An example of a complete progression for teaching a skill is shown in Figure 3.2. The skill presented is that of kicking a ball. Each step builds upon the previous step. It should be noted that each step is a complete skill in itself, and that each step is more complex than the previous one. Each step in the progression prepares the student to attempt the next one.

The progression for teaching single skills, or combinations of skills, may also be approached from the standpoint of using performance objectives. After the performance objective is identified, the instructor lists the various stages leading to the correct performance of the objective. Next the stages are structured so that the student practices them in progressive steps. In Figure 3.3, the performance objective, "in a game, the student will be able to move to meet the ball, catch it, and throw to a designated spot," has been identified. Then in a sequence of progressively more difficult tasks, the student is taught to run, throw, catch, and move, until in the last step of the progression, the performance objective is performed satisfactorily by the student. Again it should be noted that each step is a complete movement experience, moving the student toward the satisfaction of the performance objective.

Intra Sport Progression

In the previous paragraphs we have observed how there should be progression in the teaching of a single sport skill or a combination of sports skills. However, most sport skills are not employed singly but are part of an organized game or sport, and any particular skill must be learned in conjunction with numerous other skills. Furthermore, the entire group of individual skills comprising any one sport must be incorporated into the playing of that game or sport. Fundamentals, rules, strategy, and means of organized participation must be learned.

In teaching any sport, then, the instructor must identify the skills and body of knowledge the students are to learn, and plan the correct progression. Most often the progression should begin with presenting the students with the concept as a whole, so that they may comprehend the task to be accomplished. This may be accomplished in a variety of ways. The concept may be introduced by presenting a demonstration performed by the teacher, a student, or someone from outside the class. A film which illustrates the performance of the complete task may be used to introduce the concept. There are some instances in which the concept may be presented by having the students perform the activity even though they are limited in their capabilities. Once the concept of the activity is understood, the students may work through the remainder of the progression of the complete activity which they have now conceptualized.

Figure 3.4 presents an intra sport progression in tennis. This progression should not be considered the same as a unit of instruction and, in reality, may span two or more units. Various tennis teachers will disa-

---

TENNIS PROGRESSION

---

1. Present the concept of tennis through a film, demonstration, or even having the students attempt to rally the ball back and forth over the net.
2. Introductory activities such as dribbling ball with racket and bouncing ball in air.
3. Forehand grip.
4. Forehand drive from a position standing sideways to the target.
5. Ready position.
6. Forehand drive from the ready position.
7. Lead-up game using only the forehand drive.
8. Backhand grip.
9. Backhand drive from a position standing sideways to the target.
10. Backhand drive from the ready position.
11. Lead-up game using only the forehand and backhand drives.
12. In a formal setting, cover the rules and scoring system in tennis. This will prepare the students for playing the complete game of tennis.
13. Service stance and grip.
14. Basic serve.
15. Lead-up game using the serve, forehand drive, and backhand drive.
16. Net volley.
17. Beginning strategy for tennis.
18. Games of tennis using all skills known and all rules.
19. Lob.
20. Half volley.
21. Overhand smash.
22. Advanced serves.
23. Games of tennis using all skills known and all rules.

Figure 3.4   Sample intra sport progression.

gree about the exact order in which specific skills should be learned, so the order presented in this figure is simply an example of one possible progression. There are several important points to be derived from this example. It should first be noted that the total concept of tennis is presented before students perform any specific skills. This will enable them to progress toward a final goal as they practice individual skills. Each skill is presented as a complete skill in itself, which prepares students for completion of the next step in the progression if the steps are an actual advancement. For example, having students hit a forehand drive while standing in a side position to the net or fence is a complete skill, but it also prepares the students to perform the forehand drive while standing facing the net in the ready position. On the other hand, it is a matter of opinion as to whether the forehand drive or volley should be taught first. Where there is no clear cut progression involved the teacher should determine which skill will provide the earliest success.

Another idea in this progression is that specific skills may be presented periodically in the form of lead-up games. Each lead-up game involves more skills than its predecessor, but each one is considered "tennis" at that point in the progression. At the completion of the progression the students are playing tennis in its complete form.

Intra Program Progression

The third type of progression presented is that of progression within the program, or more specifically, within the physical education curriculum. Any unit of work presented to physical education students should be identified as to its difficulty. If a unit of work in soccer is presented to a class that has no previous instruction in that sport, it should be identified as "beginning soccer." If a second experience in soccer is presented to the same students in a succeeding year, it should be presented at a level that is more difficult than the first. The students taking soccer for a second time should no more be burdened with a repeat of the first experience than beginning students should be confused with the strategy and tactics of competitive soccer during their original introduction to the sport.

The task of the physical educator, then, is to identify the skills and knowledges appropriate for the beginner, intermediate, and advanced performer. They are then appropriately incorporated in the correct levels, and presented to the class that is enrolled in that level of difficulty. An appropriate progression to be used within the program of gymnastics, in which three levels of difficulty are to be taught, may be found in Figure 3.5.

Level I	Level II	Level III
The student will learn proper warm-up exercises. The student will be able to perform the basic body positions when called by the correct terminology (these include the squat/tuck, straddle, stoop/pike, wolf, and stretched/layout). The student will be exposed to the following skills and skill groups;		

Balances
  tri pod
  tip-up
	Balances
	  squat stand
	  head stand
		Balances
		  headstand variations
		  handstand

Rolls
  forward shoulder
  forward squat
  forward straddle
  backward rocker
  backward shoulder
  backward squat
  backward straddle
	Rolls
	  forward stoop
	  squat dive
	  headstand
	  backward stoop
	  backward to lunge
		Rolls
		  handstand
		  standing dive
		  running dive
		  backward to headstand
		  backward to extension
		  backward to fish-flop

Cartwheels
  elementary
  bent knee
  side to side
  lunge to lunge
	Cartwheels
	  far arm
	  near arm
	  step in
	  roundoff
		Cartwheels
		  hurdle
		  dive
		  run, hurdle, roundoff

Landing and recovering from falls.
  Landing from ground through waist high heights.
  Recovering from falls from ground to waist high heights.
	Landing and recovering from falls.
	  Landing from waist to chest high heights.
	  Recovering from falls from chest high heights.
		Landing and recovering from falls.
		  Landing from one foot above chest high heights.
		  Recovering from falls from one foot above chest high heights.

PROGRESSION FROM ONE LEVEL TO ANOTHER

Figure 3.5   Intra program progression for selected tumbling skills.

RATE OF PROGRESSION

Any consideration of the concept of progression must attend to the fact that all students do not learn at the same rate. If a teacher is presenting cognitive or movement material, when a specified amount of time has elapsed, some students will be ready for the next concept and some will not. Often good teaching methodology demands that a portion of, the class spend more time on a specified concept or movement, than do other members of the same class. Thus, we see that progression is a matter of individual progress rather than class progress.

An equally important fact for the physical educator to keep in mind is that not all students start at the same level in the planned progression. In teaching the steps involved in a tennis progression, such as the one found in Figure 3.4, some students in the class will enter that unit already possessing the knowledge or ability to successfully perform the first few steps. They will then begin their progression starting at the next step. We see, then, that in this instance the progression experienced by members of the class will vary from student to student.

PROGRESSION FOR COGNITIVE LEARNING

Most of the previous discussion in this chapter has dealt with developing progressions for teaching motor skills. This was appropriate because much time in physical education should rightfully be devoted to the development of good motor skills. However, there are specific cognitive aspects of physical education that must be taught directly. Students should be taught knowledges such as game rules, scoring, and safety. They should learn to apply various strategies to the actual performance of sport skills. In addition, there are many principles of structure and function of the human body that need to be included in the physical education program.

The development of effective teaching progressions in the cognitive domain are essential if quality learning is to occur. Bloom and associates (1956) have presented one form of progression in the cognitive domain in their taxonomy of educational objectives. The domain is sub-divided into two major categories consisting of knowledge, and intellectual skills and abilities. It may be noted that each major category is further divided into classifications of intellectual behavior. The various divisions of behaviors are presented in a hierarchical manner from intellectual behaviors of a low order of complexity to a higher order. The lowest order behavior is knowledge, which is defined as simple recall of information. The domain then progresses through comprehension, application, analysis, synthesis, and evaluation. In addition to being hierarchical, the domain is thought to be cumulative. That is, there is a dependency of each level of behavior upon mastery of the lower order levels.

Sometimes physical education teachers are so dominated by movement experiences that we do not give sufficient thought to cognitive learning. The two concepts outlined in Bloom's taxonomy (hierarchical and cumulative) should be incorporated into progressions for cognitive learning. Lower order information should be presented before higher order. This would involve proceeding from easy concepts to those more difficult. It may also involve proceeding from single component concepts to multi-component concepts. These require students to not only understand factual information, but also to understand relationships between the pieces of information. The dependency of each level of intellectual behavior upon mastery of lower levels must also be considered. This simply means that cognitive experiences build upon the students' having learned intellectual concepts previously presented.

SUMMARY

Each teacher should plan and organize practice sessions which accomplish the objectives and goals of physical education through a series of skills that are progressively ordered and developmentally sound. Teaching that follows progressions results in the best possible learning. Teaching with progression aids the teacher in presenting the subject as clearly as possible. It also allows students to enjoy successful experiences while their safety is maximized.

Several factors affect the development of skill progressions. These include the type of skill that is to be learned, the requirements of the skill, and the necessary prerequisites. Each factor should be examined to determine its relationship in the development of the skill progression.

There are several ways in which the concept of progression may be approached. Each approach should enable skill development to be progressive or additive. These approaches include proceeding from simple to complex, stationary to moving and self-paced to externally paced. Types of progression should include these within their planning. The three types of progressions presented are the intra skill, the intra sport, and the intra program. They are not independent of each other but should be used concurrently.

Additionally the physical education teacher should present cognitive learning experiences in a progressive manner. In the same way that mastery of lower level motor skills leads to higher level skill mastery, students who learn simple concepts first are more receptive to those which are more complex.

SELECTED READINGS AND REFERENCES

Adler, Jack, "Stages of Skill Acquisition: A Guide for Teachers," *Motor Skills: Theory into Practice*, 1981, 5, pp. 75-80.

Bloom, B., et al., *Taxonomy of educational objectives, Handbook I: The Cognitive Domain*, David McKay Co., Inc., New York, 1956.

Caskey, Sheila R., "A Task Analysis Approach to Teaching," *JOPERD*, January, 1982, pp. 59-60.

Corbin, Charles, "First Things First, But Don't Stop There," *JOPERD*, June, 1981, pp. 12-13.

Gentile, A. M., "A Working Model of Skill Acquisition with Application to Teaching," *QUEST*, 1972, 17, pp. 3-23.

Riley, Marie, "Developing Skillful Games Players: Consistency Between Beliefs and Practice," *Motor Skills: Theory into Practice*, 1981, 5, pp. 123-133.

Safrit, Margaret, *Evaluation in Physical Education*, Prentice-Hall, Inc., Englewood Cliffs, New Jersey, 1981.

Photo by David Brittain

53

Photo by David Brittain

PLANNING THE DAILY LESSON

The most important ingredient required of a physical educator who wishes to be a competent teacher is to have a "professional" attitude, for this affects everything that follows. However, successful planning for the daily lesson comes in a very close second. One might even say that expert planning is part of the requirement to being a real professional. Lesson planning is essentially an experience in anticipatory teaching. It is living through, in advance, mentally and emotionally, the classroom experience as the teacher visualizes it.

TYPES OF PLANNING

It is through careful planning that the teacher leads the students to the stated objectives by providing appropriate experiences in the proper sequence. Planning for teaching may be divided into curriculum planning, unit planning, and lesson planning. Only lesson planning will be dealt with in depth in this book, but a brief reference to each of the other types of planning is warranted.

Curriculum Planning

Curriculum planning is the least specific type of planning. It is generally considered to be the planning of objectives and the types of learning experiences used to meet the objectives over a period of several years. The curriculum may be planned for the entire physical education program (grades K-12), the elementary school physical education program (grades K-6), the junior high school physical education program (grades 7-9), or the senior high school physical education program (grades 9-12).

Unit Planning

Most physical education programs are built upon the unit concept. That is, instruction is given for a period of a few weeks which is clustered around a central theme of interest. This theme may be an activity; i.e., volleyball or tennis, or it may be a concept such as physical fitness or Olympic competition. Unit planning encompasses a detailed preparation of objectives, learning experiences, teaching methods, media, equipment, and the evaluation to be utilized in the unit of concern.

Lesson Planning

Lesson planning consists of the detailed planning that must be done for a single lesson. The remainder of this chapter will deal with this very important type of planning.

LEVELS OF OBJECTIVES

The first step in planning at any particular level is a review of the appropriate objectives. Objectives are found on three levels which coincide with the three types of planning. The three levels of objectives are developmental, performance, and lesson.

Developmental Objectives

Developmental objectives were discussed in Chapter 1. By way of review, listed by title, the developmental objectives are:
1. Organic development.
2. Neuromuscular development.

3. Perceptual-Motor development.
4. Intellectual development.
5. Social-Emotional development.

Performance Objectives

Performance objectives are specific statements of observable and measurable behaviors that the teacher expects the students to accomplish. Refer back to Chapter 1 for a more detailed discussion of performance objectives.

Lesson Objectives

Each day's lesson should be approached with meaning and purpose. Every word that is spoken and every movement made should focus on the objectives for the day. These specific objectives, stated for the single lesson, are called *lesson objectives.* They may be thought of as statements which give focus and direction to the instruction by the teacher and the learning by the student. Lesson objectives will be completed by the end of the lesson, but, unlike performance objectives, they are not stated with specific performance levels. Perhaps some examples of lesson objectives contrasted with performance objectives will best clarify their purpose.

Unit — Basketball

Performance objective — Each student will, by the end of the unit, make five out of ten lay-ups with the non-dominant hand when shooting from the appropriate side of the basket.

Lesson objective — Each student will continue to practice and improve upon shooting the lay-up with the non-dominant hand.

The lesson objective calls for continued practice on the lay-up shot using the non-dominant hand with the aim being improvement. The expectation is that this improvement for the day will lead toward the accomplishment of the performance objective by the end of the unit.

There exists a relationship between the type of planning and the level of objective. This relationship can be shown in the following manner:

Type of planning	*Level of objective*
Curricular planning	Developmental objectives
Unit planning	Performance objectives
Lesson planning	Lesson objectives

As can be seen, broad curricular planning encompasses developmental objectives to guide the selection of concepts and activities to incorporate in the total program of physical education. Unit planning is based upon the type and level of performance desired from the students at the completion of the unit. Hence, performance objectives are consistent with and lead toward satisfaction of the broad developmental objectives. The lesson planning process is built upon specific experiences which are aimed at satisfying the lesson objectives. The lesson objectives, of necessity, do not always meet terminal behavior. They often only lead toward the behavior desired at the completion of a unit. The interdependency of the three levels of objectives is shown as:

Satisfaction of lesson objectives	leads to	Satisfaction of performance objectives	leads to	Satisfaction of developmental objectives

NEED FOR PLANNING

Each lesson taught, and every period spent in a physical education class, is to accomplish something positive in the education of the students experiencing it. The reason that planning is required is to identify two concepts:

1) what the teacher wishes to accomplish during a particular class period, and (2) what methodologies will be employed to be successful. Years ago many physical education classes were merely play periods. More recently a large number have been simply exercise periods. The modern concept of a physical education class is that it has rich potential to educate in many ways.

Whether or not a lesson is successful is largely dependent upon the planning that has been put forth. Teachers, both experienced and inexperienced, should carefully plan each day's lesson to gain the maximum from their own abilities and to extract the best learning efforts from their students. It would be improper to assume that the experienced teacher needs to do the same amount of formal planning as the novice teacher. The experienced teacher has perhaps been "down the road" many times and has many ideas tucked away to be called forth upon demand. The novice teacher does not have that pocketfull of knowledge and experience from which to draw. The new teacher, therefore, must dedicate himself to the arduous task of detailed lesson planning.

Just as it would be improper to think the experienced teacher needs

58

to spend the same amount of time planning as the novice teacher, it would be equally improper to think the experienced teacher does not need to plan at all. The same thought process must occur, but the same amount need not be written down. Whereas the student teacher and first year teacher may go into class with a two-page lesson plan, the five-year veteran teacher may appear with a five-by-eight inch card containing notes to guide the day's lesson.

Another thought needs to be injected here to show the need for expert planning, and that is the great deal of heterogeniety seen in most classes. Typically classes include both boys and girls; mature students and immature students; those motor-gifted, and those with little motor ability; students acutely interested in sport and the world of human performance, and those whose interests lie elsewhere. To teach a lesson where objectives are met with such a heterogeneous class requires a great deal of planning.

And finally, when we analyze the variety of environments, facilities, time allotments, and equipment and supplies available, it isn't difficult to see that detailed, specific planning is necessary for each class period.

VALUES OF LESSON PLANNING

Regardless of the age or experience of the teacher, prepared lesson plans serve the teacher and students in several ways. The values of a written lesson plan may be identified as:
1. It helps the teacher organize his or her thinking.
2. It is an aid against forgetting.
3. It helps the teacher feel secure and confident.
4. It prevents over-emphasis on one area to the detriment of a second area.
5. It helps insure the availability of needed materials.
6. It reduces wasted motion and wasted time.
7. It helps in providing continuity from one lesson to another.
8. It aids in the making of future plans.
9. It provides a record of progress along the way.
10. It serves as a basis for evaluation.

CONSTRUCTION OF THE LESSON PLAN

The plan that is necessary and that is to be developed on these pages is the written lesson plan. It might sound redundant at first to say written lesson plan. But the truth is that the vast majority of physical education teachers approach their daily classes without one. Questioned on this they remark that they know what they are going to do, and they have thought it out ahead of time and have the plan "in their head." It is our belief that in order to realize a preconceived list of objectives within the complexities of a heterogeneous group and all the variables that exist, a written plan is absolutely necessary. One of the best proofs of the need for a written plan may be seen by observing athletic coaches. In many years of observing athletic coaches, none have been seen going to practice sessions without a written lesson plan. Knowing they must put their product on public exhibition once or twice a week motivates them to plan as accurately as possible. This of course means a written practice plan. If physical educators are as serious about the quality of their finished product, they too, must have written plans.

The daily lesson plan should be constructed after the previous lesson has been completed. Consideration should be given to: what has been accomplished; individual problems of students in the class; available equipment, supplies, and facilities; time allotment; and the objectives to be accomplished. All of these factors need to be considered, as many of them change from one class period to the next.

Lesson plans will vary from teacher to teacher and from day to day. This would seem obvious since the plan is developed for a specific class for a specific lesson. Even though lesson plans may change from day to day, the following procedures and contents should be constant:

1. Lesson plans, no matter how extensive, should be written. The amount of time and effort put into planning will be in inverse proportion to the knowledge and experience of the teacher.
2. Begin the planning process by planning the objectives for the day. The objectives should reflect the specific needs of the class and should precede the planning of any activities and class experiences.
3. Include provisions for experiences to be taught, organization of students, formations, time allotment, sequence of material presentations, and other pertinent pieces of information.
4. The majority of time in most classes, and at least some time in every class, should be devoted to instruction and learning. The plan is being prepared for physical education, not physical recreation.
5. Include in the lesson plan some provision for evaluation of the lesson, the students, and the teacher.

Each lesson plan should consist of three separate periods of time. The three time periods are the set, body, and closure. The *set* is the beginning of the class and serves to establish the mood for the class and create an interest in the lesson. The set could range from a short film about a sport to a brief discussion of current events in a sport to a demonstration by the teacher, a class member, or an invited guest.

The *body* of the lesson is by far the major part of the lesson. Included in this part of the lesson are the demonstration, explanation, practice, and usually the performance elements of the lesson.

The *closure* is the culmination part of the lesson. It is a way of concluding the lesson and perhaps providing a lead-in for the set on the following day. The closing, or summary section of the period, is usually about three or four minutes in length. The students should cease whatever activity they are doing and reassemble themselves with the teacher. The teacher can then ask the group if there are any questions pertaining to what was taught that day. If there are no questions the teacher may ask some predesigned questions to see if the desired learning took place. Also, at this time the main points of the day's lesson can briefly be reviewed. Depending upon the imagination of the teacher, there are many ways to employ closure in the lesson.

PLANNING FOR PRE-CLASS TIME

In a secondary school there may be a variation of one to twelve minutes in the time that the individual student reports to class. The authors have observed classes where students arriving early have sat on the sidelines and waited with nothing constructive to do for several minutes. This is a tremendous waste of time, and it contributes to the student's dislike of the class. This pre-class time should be considered part of the daily lesson plan. It should be planned for two reasons: (1) to make it a safe time, and (2) to make it a learning time. Suggestions to help plan for the pre-class time include; give students handouts to read, have students read task cards posted on the wall, observe audio-visual material, begin individual conditioning, begin practicing a skill learned yesterday, have the students go to specific teaching stations, and have question and answer periods.

PROVISIONS FOR INDIVIDUAL DIFFERENCES

Nothing indicates poor teaching more than to have all students in the class practice the same material (drill or skill) for the same time, at the same speed, and using the same level of difficulty. With thirty students in the class it is possible to have just as many different levels of skill. We know that it isn't possible to have thirty different skill levels organized profitably in a class with one teacher. What does work well, however, is to plan for at least three groups; the beginner, intermediate, and skilled.

This three-in-one concept may be developed without much difficulty. The first step is to plan a lesson for a particular age class in the appropriate activity. Secondly, within this lesson, the teacher plans for the beginner, the intermediate, and the highly skilled. Third, plans are made for the special student who may have a physical handicap, the student who is behind his classmates in motor development, or at the other end of the spectrum, the student who may be a highly gifted motor performer. Failure to structure the day's lesson so that it considers all of the above students indicates a weak lesson plan.

SELECTION OF METHODOLOGY

It is a well accepted fact within educational circles that the use of a variety of teaching methods or techniques will enhance the students' interest. Nothing will dampen the enthusiasm and interest of students faster than to do "the same old thing" day after day in the class. Certainly this is true in the physical education classroom — be it in the pool, gymnasium, or play field.

This discussion cannot specify the method to use but it can urge the teacher to consider and use the great variety of methods that are available. A list of methods from which the teacher may select two or three for use in a single lesson are:
1. Verbal presentation of a concept by the teacher (lecture).
2. Demonstration of a skill or task to be learned.
3. Explanation of the performance criteria for a particular activity.
4. Student project (individual or group).
5. Laboratory experiment.
6. Contract teaching.
7. Independent study.
8. Team teaching.
9. Library research.
10. Guest teacher or helper.
11. Self-testing activities.
12. Problem solving activities.
13. Use of competitive activities.
14. Use of non-competitive activities.
15. Use of audio-visual materials.

The methods presented above are only meant as a sampling for the teacher. Some of these and others are further discussed in Chapter 6.

SELECTING A LESSON PLAN FORMAT

In writing the lesson plan the teacher must use a format that is complete, lends itself to usability, and represents a design with which the teacher is comfortable and familiar. There is no one format recommended for all teachers. The teacher should design or adopt one that is liked and preferred by the individual. No matter which format is selected by the teacher, the following suggestions may prove helpful.

1. Duplicated copies of the form should be available so that each lesson plan simply requires filling in spaces. A ready supply of these forms should be available in the teacher's desk.
2. Design the plan so that the activities of the teacher and students are aligned longitudinally to show what each person in the class is doing at any specific time.
3. Design the plan so that the activities of the teacher and students are shown in their proper sequence going down the page.
4. Time allotments should be viewed as approximations and should set parameters but not dictate.
5. Words and phrases should be used rather than complete sentences to guide the teacher through the lesson. Phrases can be read at a glance, whereas, sentences will require the teacher to divert attention from the class.
6. Symbols should be used to represent students (X), teacher (T), and student assistants (A) in showing formations, drills, and alignments.
7. The lesson objectives are specific to the lesson and should be reflected by the lesson planned.
8. The amount of information on the lesson plan should always be adequate and appropriate to the experience and specific knowledge of the teacher. It is far better to have more information than is needed rather than to have less than is needed.
9. Evaluation should be provided for the lesson, students, and teacher. This evaluation will aid immensely in designing future lessons on the same subject. A specific space for this should be provided on the form.

Sample Lesson Plan Format A

Lesson plan format A is shown in Figure 4-1. Format A requires that two separate pages be prepared; the one with the "aim of physical education" shown at the top of the page, and the one with the closure and evaluation shown at the bottom of the page. In analyzing this format, several subdivisions must be discussed.

Activity. This is to note the activity, sport, and experience planned for the day. An example might be tennis, and the word "Tennis" would be written in the blank.

Level. This refers to the level of difficulty for which the lesson is planned. The teacher writes in beginning, intermediate, or advanced. One of the most common errors in teaching is for the teacher to ignore progression.

Format A

DAILY LESSON PLAN

Activity _____ Level _____

Composition of the Class_____ Day of Unit_____

The aim of physical education is to develop *each* student to *their* optimum, physically, mentally, socially, and emotionally, through human movement, so they may become an effective citizen in a democratic society.

Developmental Objectives of Physical Education:
   A.   Organic Development.
   B.   Neuromuscular Development.
   C.   Perceptual-Motor Development.
   D.   Intellectual Development.
   E.   Social-Emotional Development.

Lesson Objectives:

Facility Needed:

Equipment and Supplies Needed: (Number of each).

Activity	Time	Methods, Techniques, and Teaching Procedures
Closure		

EVALUATION:
   A .   Of Students:

   B.   Of Teacher:

   C.   Of Lesson:

Figure 4-1   Sample daily lesson plan format.

64

Composition of the Class. This item denotes the grade level of the class, and if it is coeducational.

Day of the Unit. This item is simply an aid to the teacher in keeping track of where they are in the alloted number of days for each planned experience.

The Aim of Physical Education. Some educators believe that most teaching that lacks quality does so because the teacher is not aware of, or forgets, what is trying to be accomplished. The statement of the aim, dittoed near the top of each lesson plan, serves as a constant reminder that the teacher is trying to develop all students to their maximum through the experiences planned for that day.

Developmental Objectives of Physical Education. The suggestion is made to list the developmental objectives immediately after the aim in order to provide one further step to aid the teacher in his or her planning. Since the aim is a lofty and philosophical statement, the developmental objectives provide a connecting link between it and the day's lesson.

Lesson Objectives. In this space teachers write what they hope to teach, or accomplish in this single lesson. Unlike the developmental objectives, which are the same every day, the lesson objectives change each day. In a tennis unit, for example, the lesson objectives for a day might be to teach the stroke and footwork for the backhand. It would then not be a lesson objective for any other day.

Facility Needed. The major installation needed for the lesson is identified. The teacher will also be reminded to reserve it, or make arrangements for its use, if it happens to be one not regularly used by the school, or if it is sometimes used by other components of the school. Examples of facilities are pools, tracks, gymnasiums, and golf courses.

Equipment and Supplies. It is important to specify what pieces of equipment and what supplies are needed in order to have them ready; be sure they are serviceable, and have enough of them. This item is directly related to the methods or teaching techniques the teacher plans to use. For example, if the class is to be divided into five squads, enough equipment or supplies are needed to equip each of the squads. If a partner ball throwing experience is planned, a ball is needed for each pair of students.

Activity. This is to identify what will occupy the students for a certain length of time. It could be to practice on ground balls, to engage in flexibility exercises, to compete in two-on-two basketball, or to listen to the teacher explain the safety factors in weight lifting.

Time. In denoting the time allocated to each activity, the teacher is parcelling out portions of the period appropriate for each phase of the lesson. It needs to be well thought-out. Ten to twelve minutes is enough for any phase in order to prevent boredom. Written on the lesson plan should be the "clock" time, and not the words, ten minutes. In the middle of the class, with all the attendant diversions, the teacher does not need to stop and figure out when a session should start or end.

Methods, Techniques, and Teaching Procedures. This is the most important, and the largest part, of the lesson plan. Here the teacher decides such things as, will there be a demonstration, will there be a skill practice session, what formation will be used, the involvement of student leaders, the division of the class into stations, units of competition, caring for individual differences, and other possible methods the teacher may employ.

Closure. The closure is to end the class in an orderly fashion, and review the most important points covered in the lesson.

Evaluation. After the lesson the teacher makes notes relative to the effectiveness of the lesson. Comments are written about the students, observations made, and feelings about what has just happened. These comments are especially valuable for improving the lesson the next time it is taught, and as an evaluation of both the teaching method and the content of the lesson.

Sample Lesson Plan Format B

Lesson plan Format B, shown in Figure 4-2, includes almost all of the same important elements found in Format A. This lesson plan format is also designed so the teacher will have duplicated copies of the form on hand. Planning the lesson then requires that the teacher fill in the blanks and spaces for the various aspects of the daily lesson. Many of the same meanings are repeated so only four new designations are needed to explain Format B.

Teacher Activity. All of the verbal and physical activities of the teacher are included in this column. The explanation, demonstrations, and activities that the teacher presents are described. For example, the teacher would write "lead exercises" in the column and then list the exercises to be led and the number or duration of each.

Student Activity. The particular activity of the students is recorded in this column. In the example used, the teacher would write "do exercises as led by teacher" in the column. The information included here would be aligned with the appropriate entry in the teacher activity column.

Formation. The formation used in a particular activity or drill is shown in this column. In the above example, a sketch identifying students with the letter X, would show the students in a circle, spread formation, or squad formation, and the position of the teacher would be shown with the letter T. The formation shown in this column is lined up with the appropriate entries in the two previous columns. A new entry

Format B

DAILY LESSON PLAN

Activity _____ Level _____ Day of Unit _____

Lesson Objectives:

Equipment:

Time	Teacher Activity	Student Activity	Formation	Notes

Evaluation:

Figure 4-2   Sample daily lesson plan format.

for formation needs to be made only when a new formation is used. Otherwise, it is assumed the same formation is used for the new activity.

Notes. This column is available for the teacher to include personal notes such as safety tips and teaching keys or to write down notes as the class progresses.

SUMMARY

Any successful endeavor requires planning. For the physical educator to ignore this is a serious offense, yet use of the written lesson plan is circumvented all too often. Beginning teachers, as well as veteran teachers, must first think through and write down the necessary information which will guide them and their students through the planned experiences.

All lesson planning must begin with the development of lesson objectives. These objectives guide the teacher in selecting the proper learning experiences which will meet the objectives. The teacher must plan for various time frames within the lesson, including the pre-class time as well as the more formal class time. Also, the various skill levels within the class must be given consideration. To put this planning into a functional tool to aid in teaching, the teacher must select a usable format for the lesson plan.

Evaluation is the means by which the teacher can monitor the progress of the students as well as his or her own peformance, thereby constantly improving as a teacher. Therefore, the teacher must make provisions in the lesson planning process to evaluate the students, lesson, and teaching process.

69

MAXIMIZING STUDENT PARTICIPATION

5

There must be a way
to increase participation!

The physical education class begins and after ten minutes of opening calisthenics the teacher divides the class of fifty-five students into eleven basketball teams of five each. Two teams were selected to take their places on the floor and the teacher announces that they will scrimmage full-court against each other until one team scores twice. The loser will then leave the court and a new team will come out to challenge the winners. The game will proceed in the same manner, with the loser of each game leaving the floor. The forty-five students who are not involved in the scrimmage are perched on top of a long, rolled-up wrestling mat that lies along one side of the gymnasium.

In another physical education class the teacher is presenting a track and field unit. Today's activity includes the long jump. The first five minutes the students are gathered around the teacher while the correct technique of the jump is explained. The students are then arranged in a single file line behind the approach to the long jump pit and they take turns at the jump.

Initially it appears that these classes were well taught. The students were given instruction, warmed-up and then proceeded with the lesson. The class was organized and orderly.

Let's take a closer look. In the first example the teams, winners and losers, shuttle on and off the court for about five minutes when a more talented team than the others appears on the floor. The new team wins each scrimmage for the rest of the period, with the remaining fifty students sitting on the wrestling mat until the time arrives for their team to go on the floor once again. Except for the talented team each player is involved in activity for approximately four minutes during the entire portion of class that follows the exercise period. During their time on the floor it is possible that some individuals may never handle the ball before the game is over and they leave the court.

In the second example, if we watch closely during the thirty minutes spent on this activity, each student gets four chances to jump and is involved in activity for about forty seconds.

The two incidents described above are actual class sessions that have been observed. Unfortunately, they are not unique to a particular school or teacher. Rather, they represent the type of class organization and teaching that occurs in far too many schools on a regular basis. The teachers of these two classes were guilty of a common error in teaching physical education — they did not maximize participation for their students. Limited participation, due to long lines and sitting while others play, harms students by not allowing adequate advancement and could contribute to behavior problems due to boredom.

NEED FOR MAXIMUM PARTICIPATION

Maximum participation by the students brings about several benefits. The most important benefits are to be found in increased student learning, more enjoyment by the students, and a greater contribution to their health-related fitness.

Increasing Student Learning

Learning is composed of a rather complex series of events that occur within and to the students. The amount of learning that will occur is influenced by numerous factors including the teacher, environment, student capability, interest, and effort. The student will bring to the learning task a specific ability and interest. It is now in the hands of the teacher to organize the subject matter and environment in such a way as to bring about learning by the student. The way the teacher presents the subject matter in the form of demonstrations and explanations is very important. Even more important, especially involving motor skills, is the manner in which the teacher organizes the practice and performance aspects of the lesson for the students. Motor skills are truly "learned by doing." It would seem rather obvious then, that to learn well, the students must be given the opportunity to actually do the skill being learned. The more times the student can attempt the skill, under the watchful eye of the teacher, the greater the chance that learning will take place. Therefore, organizing the class for maximum student participation will increase the opportunities for learning.

Improving Student Enjoyment

Students come to their physical education class with an expectation of participating in sport and activity. Too often they are disappointed by the lack of activity they actually experience. Being the fifth player on a basketball team that uses only four players, standing in long lines awaiting their turn on the balance beam, and waiting for the teacher to finish roll call will dampen the enthusiasm of most students. Every effort should be made by the teacher to increase participation opportunities for each student so that they will be able to enjoy the experience.

Contributing to Health-Related Fitness

The positive relationship between physical activity and physical fitness is unquestionable. The important thing to remember is that the relationship is between physical fitness and activity — not simply being in the class. The inactive student will not enjoy the benefits of enhanced physical fitness. Therefore, the teacher should strive for maximum participation which may contribute to health-related fitness.

DETERMINING THE AMOUNT OF STUDENT PARTICIPATION

One can easily be mislead concerning the amount of participation in a class. A class may be observed in which there appears to be a lot of movement taking place because various students are running here and there and throwing objects in a seemingly organized fashion. The participation should not be measured by the amount of movement by the class as a whole, but rather by the amount of movement by each individual. A teacher would do well to have an observer use a stopwatch to time the actual amount of movement of a few individuals within the class. The observer simply starts the watch when the student begins movement and stops the watch when the movement ceases and continues to do this throughout the period. If this is repeated on three or four different students, the teacher will have a reasonably accurate estimate of how much participation actually occurs in the class. Another excellent means of evaluating the participation of the students may be accomplished by video-taping a class and then studying the tape.

It may surprise the reader to know how little time is often devoted to movement by each individual. In our experience we have observed countless classes in which an individual's activity time would be less than five minutes out of a forty-minute class period. This is inexcusable and is largely due to poor class management procedures being employed by the teacher.

MEANS OF INCREASING STUDENT PARTICIPATION

In this description, participation is defined as the active involvement of the student with the equipment and subject matter planned for the class. The passive time spent by the student in the class is not considered participation. The student standing in squad formation while the teacher calls roll is not participating in physical education learning. The student waiting for a turn to practice on a piece of equipment is not an active participant in the class. Even the student passively trotting up and down the basketball floor, but never touching the ball, should not be considered an active participant. Although this student is receiving some movement, he or she is not actively participating in the learning experiences planned for the basketball unit.

There are many ways in which the physical education teacher may increase the active participation by each student in the planned learning experiences. Following are suggestions for increasing the quantity and quality of student participation in seven different areas. It is important for the reader to remember that the concern is with the participation of the individual within the class and not the amount of total group participation.

Streamline Class Management Procedures

Students may be robbed of participation time if an inordinate amount of class time is spent on class management procedures. These procedures are important but are not necessarily learning experiences, so the required time for their accomplishment should be kept to a minimum.

Taking roll. Roll taking procedures should be used which take an absolute minimum of time. The less time used for taking roll, the greater amount of time will be available for student active participation. Roll taking should be limited to no more than thirty seconds of class time. Specific time-saving methods of taking roll are discussed in Chapter 7.

Equipment handling. Setting up, moving, and taking down equipment can use a lot of class time. Participation time can be preserved by setting equipment in position prior to the beginning of class. Moving equipment and taking equipment down can be organized so that the students handle the equipment, thus using a minimum of time. Effective equipment handling will increase the amount of time available for student participation.

Pre-class time. Much participation time may be available before class ever begins. Many students arrive at their physical education class early. If they can immediately begin activity they will be motivated to arrive early every day. This time can be valuable participation time even though it is prior to the actual beginning of the formal class. Structured activity may be planned by the teacher, or the students may simply be given the opportunity for self-improvement participation. More details pertaining to the pre-class time are given in Chapter 4 on lesson planning.

Standardize procedures. Standardizing procedures so that repeated explanation and organizing may be eliminated will save time which may then be used for student participation. Movements of class members which are common from day to day should always be done the same and the students should know what and how they are to do it. Routines for lining up, getting in squads, etc., may be standardized so that time is not lost for such functions on a regular basis.

Avoid the "Let's Play" Plea

One of the primary purposes of physical education is to provide opportunities for students to learn motor skills. These opportunities are reduced when teachers give in to the cry of students to "play the game." Normally the game play is dominated by the better skilled individuals so that the other students don't really have much opportunity to actually do the motor skills involved. The teacher may insure that all students have the opportunity to learn motor skills if the majority of practice sessions are organized in the form of drills and lead-up activities. In this way, each student is guaranteed the chance to perform the skill a number of times before applying it in competition.

Select Appropriate Activities

Some activities are more appropriate than others in providing opportunities for maximum participation. The teacher should, where possible and feasible, select activities that provide for a maximum amount of active participation. The criteria that can guide the teacher in selecting appropriate activities are: (1) How many participants may be active at any one time in this game or activity? (2) How much active movement is involved in the activity? and (3) What are the requirements of the activity for space and equipment?

It must be understood that there may be some activities that the teacher feels should be taught which do not meet the above criteria for maximum participation. This problem can easily be alleviated by utilizing some of the other means of maximizing participation mentioned later in this chapter.

Modify Activities to Increase Participation

Many sports were designed for a very few individuals to participate in a specialized environment using specific equipment. The physical educator, on the other hand, works with large numbers of students in rather confining environments with rather ordinary pieces of equipment. The teacher should not hesitate to modify the rules, equipment, or conduct of a game so that it will increase student participation or make the activity more appropriate for the particular age students involved. A few examples of modifying activities to increase participation are as follows:

1. Allow the softball team at bat to provide their own pitcher to speed up the game.
2. Allow only one pitch in softball and have the batter run whether or not the ball is hit.
3. Play volleyball with eight or nine players on a team.
4. Allow more than three hits on one side of the net in volleyball.
5. Lower the volleyball net for younger students so they can learn the basics of spiking.
6. Lower the basketball rim for younger students so they can have a chance to make a basket and develop good shooting form.
7. Play three-on-three or four-on-four half-court basketball rather than five-on-five full court games, thus increasing the number of players as well as the amount of participation by each individual while on the court.
8. Play tennis with four players on each side of the net.
9. Allow more than two attempts on the tennis serve if you're stressing the serve in a particular lesson.
10. Begin the tennis game with a ground stroke if the serve is not of importance at that particular time.

Make Maximum Use of Facilities

Oftentimes student participation is lost because the instructional facilities are not used to their fullest extent. The teacher should purposefully examine all of the school facilities to determine if there are opportunities not being utilized. The best approach for this would be to identify all facilities and spaces that are available, and then determine how those spaces and facilities may best be used.

Maximize students in available space. The teacher should study the space available and determine if more students should be participating in that space. Increasing the number of participants in an available space eliminates students sitting out and waiting turns, although the teacher must be aware of needed safety precautions.

Use walls, folding doors, and the floor as facilities. As teachers we are sometimes limited in our scope of available facilities. One teacher may see the large folding door down the middle of the gymnasium as a hindrance, whereas, another teacher recognizes that same door as a tennis wall, handball front wall, or a volleyball volley wall. The walls and folded bleachers provide many wonderful aids if they are only used. Lines and targets painted or taped on walls may serve as a tennis net, badminton net, volleyball net, basketball goal, or passing target. The only limitation upon how the walls and other such surfaces may be used is the willingness of the teacher to search for uses. Many teachers view the gymnasium with its four or six baskets as the reason why only six basketballs can be used in a shooting drill, and why only six students can be active at any one time. Short lines on the wall at a height of ten feet provide nice substitutes for baskets. In addition, two students may work on their form in shooting by shooting back and forth to each other completely away from a basket or wall.

Use space not originally designed for physical education. On Friday evening the drama class presents a play on the large stage of the school auditorium. On Monday morning the physical education class may be involved in a wrestling or tumbling unit on that same stage. The hall outside the gymnasium is a passing hall between 10:00 and 10:05. Between 10:05 and 10:45 that same hall has become the site of a vigorous unit in hall hockey. The same hall, in another hour, may be occupied by table tennis or shuffleboard players. These are but a few examples that have been actually observed by the authors where imaginative teachers have refused to let a lack of facilities discourage them from presenting a good, active physical education program. Classrooms are another example of a facility that may be used by the teacher for some modified activity. The teacher should also be aware of the many physical education teaching stations that may be located off campus in the community.

Increase Equipment Where Feasible

A sad sight in a physical education class is four lines of nine students each awaiting a turn to dribble a basketball the length of the court and back. Each student is active for approximately twenty seconds and then stands in line for almost three minutes before receiving another turn. Simply adding two basketballs to the class would reduce the waiting time for each student by one third. Each time another ball is added to the organization it further reduces the waiting time, thereby increasing the active participation for each student.

Optimum quantity of equipment. One must be careful about simply stating that more is always better in relation to pieces of equipment. The teacher should use the greatest quantity of equipment possible within the boundaries of practicality and safety. One should never have so much equipment in use that a hazardous learning environment is created. In the same light, practicality is important to the teacher so that supervision is possible, and the available space allows the quantity of equipment being used. The teacher should always be seeking the optimal quantity of equipment. In a ball handling lesson the class would function best with a ball for each student. For a volleyball passing drill one ball for every two students would be desirable, and when working on a basketball offensive play only one ball for each team would be sufficient. To summarize, the teacher should seek to: (1) use as much equipment as possible as long as it is safe and practical, (2) use more pieces of equipment to reduce waiting time for students, and (3) use the amount of equipment that will lead to the best quantity and quality of learning.

Purchase and modification of equipment. Teachers often complain that they would like to use a lot of pieces of equipment but they simply do not have them available. If this is actually true the teacher must take steps to alleviate the problem. Every avenue should be explored for increasing the equipment available. Some logical sources of equipment might be the school budget, donations of old equipment from parents, community drives to raise money for equipment, earning equipment through advertising promotions such as turning in soup labels, and contacting local businesses such as sporting goods stores, golf corses, and racquet clubs about loaning or donating used or new equipment to the school.

In many instances the problem of too little equipment may be corrected by using equipment not specifically designed for that purpose. Where ball handling skills are involved it is only important that the students have a ball of approximate size and weight. For young children a beach ball may be equal to or superior to a volleyball for learning volleyball skills. A playground ball can be an excellent substitute in many different sports including soccer, speedball, team handball, and basketball. Nets may be replaced by ropes with streamers tied to them for easy identification in volleyball and badminton, bean bags can replace balls when a throwing skill is being developed, broomsticks cut to the proper length

78

can become a beginner's golf club, and plastic balls can replace regulation balls in golf and softball.

These are but a few of the numerous ways that modification of equipment may enhance the participation of the students. There are several books written on the specific topic of modifying equipment which are available for many more ideas and suggestions.

Increase Instructional Stations

An excellent way to increase student participation is to increase the number of instructional stations in the class. This concept involves organizing the students into small groups which practice skills in various locations with each group independent of the other groups. The reader is referred to Chapter 6 for a detailed discussion and several examples of how the small group pattern of teaching may be applied. There are three applications of the small group pattern. They are the multiple station application, the multiple skill application, and the multiple sport application.

The multiple station application. The multiple station application involves dividing the class into several small groups which practice the same skill at different locations in the learning environment. The main advantages in this application are space utilization and the use of many pieces of equipment.

The multiple skill application. The multiple skill application involves dividing the class into several small groups with each group practicing a different skill. This application is very useful in most units. It may be especially useful in such activities as swimming and gymnastics which use equipment that is stationary (diving board), difficult to move, or available in small numbers (parallel bars). Several examples of this arrangement are presented in Chapter 6.

The multiple sport application. The multiple sport application involves teaching a class in which more than one sport or activity is taught concurrently. An example would be teaching archery on one end of the gymnasium, with badminton and table tennis participation on the other end of the gymnasium. The primary reason the teacher would use the multiple sport application would be a shortage of equipment, facilities, or space for a particular sport or activity. Therefore, rather than have many students awaiting their turns with the equipment, there is more than one activity going on at the same time. In this way all students will remain busy, even though they may be working at different locations on different sports. Several additional examples of this application may be found in Chapter 6.

Maximizing Participation in Selected Activities

On the following pages are ideas for maximizing participation in some selected activities. In each activity the ideas presented are based upon one or more of the principles presented in this chapter for increasing active participation time for each student.

Maximizing Participation in Badminton

1. Practice skills against walls while some students are practicing on the courts.
   A. Practice the short serve by hitting toward a line painted or taped on the wall at the height of a badminton net.
   B. Practice the smash and long drop by hitting toward a line painted on the wall. The shuttle is set up by a partner.
   C. Practice the underhand clear and overhead clear by hitting successive shots against the wall.

2. Use multiple-skill drills on one court. Drills of this type use a maximum number of players and therefore require a minimum number of courts.

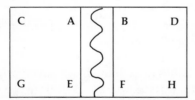

A hits short serve, B hits underhand clear, C hits overhead clear, and D hits overhead clear.
E, F, G, and H duplicate the same series of strokes on their half of the court.

3. Students share equipment in skill drills. These procedures allow practice with a shortage of equipment.

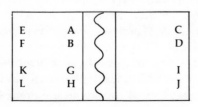

A hits long serve, C hits clear, E hits long drop.
B, D, and F then use the same rackets and repeat the same series of shots.
G, H, I, J, K, and L duplicate the same series of strokes on their half of the court.

4. Use continuous action rotation drills.

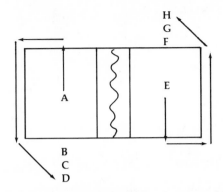

A hits to E and moves off the court to be replaced by B.
E returns to B and moves off the court to be replaced by F.
This rotation continues.

5. Play double-doubles.

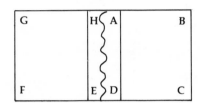

Play a game with four players on each side of the net.

Maximizing Participation in Tennis

1. Practice skills against the tennis fence or rebound wall or against a wall in the gymnasium.
   A. Practice the forehand and backhand by dropping and hitting the ball into the fence.
   B. Practice the serve by tossing and hitting into the fence from a distance of 12-15 feet.
   C. Practice forehand and backhand strokes by consecutively hitting the ball against a rebound tennis wall or a gymnasium wall.

2. Skills may be practiced in large groups.
   A. The teacher may lead the entire class through the practice of strokes without using any tennis balls.
   B. Students may dribble the tennis ball on the court with their rackets.
   C. Students may dribble the tennis ball into the air using the forehand and backhand faces of their rackets.

3. Practice skills with an increased number of participants on a court.
   A. Partners may rally across the court.

```
X | X  X  X | X  X  X | X
I | I  I  I | I  I  I | I
I | I  I  I | I  I  I | I
I | I  I  I | I  I  I | I
I | I  I  I | I  I  I | I
X | X  X  X | X  X  X | X
```

   B. Partners may rally between the net and baseline and also use the
       space between the courts.

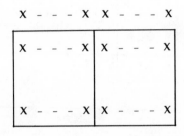

4. Use rotation drills where there is a shortage of space and/or equipment.
   A. Two lines of students may rally across the net and rotate to the
       end of the line.

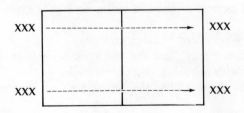

B. Students may practice the volley by tossing and volleying or continuously volleying over the net.

T	H
T	H
T	H
T	H

T = Tosser
H = Hitter

	H	H
	H	H
	H	H
	H	H

C. Students may practice strokes by using the hitter-tosser-retriever arrangement

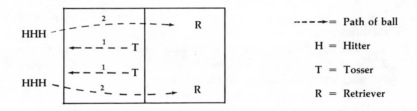

- - - ► = Path of ball

H = Hitter

T = Tosser

R = Retriever

After the hitter has hit two balls they rotate in the following manner: H ⟶ T; T ⟶ R; R ⟶ End of H line.

5. Lead-up games may be used to practice skills in a competitive setting.
   A. Two players may alternately hit one ball against a solid wall in a game similar to racquet ball.
   B. Individuals may continuously hit a ball against a solid wall to see how many can be hit in 30 seconds.
   C. Students may play trio tennis or double-doubles tennis.

Maximizing Participation in Basketball

1. Modify equipment to be used in basketball where there is a shortage.
   A. Use playground balls of approximately the same size as a basket-ball for drills.
   B. Paint or tape marks on the walls to serve as baskets for shooting drills.

C. Play half-court basketball at each available basket rather than full-court.
2. Modify the rules to allow more participation.
   A. Eliminate jump balls. Teams alternate taking the ball out of bounds.
   B. Eliminate free throws. Award a point to a team that is fouled.
   C. Require at least four passes before a shot may be taken to cut down on the domination by one or two students and increase passing practice.
   D. Require that every player on the team handle the ball every two baskets.
3. Concentrate teacher efforts upon instruction.
   A. Practice each skill through the use of drills so each student has an opportunity to learn.
   B. Use the partner pattern of practice so one student is practicing and the partner is observing.
   C. Use the small group pattern for better utilization of the space and facilities.
      1. Tape targets on the wall for passing and shooting practice.
      2. Practice dribbling around cones, chairs, or some other markers in the middle of the floor.
      3. Practice rebounding against the wall.
      4. Use baskets for two-on-two or three-on-three games or for shooting practice.

Maximizing Participation in Volleyball

1. Modify the equipment used in volleyball where there is a shortage.
   A. A rope may be used in place of a net. Bright streamers tied from the rope make it easily seen.
   B. An official volleyball may be replaced by beach balls of the approximate size. This is especially useful for young students.
   C. Large nerf balls can be substituted for official volleyballs.
2. Modify the rules to allow more participation.
   A. Allow players to move into the court to serve if needed to get the ball over the net.
   B. Require from three to five hits on each side of the net.
3. Modify the playing court.
   A. Increase the size of one court and add players if there is more space than necessary for one court but not enough space for two courts.
   B. Increase the number of courts by reducing the size of each court. Although fewer participants will play in each court, the net

result will be an increase in the total number of participants.

C. Set up several courts around the same nets.

Each team plays against every other team at the same time. You may want to use two balls.

4. Use walls, bleachers, and folding doors as practice stations.
   A. Practice the serve by hitting the volleyball against the wall and above a line at the proper net height.
   B. Practice the set and pass by hitting to the wall or bleachers.
   C. Play rotation, competitive lead-up games against a wall or other flat surface or out in the middle of the floor away from the net.

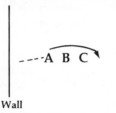

Student A tosses the ball against the wall and goes to the end of the line and the same procedure is followed by each player. This rotation continues as long as the students can maintain control of the ball.

5. Play group lead-up games that do not need a lot of space.
   A. Use one type of pass and continuously pass the ball while the students are in a circle.
   B. Continuously pass a ball to the wall and rotate to end of line.
6. Concentrate the teacher's efforts upon instruction.
   A. Practice each skill through the use of drills so each student has an opportunity to learn.
   B. Use the partner pattern of practice so one student is practicing and the partner is observing.
   C. Use the multiple skill application of the small group practice pattern for better utilization of the space and facilities.
      1. Practice the pass against the wall.
      2. Practice the repeated volley against the wall.
      3. Practice the set next to a rope with a target taped on the floor.
      4. Practice serving against a wall or over a net.
      5. Practice spiking over a net.

Maximizing Participation in Gymnastics

The following ideas can be used to increase student participation during a gymnastics unit. They should be used selectively based upon the size and age of the students, the skill or skills being practiced, the skill level of the students, and the teacher's expertise. Above all, the safety of the students should be considered.

Gymnastics unit
1. Use the multiple skill application of the small group practice pattern to station students on several pieces of equipment.
2. Use the multiple sport application of the small group practice pattern. Gymnastic and other skills taught at the same time would prevent students waiting for their turn on a piece of apparatus.

Tumbling
1. Students may tumble across the width of the mat rather than the length, thus allowing more students to be on a single mat at one time.
2. Mattresses may be used in place of tumbling mats for some skills.
3. Use capable students as spotters in the class to increase the number of performers at one time. Spotting is a skill in itself, so students must be taught how to spot correctly.

Balance beam
1. With some skills, three or four students may safely participate on the beam at one time.
2. Lines on the floor may be used to practice beam skills before they are attempted on the beam. In this way the entire class can work on the same skill at the same time if desired.
3. Carpet strips and 2" x 4" pieces of lumber may be used as substitutes for beams.
4. Mounts and dismounts may be practiced on stacked mats, a sturdy table, vaulting horse or box, or on the edge of a stage.

Single bar skills
1. Two students may practice selected skills on one bar at the same time.
2. Playground bars may be used.
3. One rail may be removed from the parallel bars for practicing single bar skills.
4. Some bar skills may be practiced on other pieces of equipment or on the floor while students are waiting their turn.
   a. The squat and squat-through may be practiced on the floor.
   b. The single leg cut, single leg squat-through, and cast may be practiced on the beam, single horse, or the edge of a stage.

Vaulting
1. Use floor vaulting.
2. Vaulting board skills may be practiced without the horse by jumping

onto a mat.

3. A balance beam or parallel bars, in addition to the vaulting horse, may be used to vault over by simply padding them with mats.
4. The student may vault onto a stack of mats, table, bleachers, trampoline, or stage.
5. The students may vault without a board if the objects are low.

Maximizing Participation in Swimming

1. Swim across the width rather than the length so more students may be in the water at one time.
2. Use small group teaching, especially in a class where there are varying skill levels.
   Example:

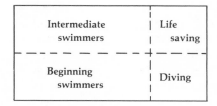

3. Use a variety of teaching methodologies so all students are busy but all do not need direct teacher supervision.

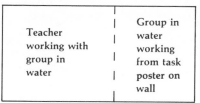

4. Use continuous swimming organization.

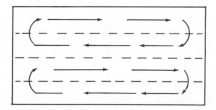

5. Use mass water games such as water tag, water polo, and water basketball.
6. Use partner practice pattern so only one-half of the class is in the water but the other one-half is busy in a teaching role.
7. Use relays with a small number of students on each team and continue for several turns by each team member.
8. Increase the amount of time available for swimming by being in the pool early and remaining after class if possible.

SELECTED READINGS AND REFERENCES

Corbin, Charles B., *Inexpensive Equipment for Games, Play, and Physical Activity*, W. C. Brown Co., Dubuque, Iowa, 1972.

Murphy, Chet. "Group Drills for Tennis Skills." *JOHPER*, May, 1974, pp. 34-37.

Murphy, Chet. "Too Many Players and Too Few Courts? Here's an Answer." *JOHPER*, May, 1974, pp. 28-31.

Werner, Peter and Lisa Rini, *Perceptual-Motor Development Equipment: Inexpensive Ideas and Activities*, John Wiley and Sons, Inc., New York, 1976.

Werner, Peter and Richard Simmons, *Do It Yourself: Creative Movement with Innovative Physical Education Equipment*, Kendall/Hunt Publishing Co., Dubuque, Iowa, 1973.

Werner, Peter and Richard Simmons, *Inexpensive Physical Education Equipment for Children*. Burgess Publishing Co., Mineapolis, 1976.

Photo by Robert Barclay

90

6

Instructional organization refers to the way educational materials, students, and the teacher are structured and organized in the classroom to bring about the most effective teaching and learning. The instructional organization used by teachers has been referred to as developing a particular teaching methodology, or teaching style.

Over the years there has been variation among educators relative to the importance of subject matter knowledge verses teaching technique in being an effective teacher. Some have believed that if one develops sufficient subject matter knowledge, the appropriate methodology, or teaching technique, will naturally occur. Other educators have believed that, although knowledge is necessary, the key to good teaching is possessing good teaching technique. Recent research in which teachers have been systematically observed while teaching seems to rather conclusively reveal that there are behaviors that separate effective teachers from those who are not as effective in the classroom. This would seem to make it clear that, although knowledge of subject matter is absolutely necessary, good teaching technique will greatly enhance the effectiveness of the teacher.

DIVISIONS OF THE LESSON

The teacher is typically responsible for organizing a lesson that spans thirty to fifty minutes in length. This period of time should be thought of as a complete lesson which is composed of three distinct parts. The three parts of the lesson are the set, body, and closure. Each part has its unique purpose in the lesson and should be specifically planned.

The Lesson Set

The set, or introduction to the lesson, is an important element because the response of the students to the set can have a positive or a negative effect upon the remaining parts of the lesson. The set is the time during which the teacher motivates and prepares the students for the material to be presented. The teacher should be enthusiastic so the students will become more interested in the lesson. One should remember that enthusiasm by the teacher is contagious to the students.

Although circumstances will vary, the students should always be placed in a position enabling them to see and hear. Preferably the students will be relatively close to the teacher so that the teacher may talk rather than shout. Experience has also taught that it is usually wise to have the students sit down during the introduction.

The Lesson Body

The body of the lesson falls between the set and closure and includes the largest amount of time. Included in the body of the lesson are the teacher presentations, student learning experiences, and most performance elements of the lesson. The body of the lesson builds upon the set and should be instructional and learning oriented.

The Lesson Closure

The lesson closure is simply a means by which the teacher draws a learning segment to a close. Closure typically occurs at the end of the class period. Its purpose is to recapture the learning that has occurred and to create an interest in what will occur in the following learning segment. The number of ways closure may be brought about is limited only by the imagination of the teacher. A few examples of lesson closures are as follows:

1. The teacher may summarize the learning that took place during the class.
2. The teacher may have the students summarize what was learned dur-

ing the class.

3. The students may be encouraged to ask questions about the lesson that has just been completed.
4. The teacher may ask the students questions about the lesson.
5. The teacher may challenge the students by asking an interesting question to be answered the following day. Example: Who won the title for hitting the most home runs in the American League in 1976? The students are encouraged to search for the answer.
6. The teacher may give a written or physical assignment relating to the lesson just completed or the lesson planned for the following day.
7. The results of the class competition may be announced and the winning teams or individuals recognized.

There are many possibilities for putting closure to the lesson. The teacher should use a variety of techniques so the students will enjoy the experience. Above all, the teacher should not simply blow the whistle and dismiss the class.

TEACHER PRESENTATION OF SUBJECT MATTER

This element of the lesson refers to the teacher giving formal instruction relative to skill, intellectual, or behavior development. Three ways in which this instruction may occur are a verbal explanation, demonstration, or a combination of the two. As an example, when explaining a complicated rule in a sport the teacher may, at the same time, set up a demonstration of the rule using students in the class. In some instances the explanation and demonstration will occur simultaneously, and sometimes one may follow the other. If one is to follow the other, the decision is made by the teacher based upon an analysis of the form and complexity of the activity.

The Explanation

An explanation includes any verbal presentation by the teacher. It may include a discussion on a particular sport strategy, an explanation of the effects of exercise upon the functioning of the heart, a clarification of field hockey rules, or a verbalization of the intricacies of performing a specific sport skill. No matter what the topic, the explanation should be well planned so that the best understanding by the students will occur. Following are a few suggestions to make the explanation most beneficial to the students.

1. Plan the explanation carefully so that all of the important ingredients of the presentation are adequately covered.
2. The best learning will occur if the points in the presentation are pre-

sented in the proper sequence. Some effectiveness is lost each time the teacher has to say, "Oh, I forgot to mention . . ."

3. Point out where there are relationships in what is being taught to what the students already know. Transfer can make the learning occur much easier and faster. Refer to Chapter 11 for more discussion of the topic of "transfer of learning."

4. Speak in a slow, well modulated tone so that the students can easily understand what you are presenting.

5. Watch the faces of the students to discern signs of misunderstanding.

The Demonstration

Although a demonstration may be applicable in many other instances, it is primarily associated with presenting a movement or skill. It is appropriate to use a demonstration when the movement or skill being presented has a "right" way of being performed, or if there are specific principles which are common to all who perform the skill. The demonstration sets forth precise performance criteria for the students to follow. Therefore, these criteria must be clearly illustrated for the students. The demonstration must be accurate and well performed, since students tend to give much more attention to what they see than to what they hear. A poorly conducted demonstration may actually lead to the development of incorrect motor skills.

Some guidelines which should be adhered to relative to the demonstration are:

1. Each student should be in a position to see and hear the demonstrator. Having the students sit down while the teacher remains standing or even stands on a raised platform is usually helpful.

2. The demonstration should be repeated a number of times.

3. If the skill is rather complicated, the demonstration may be viewed from different directions by the students.

4. The first presentation of the demonstration should be at the normal performance speed. Repeated demonstrations may be slowed down to aid the students in observing details of the skill.

5. The students should always be instructed to carefully observe and study the demonstration.

There are times when the teacher is unable to perform a good demonstration or prefers to have someone else demonstrate. Possibilities for a substitute demonstrator include a good performer in the class, a highly skilled athlete in the school, another teacher in the school, or a person from the community with the needed expertise. In addition, audio-visual aids such as films or video-tapes may be used to give the students a view of the skill to be attempted. Additional information on audio-visual aids is presented in Chapter 12.

STYLES OF TEACHING

A style of teaching can best be described as an identifiable set of teacher behaviors. This set of behaviors is designed to nurture certain student behaviors and outcomes. Early attempts at classifying teaching styles identified a teacher-centered style and a student-centered style. In some instances there was a style in between these two which was not clearly defined.

Mosston (1966) identified seven teaching styles which were based upon a set of decisions made within the complete teaching act. The different styles were to emerge as decision making responsibilities shifted from the teacher to the students. The seven styles identified were command, task, reciprocal, small group, individual program, guided discovery, and problem solving.

There are three categories of teaching styles presented in this text: direct instruction, task teaching, and inquiry teaching. We believe Mosston's (1966) seven styles may be included in these three categories in the following manner: the command style would be closely related to direct instruction; task teaching would include the task, reciprocal, small group, and individual program styles; and the inquiry teaching category would include guided discovery and problem solving.

Direct Instruction

Direct instruction is the teaching style that has been associated with effective teaching in the research. It is a manner of teaching which is academically focused and teacher directed. The primary purpose of direct instruction is to keep students engaged in academic learning experiences a maximum amount of time. The ten categories of behaviors associated with direct instruction were presented in Chapter 2 under the topic of the effective teacher. The reader is encouraged to review those behaviors as important elements of direct instruction. Of the ten categories of behaviors, three are associated with the teacher creating a nurturant classroom climate, six are directly associated with instruction, and one is a class management function.

Creating a nurturant classroom climate. The climate created by the teacher is one that is task oriented, warm, and high in expectancy from the teacher. The task-oriented aspect is developed by placing emphasis upon meeting the objectives of the class by covering the course content effectively and efficiently. There is also insistence by the teacher upon promptness and moving from one learning experience to another with a minimum of lost time. In addition to being task-oriented, the teacher expects good quality work from the students. This high expectancy is shown by moving through the course content at a fast pace and by assigning a lot of practice and homework.

The teacher, while at the same time being task-oriented and high in expectancy, creates a warm and friendly classroom climate. This warm climate is created by being sincerely interested in the students and letting them know that they are cared for.

Instructional behaviors. In direct instruction the teacher carefully structures the lesson. This includes giving clear instructions about what is to be learned and how the students will go about learning it. Students are given few choices concerning what they are to do in the classroom, and the teacher gives a lot of immediate, non-evaluative, and task-relevant feedback. More work is done with students in groups rather than individual instruction.

Class management behaviors. The class management dimension of direct instruction is focused on keeping students working on-task rather than dealing with behavior problems. This is accomplished by careful monitoring of the students by the teacher, and when they stray off-task the teacher refocuses the attention of the students instead of using direct disciplinary measures.

Task Teaching

The main feature of task teaching is that it can easily be self-paced for the students rather than under the direct control of the teacher. The task to be accomplished by the students is made available by the teacher, and the students then proceed to do the task at their own pace and, to a certain degree, in the location of their choice. The task is often written on a poster, card, or sheet of paper that the students may refer to as they work on the task.

Since the students are working on individual tasks with written instructions for guidance, the teacher experiences a freedom to mingle with and help students on an individual basis. The tasks may be organized so the students are working as individuals, with a partner, or in a small group.

Inquiry Teaching

Inquiry teaching is best exemplified by the guided discovery and problem solving styles described by Mosston (1966). Unlike other styles, the inquiry and problem solving styles encourage the students to arrive at goals through guidance by the teacher. The emphasis is placed upon the process that the students go through to reach the goal. Some teachers believe this is a desirable experience for the students to encounter.

Guided discovery involves the teacher guiding the students through a carefully planned sequence of questions or experiences designed to lead the students to a pre-determined goal. The goal could have been reached by more direct means, but the importance of the style is thought to be the process the students go through to arrive at the goal.

Problem solving is a style of teaching in which the teacher sets a problem. The students are then asked to find a solution to the problem. Different solutions by different students are encouraged. Once a solution is discovered the student may be asked to find another solution.

Teaching Style and Practice Patterns

Various practice patterns are presented in detail on the following pages of this chapter. The practice patterns presented are the large group pattern, small group pattern, partner pattern, and individual pattern. All of the practice patterns are not appropriate for each of the teaching styles.

Direct instruction may, at various times, utilize all four of the practice patterns, whereas the task style would utilize the small group, partner, and individual patterns. Guided discovery would most often employ the large group pattern, and the problem solving style would work well with any of the four practice patterns. Figure 6.1 summarizes the various teaching styles and the appropriate practice patterns.

Style of Teaching	Appropriate Practice Pattern
Direct Instruction	Large Group Small Group Partner Individual
Task Teaching	Small Group Partner Individual

Inquiry Teaching
  Guided Discovery
  Problem Solving
	
	Large Group
	Large Group
	Small Group
	Partner

Figure 6.1   Summary of Teaching Styles and Appropriate Practice Patterns.

97

PRACTICE PATTERNS

Simply observing a demonstration and hearing an explanation will not enable a student to correctly perform a skill. There must follow a period of time in which the students practice the skill under rather careful direction by the teacher. Four different organizational patterns which can be used to achieve guided practice for the students are the large group pattern, small group pattern, partner pattern, and individual pattern. The order of presentation is not to represent any preference by the authors or sequence that should be followed in their use. The teacher should become familiar with each pattern and use them selectively as various lessons are planned.

The Large Group Pattern

The *Large Group* pattern, shown in Figure 6.2, is used when the teacher wants the entire class, or a majority of the class, to practice the same skill all at the same time. The arrangement allows the teacher to act as a model for the students. While standing in front of the class, the teacher or other leader goes through the movement, and the students imitate the movements of the teacher. Some teachers also help to guide the movements by giving verbal cues which correspond to small parts of the movement. For example, the teacher may give the following cues and their meanings to the class learning a tennis forehand:

Turn — From the "ready" position the students pivot on the rear foot, turn the body sideways and move the racket back.

Stroke — The students step toward the net with the front foot, shift the weight toward the front foot, and stroke with the racket.

Recover — The students return to the "ready" position.

The teacher then calls out the cues, and the students do the various movements that are specified. In this way the students have a model (the teacher) to follow and, at the same time, can experience the "feel" of the movement. This procedure is repeated a sufficient number of times until the students are capable of performing the movement independent of the teacher's directions. The teacher controls the amount of movement associated with each cue and also the speed of the movement by giving the cues as fast or slow as desired. At any point in the lesson the teacher may increase the amount of movement allowed with each cue, and the speed may be increased.

When the learners reach the point where they no longer need to practice the skill under the direction of the teacher, they may practice the skill on their own. This can best be accomplished by setting up drills which involve one or more students working cooperatively on a skill or a

```
X          X          X          X          X
     X          X          X          X
X          X          X          X          X
     X          X          X          X
X          X          X          X          X
                      T
```

Figure 6.2   Arrangement of teacher (T) and students (X) in the large group pattern.

combination of skills. The organization of this practice will depend upon the space available, the equipment available, the number of students in the class, and the number of people necessary to accomplish the practice task. For example, if the students are to practice the forehand stroke in tennis, each student may take a racket and a ball and drop the ball and stroke it against the fence. Later in the progression this practice may involve two students stroking the ball back and forth over the net using the forehand stroke.

Having students practice in one large group or "by the numbers" has been criticized for being too formal or regimented. Some have thought that it unduly tries to stamp every student out of the same mold. It is suggested by the authors that this practice pattern not be used exclusively. There are other practice patterns presented, and the teacher should selectively use the practice pattern that best suits the situation.

The Small Group Pattern

As the name implies, the *Small Group* pattern consists of the class being divided into several small groups. The number and size of each group varies with each specific application. Each group is then assigned to a specific "station" to practice. Following are three applications of the small group pattern.

Multiple station application. The most basic application of the small group pattern is where the teacher desires to divide the class into smaller groups, but have all of the students practice a common skill. This arrangement of students practicing the same skill at different stations is referred to as the *Multiple Station* application. Figure 6.3 shows six groups of students arranged at various practice stations around the gymnasium. All of the groups are practicing the basketball jump shot. Since all students are practicing the same skill, there will be no reason to rotate the various groups through other stations. The advantages of this application are that the students may easily be ability-grouped at the various stations if the teacher so desires, and the single large class may be dis-

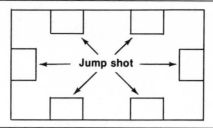

Figure 6.3   Multiple skill application of the small group pattern.

tributed into small groups so that equipment and facilities may be better utilized.

Multiple skill application. The *Multiple Skill* application of the small group pattern involves dividing the class into several small groups, with each group practicing a different skill. Four representative examples of the multiple skill application are given in Figure 6.4.

The first example in Figure 6.4 shows the application of this type of arrangement with some skills appropriate to the early elementary grades. In this application the students will work on one skill for a set number of minutes and then rotate to a new station at the request of the teacher. The teacher may want to move to various skill stations and work with specific students, or he or she may elect to stay at one station so that individual help may be given to each student as they rotate through that particular station. This is one way the teacher may be certain of giving individual attention to each student. A second benefit of this arrangement is that equipment is needed in lesser amounts since only a few pieces of the same equipment are needed at a station. An individual positive outcome that may occur is that the students will remain highly motivated as they rotate to new stations periodically.

The second example of the multiple skill application displayed in Figure 6.4 would be more appropriate to a secondary level class. The same advantages apply in this application as in the previous one. The major advantage in this particular arrangement is that the typical school would have only one or two sets of rings and probably one set of parallel or uneven bars. By using the multiple skill application, students may be practicing at various locations so there is a minimum of standing and waiting for a turn. The teacher has the option in this application of having the students practice only a few minutes at each station and then rotate to a new station, or the students may spend an entire period at one station and then rotate to a new station the following day. Additional examples of the multiple skill application are included in Figure 6.4 to show the use of the application in various environments.

100

Developmental activities.

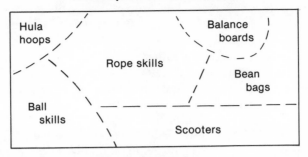

Gymnastics

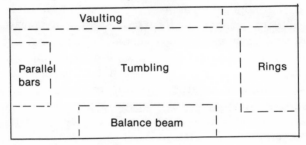

Track and Field

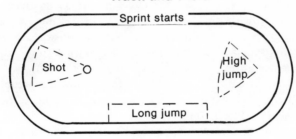

Softball

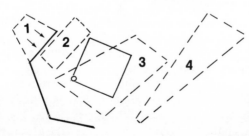

1 = Batting
2 = Lob pitching
3 = Ground balls
4 = Fly balls

Figure 6.4   Examples of multiple skill applications of the small group pattern.

101

Multiple sport application. The *Multiple Sport* application involves teaching a class in which more than one sport or activity is taught concurrently. The primary reason causing the teacher to use the multiple sport application would be a shortage of equipment, facilities, or space for a particular sport. Therefore, rather than have many students waiting their turns with the equipment, there is more than one sport going on at the same time. In this way all students will be busy, even though they may be working at different locations on different sports.

Some examples of the multiple sport application are shown in Figure 6.5. The first example may involve a situation where the teacher has a shortage of tumbling mats and table tennis equipment. Rather than offer separate units where the students would be forced to wait for their turns, the multiple sport application allows the teacher to have students working at three different locations on three different sports; namely tumbling, table tennis, and volleyball. Since the students are practicing different sports it will be necessary to rotate the groups at the appropriate time. Possible rotations are: (1) at the end of each day the students would rotate to a new station, or (2) after a week or more they may rotate to a new station. One other excellent use of this application is that it allows for competition among the students after they have gone through the skill acquisition phases of each unit.

Guidelines for rotating stations. Rotation from station to station is necessary in each of the aforementioned practice arrangements except the multiple station application. The general guideline to follow would be to rotate students so that they all have equal opportunities at each station, and that students spend sufficient time at each station to be able to accomplish the expected learning. The following conditions will help to determine the time to be spent at each station in different situations:

1. Age and school level of students. The younger the student, the shorter time to be spent at each station.
2. The number of class meetings per week. The more times the class meets per week the longer the time that can be spent at each station.
3. The length of each class period.
4. The number of students in the class, which determines the number of students at each station.
5. The amount of equipment and the type of facilities available.
6. The number of activities in a given program.
7. The physical education background and abilities of the students.

Dispensing instructions in the small group pattern. The practice instructions that the students are to follow must be given to them before they are dismissed to their separate stations. Unlike the large group pattern in which the teacher leads the students through the initial practices, in the small group pattern the students will practice largely independent

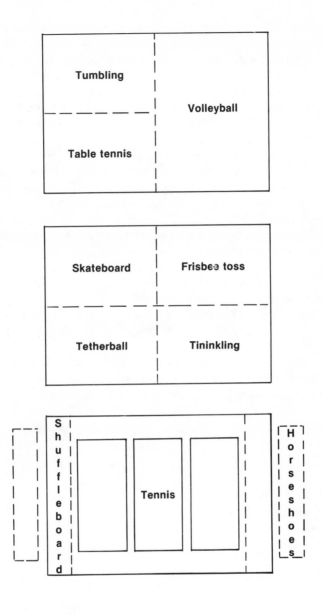

Figure 6.5   Examples of multiple sport application of the small group pattern.

of the teacher. Therefore, the instructions must be planned so that they are clearly presented to the students. There are two ways that the instructions may be presented. The instructions for practice may be given verbally by the teacher, or they may be written down and given to the students. If the practice is to be very short and simple, the teacher may verbally present the instructions for each group. However, most often the instructions will be too complicated and/or too long to be remembered by the students. Therefore, it is recommended that the practice instructions be written down and made available to the students.

One of the best ways to guide the students through the small group pattern is to place the practice instructions on a poster. The poster should then be placed in a prominent position near the station so that it can readily be seen by all the students in the group. This means that the teacher will prepare one poster for each station. Some suggestions for the preparation of the poster are:

1. The poster paper should be large enough to hold a considerable amount of information, and it should be durable enough to hang on the wall and to be stored for later use.
2. The lettering should be large and colorful so it can be read from a distance. This prevents students from crowding around the poster to read it.
3. If the poster is to be used with students where reading is a problem, the instructions may be illustrated with drawings. Figure 6.6 is an example of a simple poster for a station in a gymnastics unit.

STATION 2: TUMBLING

Instructions: Do steps 1 and 2 going across the single mats and steps 3 and 4 going the length of the triple mats.

1. Do 3 single forward rolls.
2. Do 3 single backward rolls.
3. Do 2 forward rolls, ½ turn, 2 backward rolls.
4. Do 2 combinations of forward roll, ½ turn, back roll, ½ turn, forward roll.

Figure 6.6 Sample wall poster.

With the use of instructional posters in the small group pattern, the teacher will find a rare freedom to move about the class and still know that the students are busy learning. This freedom can be utilized by the teacher to give additional instruction at stations where it seems desirable. Perhaps the greatest benefit is that the teacher can give assistance to individuals in the class without stopping the practice of others.

The Partner Pattern

In the two previous practice patterns the class practiced as a whole in the large group pattern and as a series of small groups in the small group pattern. Another logical pattern would seem to be an arrangement where the students practice the movement in pairs. There are several possible advantages to the *Partner Pattern* including: (1) one student in each pair can be performing the skill, and the other student may act as a student-teacher by evaluating and correcting, (2) safety can be enhanced in activities such as swimming and gymnastics, (3) students may gain in self-concept as they take on the responsibility inherent in the pattern, and (4) less equipment may be needed since only one piece of equipment is needed for each pair of students.

It is essential that the reader is reminded that in the partner pattern, as in previous ones, a demonstration and explanation of the skill to be attempted has been given. Therefore, the students enter the practice time with considerable information regarding the skill to be performed. The distinguishing characteristic in the partner pattern is that one student will perform the movement while the other student observes. The observing student has the responsibility to evaluate and correct the performance of the partner. It would be naive to assume that the observing student has the capabilities to completely evaluate and correct the performing student. The extent of correction is usually limited to the information presented to the students by the teacher during the demonstration-explanation phase of the lesson. Additionally, the teacher may provide the students with a worksheet which describes the task of the performing student and also presents evaluative criteria for the observing student. Each pair of students works independent of other students. The partners take turns in the roles of performer and observer. Figure 6.7 illustrates a worksheet that is appropriate for the partner practice pattern.

The teacher's role in this pattern of practice is slightly different than in the other patterns. The teacher does not directly correct errors of performance noted in the students. Rather, since one possible advantage of this pattern is to enhance the self-concept of the students by giving them some evaluation responsibilities, the teacher must use care not to infringe upon that responsibility more than is necessary. Where there are performance errors noted, the teacher should approach the observing student and discuss the errors. In this way the student observer retains his or her role as evaluator.

The order of events when using the partner pattern is as follows:
1. The students hear and see a complete explanation and demonstration of the skill to be accomplished during the instruction phase of the class.

Task: Learn to perform the tennis forehand stroke.
Practice pattern: Partner.
Equipment needed: 1 racket and 1 ball for each pair of students.
Directions: Practice with your partner at a marked area along the wall.

Step 1 — Drop and catch the tennis ball in a stroking fashion by:
    a. Standing sideways to the wall with your racket hand farthest from the wall.
    b. Dropping the ball from your non-racket hand and stroke your racket hand forward and catch the ball. As your arm is moved toward the ball the weight is shifted toward the wall.
    c. Repeat 10 times.
  Observer: Look for a stroking motion with the arm and a shift of weight from the back foot to the forward foot.

Step 2 — Drop and stroke the tennis ball against the wall by:
    a. Standing sideways to the wall.
    b. Dropping the ball and stroke it with your racket and shift your weight toward the wall.
    c. Following through with your racket hand to a position in front of the opposite shoulder.
    d. Repeat 20 times.
  Observer: Look for a smooth stroke, shift of weight, and high follow through.

Step 3 — This and additional steps will complete the intended progression.

Figure 6.7 Worksheet for partner pattern.

2. Partners are selected either by the students or by the teacher.
3. The worksheets are distributed to the students. The teacher provides the necessary instructions of how to use the worksheet and answers any questions from the students.
4. The necessary equipment is distributed.
5. The students move to the appropriate location and begin practice.

The Individual Pattern

The *Individual Pattern* has as its unique contribution the capability of personalizing a practice or program to the needs of each student. The two prominent ways in which a practice pattern may be personalized to the individual are through the teacher presenting a range of skills, and through the student developing a personalized practice program.

The first and simplest way is to have the students select an entry practice point on a range of skills presented. The skills presented should range from simple skills appropriate to the least skilled, to skills beyond the capabilities of the most advanced student in the class. Students, through previous knowledge or by trial and error, determine their present skill level. From that entry point the student practices the movements

Basketball Dribbling

Each student working on this task should take a basketball and practice in the appropriately marked area of the gymnasium.

Step 1 — Using your preferred hand, dribble the basketball until you can progress one length of the floor without an error or loss of control.

Step 2 — Using your non-preferred hand, dribble the basketball until you can progress one length of the floor without an error or loss of control.

Step 3 — By alternating hands on each bounce, dribble the basketball two lengths of the floor without an error or loss of control.

Step 4 — Dribble two lengths of the floor in the pattern: dribble five times with your preferred hand, dribble between your legs, dribble five times with your non-preferred hand, dribble between your legs, and continue the pattern until you can do it without error or loss of control.

Step 5 — Repeat step 4 except dribble behind your back in place of dribbling between your legs.

Step 6 — Dribble the basketball using the pattern: bounce, bounce; between your legs; bounce, bounce; between your legs; bounce, bounce; behind your back, bounce, bounce; behind your back. Repeat this pattern two lengths of the floor.

Figure 6.8 *Worksheet for the individual pattern with a range of skills.*

presented in the range of skills.

One can see that this pattern may serve as a self-assessment tool to determine present abilities among individuals. Some students will probably lack the ability to make an initial correct assessment and will, therefore, need the guidance and assistance of the teacher. Not only does the individual pattern serve as a means of assessing present performance capabilities, but it should also encourage self-improvement within the students. The presentation of a range of skills tends to be an appropriate method of achieving individual practice for most traditional sports skills and movement education experiences. Figure 6.8 shows a worksheet for the individual pattern range of skills. A worksheet of this type could also be presented in the form of a wall poster.

The second use of the individual pattern is with such developmental programs as exercising and weight training. It seems obvious that the same number of sit-ups would not be appropriate for all students in the class. Also one would never expect all students in the class to be able to bench press the same amount of weight. It would not be reasonable to think the teacher could plan an individual practice program for each student. The technique is for the teacher to develop standards which will be individualized to the capabilities and present status of each individual in the class. All students receive a similar worksheet which is completed according to their abilities. Reference to Figure 6.9 will show how this can be accomplished.

INDIVIDUAL WORKSHEET — DEVELOPMENTAL EXERCISES

Name _____**Class** _____**Date**_____

Instructions:

1. For each of the exercises listed below determine the maximum (M) that you can perform and record it.
2. For the first 8-10 days (Stage 1) of the unit do 3 sets of each exercise with the set consisting of .5 X M.
3. For the next 8-10 days (Stage 2) of the unit do 3 sets of each exercise with the set consisting of .7 X M.
4. For the next 8-10 days (Stage 3) of the unit do 3 sets of each exercise with the set consisting of .85 X M.
5. At this point you should check M again and repeat the sequence for each exercise.*

	M	Stage 1	Stage 2	Stage 3
A. Sit-Ups. Lie on your back with legs raised so knees are at approximately 90° and the arms are crossing the chest with the hands near the shoulders.				
B. Push-Ups. Use number 1 or 2. 1. Body in support position and straight with arms straight and hands shoulder width apart. 2. Knees on floor and body straight with arms straight and hands shoulder width apart.				
C. Next Exercise.				
D. Next Exercise.				

*Note to the teacher. Increases may also occur in the number of sets.

Figure 6.9   A sample worksheet for the individual pattern.

STUDENT PERFORMANCE

The performance segment of the class is designed to permit students the opportunity to utilize the skills they have been practicing during guided practice. The performance should not be thought of as being void of practice and improvement, but rather the emphasis has simply been shifted to that of performance. Students should be encouraged to use the level of skill attained during the practices to perform the movements to the best of their ability.

One should keep in mind that there is some conflict between learning and performance. Research indicates that learning occurs best when there is a lack of intense competition and performance tends to increase with at least some competition. The implication would be that while students are in the early stages of learning a new skill, the performance element of the lesson may be improved through the use of less intense competitive situations. Lead-up activities tend to work well to provide the desirable level of competition. The following example shows the relationship between instruction, practice, and performance for selected days of a badminton unit.

Day 1

Instruction: Instruction on the forehand grip and long serve.

Practice: Large group practice and checking of the grip by the teacher. Partner practice by students hitting long serves which drop to the floor.

Performance: Lead up game in which the server scores a point and continues serving if the shuttle falls within three feet of the back boundary line and within the legal court. High score at the end of class wins.

Day 2

Instruction: Review of the grip and long serve and instruction on the overhead clear.

Practice: Partner practice of long serves. One player long serves and the other player overhead clears the shuttle.

Performance: One player long serves and the other player clears the shuttle and both players continue to clear the shuttle back and forth until one player is driven off the back of the court. The player that forced his opponent off the court wins the rally. (The objective is to get the students to hit strong, deep clears.)

Day 10

Instruction: Demonstration-explanation on court coverage using the side-by-side formation.

Practice: Four students on each court practice the side-by-side formation by carefully hitting or tossing the shuttle to various spots on the opposite side of the net to emphasize which player would return it.

Performance: Four players, in a side-by-side formation, on each court play a regulation game of badminton using all of the performance skills they possess.

As can be seen in the illustration, the level of competition is very mild on day one and only slightly stronger on day two. However, as days progress the competition also increases until the game is played under highly competitive circumstances as is shown on the tenth day.

SPECIFIC INSTRUCTIONAL METHODOLOGIES

Understandably, the majority of instructional time in physical education is carried on in the gymnasium, pool, or on the field involving physical movement. However, there are many occasions where instruction should take place in the classroom, or at least in a non-activity environment. With this thought in mind, some selected techniques appropriate to the various instructional climates of physical education are presented. The teacher should select from the various techniques those which best accomplish the intended purpose. A general recommendation is that the teacher should attempt to use at least two of the techniques in each class meeting.

Committee project. The assignment of class members into groups for the purpose of conducting research or group study on a selected topic. The procedure may bring about group cooperation and reliance.

Contract teaching. A written agreement between the teacher and student which describes the learning activities the student is to follow. Usually included in the agreement are the learning objectives, student activities and evaluation criteria.

Creative endeavors. The students may work as individuals or in small groups. The purpose is to stimulate creativity within specified parameters. Examples could be designing a new game, alteration of rules for specific purposes, and formulating a movement to accomplish a purpose.

Demonstration. The presentation of a technique or principle in front of the class by the teacher, a student, or another qualified individual.

Discussion. A verbal exchange between students, or between the teacher and students, concerning a particular topic. There is moderation of the exchange by either the teacher or a student. The technique stimulates thinking and verbal expression on the part of students.

Drill. Repetitive practice by the students of a teacher designed task for the purpose of bringing about automatic response. The drill may involve mental or physical exercises.

Experimentation/exploration. Placing the students in a simple ex-

110

perimental setting where they test various hypotheses. An example is the students determining the effects of exercise upon body functions such as heart rate and breathing rate.

Field trips. Educational trips, usually outside the school, which allow students to study their subject in its natural setting. Students could visit an exercise laboratory or play a round of golf on the community course.

Guest speaker. A guest speaker is anyone who is not assigned to teach the class. A guest speaker should be someone who can bring a special expertise to the class and add additional interest at the same time.

Instructional testing. Testing during the instructional phase of the unit for the purpose of diagnosis or self-assessment. This testing is carried out primarily by the students themselves.

Lead-up game. A game that consists of a limited number of skills on which the students are to focus. The game is usually competitive and includes a method of scoring. It is usually most effective when it involves a small number of players.

Learning aids. The use of audio, visual, and tactile instructional aids. Such aids include video-tape, films, film strips, slides, photographs, bulletin boards, tape recorders, and models. Students may not only observe these various mediums, but may also be involved in the construction of some of them.

Lecture. Formal verbal presentation of the subject matter by the teacher with little or no student participation. The students are expected to listen, observe, and usually take notes.

Lecture/discussion. This technique includes the basic elements of the lecture procedure, but in addition the students are encouraged to offer opinions and ask questions at appropriate times during the presentation. This technique is effective in disseminating information in an understandable format, as well as creating a positive learning atmosphere.

Oral reports. The verbal presentation by individuals or groups of the findings of a study project. Promotes organization skills and self-confidence in students.

Reading assignments. The assignment of reading for students to accomplish from textbooks, library books, journals, newspapers, and other pertinent materials.

Team teaching. Cooperative planning and teaching between two or more teachers. It allows the teachers in the team to take advantage of their individual abilities.

SUMMARY

While knowledge of the subject matter is essential for teachers, those who also possess good teaching techniques will create an atmosphere most conducive to learning. Each lesson plan should contain three distinct parts. These are the lesson set, body, and closure. The set is used to introduce the lesson and establish the groundwork for what follows. The body is the most important part of the lesson, as it includes the presentation, practice, and performance of the skills. The closure ends the lesson by recapturing what has taken place and creating interest in what will occur in the next learning segment. The teacher may use one of three ways to give formal instruction dealing with the skill, knowledge, or behavior of the lesson. These three are by a verbal explanation, a demonstration, or a combination of the two.

Three categories of teaching styles are presented: direct instruction; task teaching; and inquiry teaching. A style of teaching is an identifiable set of teacher behaviors designed to nurture student behaviors and outcomes. Direct instruction is one style which is academically focused and teacher directed. Task teaching is more student controlled and self-paced. During inquiry teaching the teacher emphasizes the problem solving process while guiding the students to arrive at solutions to problems.

There are four basic organizational patterns in which students may be placed during actual practice of various skills. These are the large group, small group, partner, and individual patterns.

The performance segment of a class is designed to give students the opportunity to use the skills they have been practicing. This phase is not totally separate from the practice but rather a temporary shift of emphasis. For optimum learning, students in early learning stages should be involved in less intense competition.

The majority of instructional time in physical education classes takes place in the gymnasium, pool, field, or court and involves physical movement. There are, however, times where instruction may take place in a non-activity environment. The teacher should select those instructional techniques which best accomplish the intended purpose.

SELECTED READINGS AND REFERENCES

Graham, George and Elsa Heimerer, "Research on Teacher Effectiveness: A Summary with Implications for Teaching," *Quest,* Vol. 33, 1981, pp. 14-25.

Jensen, Mary, "Teaching: An Open Skill, Implications for Teacher Training," *Quest,* Vol. 32, 1980, pp. 60-70.

Mosston, Muska, *Teaching Physical Education: From Command to Discovery,* Charles E. Merrill Publishing Co., Columbus, 1966.

Photo by David Brittain

CLASSROOM MANAGEMENT AND PROCEDURES

The primary purpose of the physical education class is to help the students to learn. If this is to be accomplished the teacher must manage the class and develop procedures that are conducive to learning. If this is done, not only will learning occur, but the teacher will also save energy and prevent confusion on the part of the students.

Management may be referred to as non-academic behaviors of teachers which are associated with organizing students, giving directions, handling equipment, changing activities, and attending to classroom routines. These functions are important to the smooth operation of a physical education class, but they are not instructional activities. Therefore, the teacher should be sensitive to the amount of time that is devoted to them.

Through observing physical education teachers in their classes, research has shown that far too much time is devoted to management functions. Representative of this type of research is the work by Godbout, Brunelle, and Tousignant (1983) who studied elementary and secondary teachers in Quebec. They found that elementary teachers were spending approximately 30 percent and secondary teachers approximately 19 percent of their class time on management functions. These are extremely high figures and teachers need to lower the percentage of time devoted to management functions. During the remaining class time the students were involved with physical education content areas. However, the researchers observed that the students were waiting for their turn to participate approximately 50 percent of the time they were involved with content areas. There is a strong implication that this ridiculously high amount of waiting time is also attributable to poor class management.

The remainder of this chapter includes means by which teachers may streamline their management functions. In addition, some suggestions for standardizing certain classroom procedures are given.

THE ORIENTATION PERIOD

One of the reasons many teachers have trouble with their class management procedures is that they fail to make them well-known to their students. Students are admonished, members of the class are confused, and precious time is wasted because the students are not sure of what the teacher wants or what the correct procedure should be. Therefore, the suggestion is made that the teacher begin each school year, or each semester if the class contains different students, with an orientation period. The purpose of the orientation period would be to acquaint the students with, and answer questions about, the various aspects of class management and class procedures. With young students the teacher may rehearse some management procedures.

The orientation period may vary in length but it should always occur at the beginning of the instructional unit. The elementary physical education teacher may extend the orientation period over several days by spending time on management functions as they are encountered. For example, the teacher may spend a considerable amount of time at the beginning of the first day on such things as how to properly enter the gymnasium, where to line up, sit or stand, and what kind of behavior is expected in the class. At the end of the class the teacher may carefully explain how the students are to prepare for and be dismissed from class. Procedures such as how to get the attention of the teacher, when to get a drink, when the equipment may be used, and other routines felt important by the teacher should be clearly explained to the students. These procedures will need to be reinforced for the students periodically. It is suggested that the reinforcement be done in a positive manner as often as possible. For example, after a few days the teacher may say something like "I am very pleased with the way you lined up quickly and quietly just as you have been asked." This technique serves as a reminder as well as a compliment to the students.

The secondary physical education teacher will most often find success with a one or two day orientation period. This should be time spent

116

in the formal classroom, and the material discussed may also be presented as a booklet or individual handouts. The teacher should inform the students of such things as dress requirements, shower policies, absence and excuse policies, class rules of behavior, the grading system, and all other procedures and policies the teacher feels is necessary. When the orientation period is complete, whatever be its length, the students should be aware of the procedures, rules, and guidelines necessary to make the class proceed smoothly. This does not mean that the teacher may not need to reemphasize some points later, or even a number of times. Repetition of material covered in the orientation period may be desirable and necessary.

STREAMLINING CLASS MANAGEMENT FUNCTIONS

There are many class management functions that must occur in the physical education class which are not important learning experiences in themselves. Therefore, these functions should take as little time as possible. The less time the teacher must devote to these functions, the more time is available for instruction and practice. Many of these functions can become routine so that the students know what is expected and can accomplish them with a minimum of lost time. This section contains a discussion of some of these functions and offers suggestions for completing them without using too much time.

Conduct Class on a Schedule

Some teachers conduct their classes on a very loose schedule, beginning class when everyone is present and everything is ready and dismissing class at a time somewhere near the proper dismissal time. This approach is very dangerous to the efficient conduct of the class. Students become ambivalent to the time schedule when the teacher does not show the proper concern. The class should begin when it is scheduled to begin, and it should end when the proper time comes. The teacher should insist that students report to class promptly and the teacher must do likewise. Students should be in the locker room dressing when the bell rings to start the period, and they should be given a reasonable period of time (3-5 minutes) to report to the instructional site. There will always be some students who arrive at the instructional site ahead of others, so the teacher must be prepared for them. Some type of activity should be planned so the students do not have to stand and wait. Some teachers have found it helpful to post the beginning activities so early arrivals know what to do. A reasonable period of time (8-10 minutes) should be given for showering and dressing at the end of the activity session, and the teacher should be careful to abide by the schedule. The most important concept here is that students should be given a time schedule, and they should be held to it.

Use an Efficient Method of Taking Attendance

The teacher must take attendance for a number of reasons. Teachers are responsible for the whereabouts of the students assigned to their class. Learning cannot take place if the student is not present. In addition, in some states the amount of money allocated to school districts for state-aid is based on the number of students present.

No matter which method the teacher selects, attendance should be completed quickly and accurately. The following section contains several methods that have been successfully used by teachers.

Squad method. In this method each student is assigned to a squad. One student in each squad serves as the squad leader and reports all absences to the teacher. This method is fast and it provides an opportunity for giving students some responsibility. Many teachers use the squad method because it can be used for general class organization, as an exercise formation, and for assignment of teams. When this method is used, the teacher should see to it that the position of squad leader is rotated among various members of the squad.

Assigned numbers. The number method utilizes a series of numbers stenciled on the wall or on the floor. Each student is assigned a number, and on cue from the teacher the student stands on or covers the number. The numbers left uncovered are recorded as absences for the day. This method is time-efficient and accurate.

Count off. Students are listed in the grade book by name and number. The students count off while standing in a line. As the students count off, the teacher hears a succession of numbers from one to the number of students in the class. Should a student be absent, for example number 12, there would be no number 12 called out. The teacher then notes this as an absence by matching the number with the appropriate name in the grade book.

Sign in. In this method the teacher provides a clipboard near the entrance with a sign-in sheet on it. Students sign their names as the enter the instructional area. After the class is completed the teacher collects the sheet and compares it with the actual class roll written in the grade book. The advantage of this method is that it takes no time at all from the instructional time, and the disadvantage is that students may forget to sign in, or they may have someone else sign in for them.

Student report. Students approach the instructor as they enter the teaching area and give their name or number, and the teacher records it in the grade book. This method is accurate, but it involves instructors taking attendance over a period of time when they could be employed more advantageously in supervision or instruction.

Name tag. Numbered tags are hanging on a board close to the entrance to the instructional area. As students enter the class they turn their tag over. The numbers that remain visible are recorded as absences. The tags must then be turned so all numbers are showing prior to the arrival of the next class.

Calling of names. This method requires that the teacher calls each name on the roll sheet and the students respond. It is very time consuming and is not generally considered to be a very good method. However, this is a good method to use at the beginning of the year when the teacher is learning the students' names. It should be abandoned in favor of a more efficient method as soon as possible.

Teach a Specific Signal for Attention

There are many times during the class when the teacher needs to gain the attention of students. Attention may be desired for instructional purposes, management functions, or for changing activities. Gaining students' attention quickly is an important time saver as well as a means of maintaining rapport within the class. When the teacher calls for attention and does not receive it, there is frustration created for the teacher, and other students experience irritation at their classmates. There are many signals that teachers may use. They include a hand clap, ringing a bell, blowing a horn or whistle, or perhaps other means. Although the whistle is the most popular means, any signal that is effective is acceptable. Students should have the signal explained to them, and they should be instructed how to react to the signal. This signal should always mean "stop what you are doing and give your attention to the teacher." The signal should never have other meanings that will confuse students. Teachers will sometimes blow a whistle to start an activity, and then they blow a whistle to gain the attention of students and cannot understand why they don't receive immediate attention. Students should be told that when they hear the signal they are to stop what they are doing immediately, and give their attention to the teacher. There should not be "one more shot" or one more of anything.

In gaining the attention of the students, the teacher should allow a reasonable amount of time after the signal is given. However, the teacher must be aware that five seconds lost with each signal may easily accumulate to over one minute in a single class period. This would multiply itself to as much as three hours over the course of a school year.

There is an important safety consideration involved here as well.

During a golf exercise one student may hear the signal, stop, and move closer to the teacher. At the same time another student wants to take "one more swing." The possible results of this situation are obvious and point out the need for adherance to the signal by all students.

Handle Equipment Efficiently

Almost all physical education classes require the use of a number of pieces of equipment. Students should be taught to have respect for the equipment and to use it properly and safely. The proper handling of equipment can significantly reduce the time devoted to class management. The equipment to be used in a particular class should be in place before the formal class begins so class time is not used for this purpose. The distribution of small pieces of equipment such as balls and racquets should be assigned to students so it can be done quickly. Movement of large pieces of equipment such as mats, vaulting horses, and so forth should be done by students. The lesson should be planned so that this type of movement is kept to a minimum.

Reduce Transition Time

The time that is spent changing from one class activity to another is referred to as *transition time*. These changes occur often during most classes. Some of the more prominent changes include moving from the attendance formation to the exercise formation, moving from one learning station to another, and rotating teams during competition. Each transition takes a small amount of time, but as the number of transitions increase the total time becomes significant. Although these changes cannot be eliminated, the transition time can and must be reduced.

The teacher should be aware of the number of planned transitions for a lesson and try to eliminate those that do not deter from meeting the objectives of the lesson. Students must be made aware of how much time can be lost, and they should be encouraged to reduce the transition time as much as possible. An excellent means of encouraging students to reduce transition time is to give positive verbal reinforcement when they respond quickly. Another way to decrease transition time is for the teacher to specify a reasonable transition time (for example, 6 seconds). Each time the class completes the transition within the specified time, the students have earned one or two minutes. On a particular day, specified by the teacher, the class is given the opportunity to use the time they have earned in an activity of their choice.

STANDARDIZED CLASS PROCEDURES

In the remainder of this chapter the authors have presented a few thoughts about several topics with which every teacher must be concerned. It is most important that teachers develop a policy regarding each of the topics and that they share that policy with the students. The most logical time to discuss these policies is during the orientation period.

Dress Requirements

Students in the elementary school normally do not change clothes for their physical education class. Therefore, it is important they dress for school in a manner conducive to participation in physical education. The students should wear appropriate activity shoes. In addition, the girls might wear slacks, or they may wear shorts under their skirt or dress. The physical education teacher will be wise to communicate this information to the students, their teachers, and parents.

Whenever possible junior and senior high school students should change into physical education activity clothes for participation in activity. Changing clothes for activity is a good practice for health reasons, for improving performance, and for reinforcing good grooming. Each school should develop a policy regarding the proper manner of dress. The basic recommendation is that students should dress appropriately for the specific content of the class. What is appropriate for one activity is not so for another. It is quite obvious that students will vary their manner of dress from swimming class to skiing class, to volleyball, to a classroom session on the biomechanics of jumping. For special activities like skiing, dressing should be part of the course content, for "layering" is an integral part of the good skiers knowledge. For aquatic classes, the school may want to furnish swim suits so that the swimming attire is modest and appropriate. For classes such as volleyball, basketball, and tumbling, the dressing requirement should state that students dress so they have freedom of movement to perform well, their clothing is not a hazard to the activity being done, and there are no offensive slogans or advertisements on the shirt. The proper type of shoe is essential for safety purposes. Since there are special shoes designed for practically every sport today, a general type of all-purpose shoe is suggested. Arrangements may be made with a local sporting goods store to handle the appropriate shorts, shirts, sweat pants, socks, and shoes, or the school may make the necessary arrangements to make these materials available to the students.

Whatever dress procedures are used, it is desirable for the students' clothing to be clean. Adolescents are occasionally lax in laundering activity clothes. Therefore, the teacher needs to set standards for correct hygenic practices regarding clean clothing for physical education.

Students will sometimes not have the proper clothing available because they forgot to bring them or they cannot afford to purchase the clothes. In either instance the teacher may provide clothing if it is available. At the end of every year several students will leave good clothing and shoes in the locker room. Those abandoned articles should be washed and stored for those situations previously mentioned.

Shower Regulations

Students in the elementary grades seldom change clothes for the physical education class and, therefore, seldom take showers after participation. Since there is less likelihood of body odor and extreme perspiration from these students, the practice would seem acceptable. However, with junior and senior high school students, the teacher should encourage them to change into activity clothes and shower regularly after vigorous activity. Taking a shower after vigorous activity is a desirable practice, and the reasons should be discussed with the students. If the teacher has presented logical reasons, there is usually no problem with getting students to take showers. The reasons for showering that the teacher should emphasize to the students are:

1. Showering is a basic health practice which should follow vigorous physical activity.
2. The students will feel more comfortable and will not be offensive to others in classes which may follow physical education.
3. Showering regularly aids in good grooming, and this is a concept which should be encouraged in the school as well as in the home.
4. Prevention of communicable diseases is helped by cleanliness.
5. There is an aesthetic "feeling good" aspect to showering after vigorously participating in activity.

Students should be encouraged to shower after active classes for basically the health reasons stated above. By the same token one would not expect students to shower after a non-active class. If students are asked to shower when there is no need then it contradicts the reasons mentioned earlier.

Locker Room Procedures

There are so many variables in the locker room procedures encountered in various schools, it would be impossible for anyone to recommend a specific set to the reader. The recommendation is made here that the teacher take into consideration all of the physical and environmental

122

factors such as the number and type of lockers, and the number of students to be serviced at peak load, and devise a system applicable to their situation. Locker assignments and lock numbers should be kept on record by the teacher. Records of lock combinations are necessary for the teacher because inevitably a number of students forget their combinations. Locker systems that use keys necessitate the teacher having a master key always available. In assigning lockers the teacher should remember that is is necessary to space locker assignments so that aisles and areas are not overcrowded. This will both speed up the dressing and undressing process, and aid in avoiding accidents and behavior problems

Role of the Student Leader

Student leaders should be used for two reasons: (1) the physical education class is an excellent laboratory for developing leadership skills, and (2) the teacher is able to do a superior job of instruction when student leaders are employed. Not all students can become full-fledged student leaders, but all students can assume some leadership function. There are many instructional strategies and class routines in which the students can become involved. The teacher should ascertain what these are considering the unit of work that is being done. The responsibilities of students serving as leaders should be shared with the entire class, along with the reasons for utilizing students. It is important for the teacher to rotate some of the leadership positions, so that all students that wish may get the opportunity to serve in this fashion. It should be remembered that there are other kinds of leaders in addition to the student with superior motor ability, such as the more mature student, the student with the natural personality to be a leader, and the student with superior mental ability. Too, there are leadership roles that demand a lot of the student, such as being in charge of a teaching station, and there are those that do not demand as much talent, such as caring for the equipment. The teacher should match the student assignment with the student's ability.

Absences and Excuses

Every school district will probably have its own set of policies regarding student absences and excuses. The physical education teacher should become knowledgeable of these policies. Additionally, specific physical education policies regarding absences and excuses must be developed so that they are consistent with school or district policies. Once the policies have been formulated by the teacher or physical education staff, they should be carefully explained to the students during the orientation period and periodically discussed as reminders. Many teachers also find it very helpful to make the parents aware of these very important policies.

Excuses from class participation present the physical education teacher with a unique problem. The school may have a school nurse to whom all requests for excuses from participation may be referred. If this is the case the physical education teacher should abide by the decision reached by the nurse. It is recommended that the physical education teacher discuss the policy and procedures with the nurse so that there is an understanding between the two people involved. Very often there is no nurse in the school, so the individual teacher must handle all requests for an excuse from participation. The teacher should always honor written requests for excuses from a parent or a medical authority. However, the teacher should periodically follow-up on these excuse requests to verify their authenticity. When students request to be excused from participation without parental authorization the teacher should treat each request on an individual basis and try to make the proper decision for the student involved.

When absences or excuses from class become a problem for a student the teacher should take corrective steps. The first realistic approach would be to discuss the situation with the student and attempt to alleviate the cause of the absences and/or excuses. If the problem cannot be corrected with the student alone, the parents of the student should also be asked to become a part of a conference. The primary focus of any conference with a student or the parents should be to discover the reason for the absences or excuses and to plan a program to eliminate the problem.

Class Formations

Teachers will use many different arrangements of students in teaching physical education activities. Each time the teacher must explain an arrangement for the students to assume it takes class time. The majority of the activities that will be done can fit into a rather small number of arrangements. For this reason the teacher should select a few formations which serve the majority of needs and acquaint the students with these. The first time a formation is used it should be explained and given a name. If this is done the teacher will only need to instruct the students to assume a particular formation as it is used in the future.

Figure 7.1 shows nine formations which may be used as they are sketched, or they may be modified to fit specific needs of the teacher. A specific formation should be chosen for several reasons: (1) the formation should allow for the best interaction for the specific activity between the teacher and students, (2) the formation should be one that allows students and the teacher to see and hear one another, and (3) the formation

Circle	Semi-Circle	Double Semi-Circle
X X X X X X X X X X X	X X X X X X X X X X X X	X X X X X X X X X X X X X X X X X X X

Squad	Off-Set Squad	Scatter
X X X X X X X X X X X X X X X X X X X X X X X X X X X X X X X X X X X	X X X X X X X X X X X X X X X X X X X X X X X X X X X X X X . X X	X X X X X X X X X X X X X X X X X X

Line	Double Line	Shuttle
X X X X X X X X X X	X X X X X X X X X X X X	XXXX XXXX XXXX XXXX XXXX XXXX XXXX XXXX

Figure 7.1   Sample formations.

must allow for safe participation in the specific activity. An example of the formation allowing good interaction would be the use of the "Double Semi-Circle" formation for talking with the class or presenting a demonstration. The teacher would stand in the open end of the circle and the front row of students may sit down while the second row kneels or stands. The "Off-Set Squad" formation illustrates a formation which allows the students and the teacher to see and hear one another. Safety is an important concern and can be shown by the use of the "Line" or "Double Line" formation for hitting golf balls. In the double line formation the two lines of students hit balls away from the other group and the teacher walks up and down between the lines to offer assistance.

SUMMARY

Effective classroom management is necessary if the teacher is to avoid wasting time, conserve personal energy, and avoid confusing the students. Management is concerned with the non-academic behavior of teachers, and how efficient they are in conducting classroom routines.

Research has shown that far too much time is spent by most teachers on management functions. The time spent can be reduced by a well-planned orientation period in which the teacher discusses with the students the various aspects of classroom management at the beginning of the school year.

Classroom management functions are not learning experiences in themselves; therefore they should be streamlined as much as possible. Suggestions for doing so include the following: (1) conduct class on a schedule, (2) use an efficient method of taking attendance, (3) teach a specific signal for attention, (4) handle equipment efficiently, and (5) reduce transition time.

There are some additional aspects to helping the class run smoothly that each physical education teacher should keep in mind. Therefore, the teacher should formulate policies regarding dress requirements, shower regulations, locker room procedures, use of student leaders, absences and excuses, and formations to be used. Some of these policies directly effect the students and should be shared with them.

126

SELECTED READINGS AND REFERENCES

Emmer, Edmund and Carolyn Evertson, "Effective Classroom Management at the Beginning of the School Year," *The Elementary School Journal,* May, 1980, pp. 219-231.

Godbout, Paul, Jean Brunelle, and Marielle Tousignant, "Academic Learning Time in Elementary and Secondary Physical Education Classes," *Research Quarterly for Exercise and Sport,* March, 1983, pp. 11-19.

DEVELOPING POSITIVE STUDENT BEHAVIOR

8

Several years ago a list of problems encountered by first year teachers was collected by a college placement office. There were fourteen different categories of problems, and eleven of them were concerned with various aspects of student behavior, class control, and class management. Since then it has been recognized that the ability of teachers to maintain a suitable learning environment plays an important role in the success of their teaching. A recent issue of the *Phi Delta Kappan* (1982) reports that lack of discipline in the public schools again heads the list of problems cited most often by survey respondents. Discipline has, in fact, been named the number one problem of the schools in eleven of the last twelve years.

The phrase "maintain a suitable learning environment" is really what the topic of discipline, or class control, is all about. Teachers must maintain control of the individuals in their classes, and be responsible for correct student behavior, if learning is to occur.

PREVENTION OF BEHAVIOR PROBLEMS

The problem of student behavior is discussed whenever teaching professionals get together. It seems the question most often asked is, "What do you do to a student if _____," and then they list some undesirable behavior exhibited by a member of their class. Or perhaps they phrase the question this way: "What punishment do you administer to a student when they _____." The profession seems obsessed with the question of what to do to students in order to "discipline" or punish them. To the writers of this text, this seems entirely the wrong approach. The preferred approach should initially emphasize the prevention of behavior problems over everything else. Isn't it logical to put this concept first? The degree to which the teacher is successful in preventing behavior problems, will determine all other action needed. Behavior problems among students do not just happen — they are caused. Therefore, if the cause is eliminated, the teacher will have been successful in preventing behavior problems from occurring.

The prevention of behavior problems must be approached in a systematic fashion. There are several aspects of the teachers' job that may contribute to, or prevent, behavior problems, depending upon how they are handled. Most behavior problems may be prevented if the teacher concentrates attention upon planning, management, instruction, and desirable personal behavior on the part of the teacher.

Preventing Behavior Problems Through Planning

The planning process entails many considerations, none of which is more important than insuring proper student conduct. Therefore, the teacher should give specific thought to planning toward good student behavior. For example, the teacher should make allowances for different skill levels when planning a lesson. It has been stated by some that almost all behavior problems are caused by students who find the class so difficult they see no chance for success, or by students who are not challenged by anything happening in class. In addition, the suggestion is made that teachers should take the students into the planning process. Very few individuals, students included, react negatively to a situation they had a hand in creating. This may be in regard to electing activities, choosing methodology, selecting facilities and equipment, or in deciding who makes up certain stations, partnerships, or teams. Notice, it is not recommended that these procedures be turned over to the students, but to positively involve them in the planning.

Preventing Behavior Problems Through Management

Class management procedures used by the teacher can have an important impact upon the behavior of the students. Procedures should be used which will not only prevent behavior problems, but which will encourage good behavior. It is quite obvious that teachers should keep the

130

physical factors of the environment in mind. If it is too hot, or too cold, or the humidity is unbearable, allowances should be made for these characteristics in their handling of the class. Likewise, the class will run more smoothly if the teacher has all the equipment, facilities, and supplies ready, in playing condition, and in sufficient quantities.

The teacher should be cognizant of students who have reacted negatively toward each other in the past, and arrange to keep them physically separated during the class period. We should not assume that students are acquainted with correct modes of behavior when they enter our class. Often students are admonished for violating desirable behavior practices, when in reality they are not aware they were behaving in an unacceptable manner. The teacher should establish behavior rules at the beginning of the class. This desirable method of behaving should then be shared with the class during the orientation period, so that the students are acquainted with what is expected of them, as well as the types of behavior that are not acceptable.

Preventing Behavior Problems Through Instruction

The instructional behaviors of the teacher that have an effect upon the development of proper student behavior are those that are directly tied to the success students experience in physical education. The teacher should use instructional behaviors that not only produce good student learning, but also result in good student conduct. The teacher should be sure the daily lesson plan is developed so that all students are involved in activities that are meaningful to them, the students are active at all times, and there are no long delays or periods when the students are standing around. Also, each day teachers should use several of the motivational techniques listed in Chapter 9. These techniques help the students keep an interest in the class and are extremely helpful in preventing aberrant behavior.

The teacher should be aware of the students' need for recognition, and provide positive ways for it to materialize. When positive behavior does materialize, it is important to see that it is rewarded.

Preventing Behavior Problems Through Personal Teacher Behaviors

How students act is often caused by the personal behavior of the teacher. The interaction between the teacher and students sets a tone within an instructional environment which contributes to the behavior exhibited by the students. The teacher should develop an atmosphere in the physical education class that will inform the students that this is a class.

131

You are the teacher, and responsible for the conduct of the class; they are the students, and are there to learn. When the teacher starts the class on time, has a prepared lesson plan, and shares the class objectives with the students, a working, educational tone is set for that period. When teachers maintain control of their emotions and their manner of speech, it helps the students to do likewise.

It is necessary for the teacher to keep a social distance between themselves and their students. Students need adult friends as models of behavior, and not "peer buddies." An atmosphere of too much informality often leads to behavior problems. The teacher should consider students' actions or comments as educational problems, and not as a personal affront.

STRATEGIES FOR DEVELOPING GOOD BEHAVIOR

The goal of every teacher regarding student behavior should be the development of good behavior patterns within students. If the teacher is successful in developing good behavior patterns, there will be less need to deal with bad behavior. Good behavior in the classroom is not something that occurs naturally, but rather is something that must be explained, taught, practiced, and reinforced.

Teachers who are compelled to spend a lot of time on petty behavior correction tasks will not be able to successfully carry out their main job of instruction. Too often the teacher spends too much time asking students to be quiet, don't bounce the ball, get back in your position, and pay attention. This situation is due to a lack of positive behavior strategies being used by the teacher, along with a lack of preparation of the students for the proper functioning of the class. In this section of the chapter are presented several strategies for maintaining good behavior within the physical education class.

Expect Positive Behavior From Students

The importance and power of expectation can be seen in this amusing story. A new teacher in a junior high school received a set of cards which contained the name, address, telephone number, and other information about each of the students. Also on the card was a number for which the teacher did not know the meaning. Assuming the number was an I.Q. measure for each child, the teacher greeted the first hour class whose "I.Q. measures" ranged between 90 and 110. These were obviously average students so the teacher expected only average performance from them, and that was exactly what was revealed. The numbers on the cards for the second period class ranged from 112 to 136. The teacher

132

smiled in anticipation of teaching this very bright group of students, and consequently made considerable academic demands upon them which were met with high degrees of success. Shortly thereafter, to the dismay of the teacher, the principal sent for the sets of class cards because the only record of the students' "locker numbers" were on those cards.

Students not only respond to teacher expectation in academic matters, but also in behavior. The type of behavior that is expected by the teacher must be transmitted to the students. This expected behavior may be learned by the students in formal ways, such as statements and written rules, or it may be learned by observing the mannerisms and informal behavior of the teacher. The teacher who takes a positive approach to the class is more likely to receive positive behavior from the students. The teacher who lists many negatively stated rules on the first day of class is indirectly telling the students that poor behavior is expected, so here is what you are not to do. It is important for the teacher to spend time with the students at the beginning of the year to establish what the acceptable behavior will be. This should be done in a manner that expresses to the students that you believe they can and will behave in the proper manner.

Have Clearly Stated Rules

Rules are important to the proper functioning of a physical education class. They establish the boundaries within which all students can function in a harmonious manner and learning may proceed. Obedience to class rules is what keeps students from infringing upon the rights of one another.

All teachers seem to have rules for their classes. However, all teachers do not handle the rules in the same way, nor do they all have the same success with making the rules work in a positive way in the operation of the class. Teachers who are effective in the classroom not only have rules, but they also make sure the students clearly understand the rules. This is accomplished by presenting the rules to the class and discussing them. In the case of early elementary age students the teacher not only presents and discusses the rules with the class, but the rules are practiced by the students. Such class procedures and rules as those for entering and leaving the gymnasium, receiving permission to go to the bathroom, and rules pertaining to the use of the water fountain would actually be rehearsed by students.

Another distinctive action of successful teachers is that they follow through with rules and deal properly with students who break the rules. In this way the students understand that the rules do have meaning, and it will cost them something if they break a rule.

133

Rules need to be written in such a way that they will be a positive influence upon the behavior of the students. A great number of harsh, negatively stated rules give students the impression that the teacher expects bad behavior and the rules become a challenge for the students. It would be best if the teacher could create a positive feeling toward the class rules. Madsen and Madsen (1974) offer the following guidelines for formulating rules.

1. The class should be involved in making up the rules.
2. The rules should be short and to the point.
3. Remind the class of the rules at times other than when someone has misbehaved.
4. State the rules in a positive form rather than negative. ("Stand quietly during instruction" instead of "Don't talk to your neighbors.")
5. Post the rules in a prominent place in the locker room. Many teachers also include the class rules as part of a student "handbook" that is distributed to each student.
6. Make different sets of rules for varied activities.
7. Keep a record of the times you review the rules with the class.

Re-Focus Students Rather Than Punish

Teachers will be able to eliminate the majority of punitive punishment and verbal reprimanding within their classes if they will learn to refocus the students upon the task at hand. Re-focusing is simply drawing the attention of students back to the task when they begin to wander off-task. This is a technique that precludes the use of punishment and, if used successfully, may remove the need for punishment entirely. The effectiveness of re-focusing depends upon the ability of the teacher to know when students need to be re-focused. This is accomplished by careful monitoring of the students by the teacher. Therefore, the teacher must develop the ability to survey the entire class and be aware of their activities at all times, including while the teacher is giving individual or group instruction.

Re-focusing techniques may be verbal comments to the student, or they may simply be gestures or body movements by the teacher. Making eye contact with the student will very often convey to the student that something needs to be changed. Sometimes eye contact accompanied by a head movement or pointed finger will bring the student back on-task. Some techniques that work well when the teacher is talking to a group of students is to simply move close to the offending student, or place a hand on the shoulder of the student who is talking or otherwise in need of re-focusing. No matter which technique is used, the important thing is that the student has been brought back into the lesson without the disruptive consequences of verbal reprimands or punishment.

THE ROLE OF RESPECT IN STUDENT BEHAVIOR

"To consider worthy of high regard" is the way Webster (1981) defines the term, respect. If there is respect for the teacher by the students, there will be a much greater chance that the behavior of the students will be proper. If students respect the teacher they will not want to infringe upon the rights and responsibilities of the teacher.

To fully understand the impact of respect upon student behavior, the discussion must be separated into "having respect for the position of teacher" and "having respect for the individual who is the teacher." It is important that both the teacher and students understand this difference.

Respect for the Position of Teacher

Teachers, along with such other positions as parents and the elderly, deserve and command respect simply because of their position. Students must learn that they are to respect the teacher, if for no other reason than that the person is a teacher. Since each teacher represents, to a certain degree, all other teachers, the dignity of the position must be maintained. Therefore, it is a responsibility of the teacher to insist upon respect from the students for the position of teacher.

Respect for the Individual Who is the Teacher

Respect for a position may be expected, but respect for a person must be earned. If respect for the teacher does actually result in better student behavior, it behooves the teacher to be cognizant of ways of gaining the respect of the students. A few suggestions of how teachers may gain the respect of their students are as follows:

1. The teacher can gain the respect of students by being well prepared and organized for each class period.
2. The teacher should have the students' best interests in mind in all that occurs in the class, and should let it show through both words and actions.
3. The teacher should treat each student with respect and dignity, and let all students know they are important.
4. The teacher should not be above apologizing to the class or an individual if it is warranted.
5. The teacher should handle all disciplinary discussions and actions with a student in private, rather than in front of the rest of the class.

SEEKING THE CAUSE OF UNDESIRABLE BEHAVIOR

If the teacher takes the above approach to student conduct, many behavior problems will never appear. However, in being realistic in this discussion, we know that some behavior problems will still emerge. It is at this time that the teacher should shift the emphasis to find out why the student behaved as he or she did. To think in terms of punishment, or "what to do with the student," is still premature. All kinds of punishment may be levied for undesirable behavior, and it will solve nothing if the reason for the student's undesirable behavior is not removed. Marten, Ishmael and Singh (1980) report, from a questionnaire responded to by 702 teachers, that the three main causes of discipline problems in the school are: (1) the home environment, where there is a lack of discipline as well as social and emotional support, (2) a general attitude of permissiveness in society, and (3) the constraints placed upon the teachers concerning disciplinary methods that may be used.

Teachers may not be able to change society or the home environment of students, but they can understand how these factors affect students. The best technique to use in attempting to find the cause of undesirable behavior is the individual conference method. The teacher may, in private conference with the student, succeed in getting the student to reveal the problem. In some cases the teacher may be able to see what the problem is, even though the student does not recognize it. The teacher's approach to the student should be one of expressing disappointment in the behavior, and confiding that the teacher had expected a more mature behavior from the student. Contrary to what is often expressed, the majority of students want their teachers to think well of them. The suggestion is made to talk to the student alone, even though there may have been a group of students involved. This is because it has often been shown that the student will talk more freely when alone with the teacher than if two or three peers are also present. If the offense is serious enough to involve the parents of the student, they should be included in the conference.

It is important that the teacher remembers the reason for the personal conference. The purpose is not to admonish, belittle, or threaten students with some dire consequences. The purpose is to better understand the student, and aid the student in understanding the teacher. An even tone of voice, calm mannerisms, and a professional, helping approach will reap much greater rewards.

THE PUNISHMENT OF STUDENTS

It is recognized that at some point in the teaching process, punish-

136

ment will need to be used. It should be kept in mind that the purpose of using punishment is to prevent the same behavior from occurring again. At the same time the teacher desires to move the student toward becoming more responsible for his or her own behavior.

Guidelines for Punishment

If punishment is to serve a useful function, it must be used in the proper manner. The use of punishment should be given the same thought and planning as other important aspects of teaching. It should only be used when teachers are in full control of their emotions and are able to administer punishment within the following guidelines:

1. The teacher should punish without being punitive or retaliatory. The teacher is not trying to get even, or show the student "you can't get away with that in my class." The teacher is simply educating the student as to what type of personal behavior is acceptable and what type is not.
2. The teacher should administer punishment as soon as possible after the undesirable behavior occurs. This should be done because the offender is more able to relate the punishment with the undesirable behavior if the intervening time is brief.
3. The teacher should administer the punishment in private, with the possible exception of having an adult "witness" in extreme cases. Punishment can be demeaning if administered in front of other students. In addition, the punished student may be more defensive about the punishment if it is done in front of peers, thus losing some of the desired results from the punishment.
4. The teacher should accompany the punishment with a statement of what the appropriate behavior should have been. The punishment should not be levied in a "void," and it should be explicitly explained to the offender what type of behavior would have been preferred.
5. The teacher should make sure the punishment is appropriate for the behavior. Severe punishment should not be administered for a minimal offense, and neither should the punishment be only remotely related to the undesirable behavior. It would not be appropriate for the teacher to dismiss a student from class for three days for chewing gum in the gymnasium.
6. Teachers should direct punishment at the undesirable behavior committed by students, and not at the students personally. The students would then understand that it was not them that the teacher was dissatisfied with, but rather the particular act they committed.
7. The teacher should administer punishment to the individual that performs the undesirable behavior, and not to the group of which that

person is a part. It would not be appropriate, therefore, to deny an entire class or squad some privilege simply because one member of the class had disobeyed some stated class rule.

8. The teacher should forget an incidence of undesirable behavior once it is past, and not label that student a trouble-maker. Often an incidence of undesirable behavior is a one-time occurrence by a student. Therefore, teachers should not necessarily expect students to behave in an undesirable manner a second time.

Proper Methods of Punishment

Once the teacher has determined that some kind of punishment is necessary, there is still the question of what the punishment should be. Some means of punishment serve a useful purpose and others only compound the problem. The acceptable methods of punishment are those that deter the student from repeating the undesirable behavior, and at the same time help to make the student understand what benefits accompany good behavior. Any punishment used should be appropriate for the negative behavior. A few acceptable types of punishment to be used are listed below:

1. Expect students to meet the responsibilities of their behaviors. Students who act in such a way as to waste time for themselves and other class members may be asked to do extra work to make up for the wasted time. Students may be asked to pay for equipment that was damaged due to their intentional destructive behavior.

2. Verbally reprimanding students for their behavior. A verbal reprimand may be adequate punishment for some students under certain circumstances. Part of the verbal reprimand may include the request for an improved standard of conduct from the student.

3. Remove privileges from students for their behavior. Both class and extra-class privileges may be removed as punishment for undesirable behavior. Such privileges as being squad captain and equipment monitor may be removed.

Improper Methods of Punishment

There are many methods of punishment that have been used by teachers which are not proper in the school setting. Punishments that result in physical abuse of students is one of these. Having students sit or stand in positions that cause physical discomfort should never be used. Verbal abuse of students is equally bad for a teacher to use, because it can be harmful to students. This demeaning type of teacher behavior is not effective in correcting the behavior of the students, and it may cause

138

lasting problems between the teacher and the student.

There are several undesirable forms of punishment that implicate the subject matter of physical education that should be avoided. The students are in physical education to participate in, and learn from, movement experiences. It is most wise for the teacher to keep punishment completely separated from the subject matter of physical education. The teacher should not use physical activity itself as a form of punishment. Assigning students to do push-ups or run laps as punishment may have the effect of turning the students against activity. They may begin to associate physical activity with the distasteful results of punishment. On the other end of the continuum, the teacher should refrain from dismissing students from class as a means of punishment. This action is obviously in direct opposition to the purposes of the physical education class. One purpose of the class is to promote activity and the removal of students defeats that purpose. Another related means of implicating the subject matter of physical education is the use of grades as a punishment. Teachers should avoid "automatically" lowering students' grades as a means of punishment.

One last area of undesirable punishment is the failure of teachers to handle their own student "discipline." Some teachers shirk their responsibilities by "sending kids to the office" for every infraction. This practice undermines the authority of the teacher, and it also causes a loss of respect for the teacher by the school administration. This may result in future lack of support from the administration. Teachers can also shirk their responsibility by allowing the class to determine the punishment for certain student offenses. This practice is rarely successful and could have destructive results.

Possible Negative Results of Punishment

Even though it may be necessary for teachers to consider the use of punishment, they should realize there are negative results that may accompany the punishment. Gallahue (1978) presents these possible negative results of punishment which the teacher should guard against.

Negative generalization. It is quite possible that the student will generalize such traits and feelings as worry, hatred, fear, and animosity toward the teacher, the subject of physical education, the class, and everything present when the punishment occurs. If this is the case, the results of the punishment will be more detrimental than the offense being punished.

Withdrawal. If the student is the victim of repeated punishment, it may cause him or her to fear school, develop an intense dislike for the learning environment, and eventually withdraw. The withdrawal may be from the teacher, students, activities, class, or in extreme cases, the school.

Increased emotionality. The student who is punished invariably has an emotional reaction to the punishment. This emotion increases with the severity of the punishment, and may reach such a state as to make it very difficult for the student to change behavior.

Aggressive behavior. Punishment is perceived differently by various students. Some students will change their behavior favorably, while in other students punishment they receive may trigger additional aggressive behavior.

Improper reaction to the punishment. The teacher using punishment may become a model of behavior for the student who was punished, as well as other students in the class. They may perceive the teacher's actions as the way to treat other people, instead of correctly interpreting the punishment as being imposed for an unacceptable behavior.

Lowered self-esteem. The self-esteem of a punished student may be influenced negatively. Since they have been punished, and the other members of the class know it, the student may then have a lower opinion of themselves. Self-esteem is definitely influenced by how students think others perceive them.

THE CONCEPT OF SELF-DISCIPLINE

No discussion of discipline, or student behavior, would be complete without a consideration of the concept known as self-discipline. This is the ultimate in student behavior, and is a state of affairs regarding the behavior of the young people in our classes that each one in the teaching profession should work for constantly.

Basically, self-discipline means the student has behaved correctly because of an understanding of the requirements, has thought over the reason for the requirements, and has made a mature decision to act in the correct fashion. The decision is not made just because an adult, teacher, or higher authority is present. This is the true type of adult behavior, and is valuable in the adult world as a participating and responsible citizen. An example of self-discipline in the adult world is the driver who obeys the speed limit even though there is no police authority in sight. This is done because the person understands the consequences of failure to obey, with all of its negative possibilities.

A teacher striving to teach the concept of self-discipline has a never-ending task. It is present in small degrees in all students, but never enough in any of the students. It becomes a continuous quest for the teacher, and is part of the life-long commitment on the part of the teacher to be a true developer of youth.

140

SUMMARY

Discipline has repeatedly been listed as the number one problem of the schools. Teachers must maintain control of individuals in their classes if any learning is to occur. Teachers should first approach the problem of correct student behavior from the viewpoint of preventing undesirable incidents from happening. If they are successful, the "desirable learning environment" needed for learning will exist. If prevention is unsuccessful, the next approach should be the attempt to find out the reason why the behavior problem occurred, for discipline problems will repeat themselves if the reason for them is not removed. Reasons for undesirable behavior may be related to factors outside the school, such as family or societal influences. Teachers who are respected tend to have fewer problems.

There are incidents of undesirable behavior that indicate some modicum of punishment is necessary. There are general guidelines available for the punishment of the student. The teacher should study this carefully so that the punishment is reasonable, fits the offense, and is not unlawful.

One of the concepts that is of extreme importance in teaching students how to behave is that of self-discipline. This concept is based on the attempt to teach students to behave correctly because they understand school requirements, and have made a mature decision to adhere to them.

The most important factor in class control is the teacher. The teacher's influence may come from employing sound teaching strategies, or it may originate from personal traits, such as speech, dress, sincerity, physique, voice, or personality.

Physical education teachers must remember that correct social-emotional development is one of the major objectives of physical education. Students who are skilled and physically fit but behave poorly leave the teacher's job unfinished.

SELECTED READINGS AND REFERENCES

Dobson, James, *Dare to Discipline*, Bantam Book, Toronto, 1970.

Dobson, James, *Hide or Seek*, Fleming H. Revell Company, Old Tappan, New Jersey, 1971.

Gallahue, David L. "Punishment and Control, Negative Results," *The Physical Educator*, May, 1978, pp. 58-59.

Gallup, George, "Gallop Poll of the Public's Attitudes Toward the Public Schools," *Phi Delta Kappan*, September, 1982, pp. 37-50.

Madsen, Charles and Clifford Madsen, *Teaching/Discipline: A Positive Approach for Educational Development*, Allyn and Bacon, Inc., Boston, 1974.

Martin, Wilfred, Ishmael, Baksh, and Amarjit Singh, "Observations from Teachers and Students on School Discipline," *The Clearing House*, October, 1980, pp. 80-82.

Spettel, Gratia, "Classroom Discipline-Now?" *The Clearing House*, February, 1983, pp. 266-268.

Wasicsko, Mark and Steven Ross, "How to Create Discipline Problems," *The Clearing House*, December, 1982, pp. 149-152.

Webster's New Collegiate Dictionary. G. & C. Merriam Company, Springfield, 1981.

144

MOTIVATION TOWARD MAXIMUM LEARNING

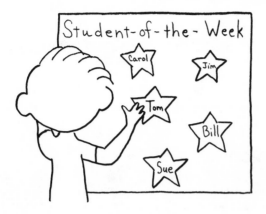

There is probably no one technique more important to the success of the physical education teacher than the ability to motivate in the classroom. Daughtrey probably states it best when he says:

> Underlying all efforts to improve the quality of teaching is the element of motivation. Motivation is the key to all learning, and teachers who are able to motivate children will find teaching more interesting and satisfying (Daughtrey, 1973, p. 253).

The ability to motivate others may largely be precipitated by a knowledge of what motivates oneself. The teacher must first be motivated and believe in what is being taught and its' inherent value. The enthusiasm of the teacher will rub off on the students just as will the lack of enthusiasm.

Even though the physical education teacher has the advantage of teaching a subject that, by its very nature, appeals to a large percentage of students, motivation is still necessary. The play urge is part of the natural make-up of most boys and girls unless something gets in its way. Unfortunately, there are many things that do get in its way, or inhibits the natural desire to play, perform, and compete. Among these are: the attraction of many other aspects of modern life available to the youth; homes where sport, motor performance, and physical activities are down-played by the parents; physical education programs that are too traditional, poorly taught, use improper teaching methods, lack progression, and offer a too meager number of activities; and the pressure of other school subjects. We should also mention the student whose main interest in life lies in another area such as music, science, or perhaps art. When we add these facts to the situation where the student who is not motor-gifted is asked to compete with the skilled students in the class, it is relatively easy to understand why the physical education teacher needs to be skillful in motivating students.

The teacher prepares to attack this problem by realizing that motivating students is one of teaching's prime responsibilities. Just as being able to demonstrate a sports skill, or correctly explain some aspect of team strategy is necessary for every physical education teacher, so is the ability to motivate students. Knowing all about a sport is not enough. Being able to perform a sport is not enough. Along with all the other requirements of a good teacher, being able to motivate students is a necessary skill.

MOTIVATION DEFINED

Motivation may be defined as an intangible which raises the individual's readiness for action. In reading this definition over and over, and thinking about what it really embodies, attention is called to the words "individual readiness." In other words, motivation is an individual, rather than a group, technique. Different motivational techniques work more or less effectively when applied to different individuals. For example, some students are inclined to perform especially well when put into a highly competitive situation, while others react negatively to the same experience. Therefore, a prerequisite to being able to motivate students, is to know them — their likes and dislikes, fears, abilities, interests, and their social and emotional state of development. Without this knowledge, even the best motivational techniques will be unsuccessful.

Sport psychologists have learned that two very important needs of students in physical activity are: (1) the need to be stimulated and have excitement — to have fun, and (2) the need to feel competent and successful — to feel worthy.

The Need for Fun

In order to have fun, optimum arousal is necessary. If our level of arousal is too low we become bored and seek stimulation. However, if the arousal level is too high we become fearful or anxious. We then try to decrease the arousal in what ever way possible.

Each individual will differ in his or her optimum level of arousal. To help the students reach this level the teacher may:
1. Fit the difficulty of the skills to the ability level of the students by using skills that challenge the student but are not too advanced so that they are dangerous or unattainable.
2. Keep the lessons exciting by offering a wide variety of activities and

sports. Letting the youngsters share in selecting the activities will also stimulate them.
3. Keep everyone active, not waiting in line for long periods of time.
4. Avoid constant instruction. Allow occasional time to just "play the game" or practice the skill and be absorbed in the activity.

The Need to Feel Worthy

In order to feel worthy the student needs to feel competent and experience success. Sports are potentially threatening, as in our society we learn early to equate self-worth with winning. Winning is perceived as success and losing as failure.

When a reasonable amount of success is experienced, it reinforces the sense of competency which encourages further pursuit of excellence. Success is the greatest form of motivation.

Just as there is motivation to achieve success, there is also motivation to avoid failure. Children accomplish this by not putting forth a full effort, so that if failure occurs it can be justified as not trying rather than being due to a low skill ability. Teachers can unknowingly reinforce both of these. If they spend more time and offer more rewards or feedback to the skilled performer, this motivates that performer to continue. At the same time, by spending less time and having lower expectations for the lesser skilled, those students are motivated to avoid failure by not trying.

Another problem that can be caused by giving greater recognition to the students with superior skills is that some students with lower skill abilities may set unrealistic goals. These goals are too high for the individual's skill level, and therefore result in failure.

Children, when left alone without teachers, coaches, peer pressure, or spectators, learn motor skills and avoid failure in very ingenious ways. If they do not attain a goal, they lower it or learn from their mistakes and try again. These self regulated mistakes are seen as just that, part of the learning process, not as failures. Once they succeed they will raise their goals and try again.

INTRINSIC AND EXTRINSIC MOTIVATION

Intrinsic Motivation

Intrinsic motivation is the sheer satisfaction of doing something. It is self fueling and not directly available for use by the teacher. It can, however, be encouraged if the teacher will accentuate the positive through the use of feedback. Success and positive feedback are strong

147

motivators to continue the effort necessary for improvement. The teacher is the most critical source of positive feedback.

Feedback

Feedback provides information, motivation, and reinforcement in the learning of motor skills. Positive feedback allows the student to profit from each practice experience. More importantly, the quality, availability, and effective use of feedback directly affects the potential for optimum performance of a motor skill.

Quality of Feedback. Verbal feedback should focus on the correct skills, behavior, or reaction in a game. An example would be telling the student he or she had a good strong serve in volleyball, rather than to say the serve was out of bounds, since that is obvious. During a game of soccer the teacher may stop the students to explain how John maintained his position correctly and was therefore able to score a goal. The use of genuine praise is extremely valuable. The praise, however, must be sincere or it loses its validity. When giving feedback it is important to observe several performances before making comments, in order to see the things that are consistently correct or incorrect. When offering a suggestion on how to correct a mistake, it should be positive and limited to one aspect of the skill. An example would be to tell Sally to step forward with her foot this time when she throws the ball.

The use of nonverbal feedback may also be important for motivation. A smile, thumb up, OK sign, and clapping are examples of nonverbal feedback.

Availability of Feedback. When students are learning a new skill they should be frequently rewarded. Generally, the greater the frequency, the faster the learning. Once the skill is learned it should be reinforced occasionally.

Since teachers cannot be with each individual student continually, they must accept the responsibility to structure and facilitate the environment to provide feedback to the students whenever possible. The use of older student aids to offer verbal reinforcement to the students when they are practicing motor skills is useful in reaching a larger number of students during the class period. The partner pattern of practicing, as discussed in Chapter 6, is also useful for additional feedback. The partners can chart each others progress during the class. As students are encouraged to give praise where it is due, as in a good performance, they will be learning both the give and take of rewards.

Effective Use of Feedback. During the instruction of skills the teacher should stress the positive aspects of each. Only the basic elements of the skill should be emphasized when introducing it (e.g., accuracy, speed, distance). Further refinements can be added slowly as a challenge after the basic skill is mastered.

The environment itself may be used to add feedback. With younger students this may be accomplished through the use of lights, bells, movements, or other agents that are incorporated into the apparatus. A clown target, whose nose lights up when the bullseye is hit by the bean bag or ball, is one example of having the apparatus give feedback. More information on feedback may be found in Chapter 11.

Extrinsic Motivation

Extrinsic motivation is when outside rewards are given for skill acquisition. An example of extrinsic motivation is allowing the entire class to earn one minute of free time each time they organize and change activities within a given time span. An individual student could earn points by completing a task leading to a skill, or by completing the skill itself. This motivates students to cooperate as a whole as well as to strive to achieve personal tasks. The points may be traded for a reward or privilege such as allowing extra time in the gymnasium, being a student leader, or having a chance to participate in a favorite activity.

Other extrinsic rewards may be trophies, medals, ribbons, or certificates. When using these types of rewards it is important to emphasize the meaning attached to them. They are just tokens for recognition of the realization of larger goals. They do not make one person better than another. The participation itself should still be the most important part of the learning activity.

MOTIVATION TECHNIQUES AT OUR DISPOSAL

Through research by the psychologist and educator, a number of motivational techniques have proven to be successful. The important thing for the physical education teacher to remember is that no single technique will work with all students. Also, the teacher should not pick out a few favorite techniques and neglect the rest. Some will work in some situations and not in others. Some are effective with certain types of students and ineffective with others. Therefore, the teacher needs to analyze the class as a whole (age, sex, skill level, stage of development, interests) and select the techniques most applicable. In a like manner, the teacher needs to study closely the individual student that needs to be motivated, and from the techniques available, choose those that are most appropriate.

It is one thing to state some practical motivational techniques, but quite another to show how these techniques can be put into practice. In the following section are presented some time-tested motivational techniques, along with suggestions for implementing them into the actual instructional program.

Follow Interest-Stimulating Curricular Practices

Offer elective as well as required physical education programs. Required physical education programs often meet with resistance just because they are required. Elective programs give the students the option of choosing to participate in the offerings or not to participate. The existence of this "freedom" often motivates the student to elect physical education. In addition to the option of taking the program or not, the majority of elective programs have, built within, the opportunity for the students to take the game, sport, or activity that they like — usually because they have had a successful prior experience. And finally, students in the elective program will work harder, apply themselves better, and progress faster, because they are a select group — both in ability and in interest.

Offer elective activities within each yearly program. Physical education teachers are continually urged to meet the needs and interests of the students. When students have a chance to elect either skiing or skating in the winter, or archery or bowling in the lifetime sports program, they are being allowed to participate in an activity they prefer over the other one offered. Their interest is being better satisfied, and the students are motivated to work harder because they like what they are doing.

Offer a variety of activities within each yearly program. Individual students are attracted to many different activities. If a program has tennis, football, and swimming, a certain percentage of the class will like those activities, and will be motivated to achieve as much as they can. If the program includes the above three activities, plus golf, volleyball, and aerobics, an additional number of students will respond positively. Therefore, the suggestions is made to include from eight to twelve activities per year, so that the interests of as many members of the class as possible are met and the students are motivated.

Offer experiences suited to the needs of the students. Students do not like activities that do not "fit" them, nor can they deal with them effectively. A teacher trying to teach a complicated basketball offense to a group of ninth graders would have great difficulty. The students would not have the necessary background, would not be psychologically ready for something as complicated, and would not see the need. Instead of this, the teacher might introduce a simple basketball offense that would be appropriate to the skill level of the class. Another example of meeting

150

the needs of students involves the junior high school student who is going through his or her growth spurt, is often gangly, and usually lacks a lot of muscular strength. The teacher, in that situation, should emphasize a program that is not dependent on muscular strength for a successful performance. It would be preferable to forego a weight program and concentrate on ball handling or eye-hand and eye-foot activities.

Use Good Instructional Techniques

Use a variety of teaching methods. A common complaint heard from students who do not find their physical education class a satisfying experience is, "We always do the same old thing." Sometimes they are referring to the repeat of the same activity over and over, and sometimes they are referring to the way the teacher conducts class. The latter case may be corrected by employing a variety of teaching techniques. This allows the students to be looking forward to what will happen next. A few examples of using a variety of teaching methods are to have a varsity player come in to demonstrate a skill, assign outside reading in interesting publications, let students do some coaching and officiating, and let students alternate in leading flexibility exercises or being team captains.

Give individual attention and instruction. There is a common belief in education that each student should receive some individual attention from the teacher each class period. Yet many classes can be observed where the teacher is standing or leaning against the wall while students are participating. During the class period the teacher should constantly be giving group instruction or paying attention to some individual in the class. It is this individual attention that motivates the student to strive for better performance. Special attempts should be made by the teacher to see that the necessary time is spent with the unskilled as well as the skilled performer.

Avoid undue amounts of student failure. Constant failure can cause students to lose their motivation for learning. Failure can be decreased significantly if skills are taught with a good progression. Matching teams and individuals of near equal ability in competitive situations also leads to less failure. In addition, the composition of teams should be changed frequently. The way scores from skill and physical fitness tests are recorded can result in success or failure. It is suggested here that in dealing with physical fitness test scores, numbers are only used to indicate a student's improvement over a previous peformance. In this way students may experience success, even though their scores are low compared to the rest of the class.

Provide the students with challenging situations. The teacher should

151

challenge students with tasks that are difficult, but attainable. These challenges may be for the whole class or for individuals within the class. The class challenges would primarily be represented by the planned curricular experiences. Individual challenges should be aimed at specific weaknesses or areas within the individual student where improvement would be desirable. Acceptable individual challenges might include having a student try to reduce his or her weight by twenty pounds, participate in a personal conditioning program three days a week for the semester, and strive to score 80% or higher on all knowledge tests for a quarter of the school year.

Include instruction and demonstration when presenting new material. Every unit will be new to some students in class. The importance of a new skill, how to perform it, and where it fits into the whole sport needs to be discussed. An example may be found in teaching the soccer dribble. Most American school children associate the dribble with basketball. The fact that the soccer dribble is done entirely with the feet needs to be explained, its importance in the game discussed, the skill demonstrated, and some pre-practice maneuvering with the ball done by the students before they begin formal practice on perfecting this new skill.

Make drills as game-like as possible. The more game-like a drill is, the better the students' effort. An example may be found where the students are working on the double play in softball. If the second baseman and the shortstop execute the double play in practice against a base runner, the increase in the speed of execution will be amazing, when contrasted with doing the same movements without a runner. Another example may be found in teaching the basketball player to dribble with either hand. If this is taught without a defensive player, small mistakes in technique go unnoticed, but if the drill pits the dribbler against a defensive player, the dribbler will pay much stricter attention to the fundamental of dribbling the ball with the hand away from the defensive player.

Show Good Non-Instructional Behavior

Be a good role model for the students. The teacher may serve as a role model in all three domains of student learning. If the teacher is physically fit, the students see that he or she really believes in the importance of a personal fitness program. Students will be more likely to run, swim, cycle, lift weights, and compete if the teacher does. Teachers who are scholars themselves will be an encouragement to their students to become more knowledgeable in the area of sport and physical education. The same is true about behavior in the affective domain. Students are motivated to accept officials' decisions, and congratulate opponents, if this is part of the life-style of the adult physical educator.

Let the students know you care for them. Knowing that their teacher cares for them can cause students to behave and try harder. Sincere interaction with students in an instructional setting is the best way to show this concern for them. In addition, the teacher can show care for the students by being friendly and personal in and out of the classroom environment. Offering to help students outside of the class and showing an interest in the things that are of interest to them will enhance this feeling of caring.

Use Performers and Audio-Visual Aids

Arrange for the class to see champion performers. Adolescent students are impressionable, and they are hero-worshippers. They will work hard to be like someone they admire. This thought puts a responsibility on the teacher to invite performers of good character as guests of the school. The suggestion is made to invite a professional athlete, Olympic candidate, all-state or all-American performer, or a local record holder to speak to, and perhaps perform for, your classes. Some sources of prominent athletic speakers are various religious organizations, commerical concerns, and speakers bureaus, as well as the school's own alumni.

Use attractive and interesting bulletin boards. Bulletin boards are a good means of creating student motivation. They should be located where they will be seen by the maximum number of students. They should be changed frequently, probably at least as often as the class changes units of activity. Students may be assigned, by groups, for the preparation of most of the bulletin boards. Special events, such as intramural tournaments or the introduction of a new sport, should receive prominence. The teacher may also seek the cooperation of the art and industrial education departments to improve the quality of the bulletin boards.

Use interesting and motivational films. Good motivational films are available through many sources. Two of the better ones are the American Alliance for Health, Physical Education, Recreation and Dance, and the Athletic Institute. Through these and other organizations, films, film strips, and loop films may be secured for almost every activity. Films can be used for instruction, as the above types are, or for building interest, such as films of the World Series or Olympic Games.

Appeal to the Cognitive and Affective Senses of the Students

Explain the benefits derived from movement experiences. Testimonials of the benefits of exercise and participation can have a great impact upon students. If these testimonials are first hand, they will be most effective, but second hand quotes will also produce the desired results. For example, if teachers run regularly, they can explain how they have reduced their weight, feel better about themselves, and have a feeling of general well-being. Second hand testimonials can be gathered from newspapers and magazines which are full of quotes from well-known public personalities advocating the playing of a sport regularly, or the advantage of personal fitness programs.

Explain the "why" of a sport or activity. Physical educators have been prone to tell students what to do, or how to do it, but have often neglected to tell them why they should participate in physical activity. This can be illustrated in relation to the calisthenics program. Students have traditionally been told to do certain exercises and to do them a specific way. In addition, the "why" should be included, so the students know what part of their body is affected, why that effect is desirable, and what happens if the anatomical part is neglected. Specifically, the teacher should relate the static stretching of the hamstrings to injury prevention. If the teacher insists that the student stays down low in line play in football, the concept of center of gravity should be explained, and the student told how the performance is enhanced when this is done.

Discuss extraordinary athletic feats. Knowing how others have overcome difficulties and excelled can be an inspiration to students. There are many recorded examples, such as the Glenn Cunningham and Wilma Rudolph stories. In many instances local triumphs may be shared which will be even more impressive to the students. The sports world is rich in feats such as blind football and wrestling competitors, the football kicker with half of his foot missing, and the baseball pitcher with a reconstructed pitching arm. Stories such as these can be used effectively in introducing new units or to encourage special effort from specific individuals in a class. Such feats could also be featured on bulletin boards.

Recognize Student Achievement and Good Effort

Employ verbal praise. Although this technique seems obvious to most readers, in actuality it is practiced very little compared to verbalization on the part of the teacher to call attention to mistakes in performance, or to unsatisfactory effort. Psychologists have reported for many years that most individuals respond better to praise than they do to criticism. Therefore, a physical education teacher will certainly have more students liking the class, the activity, and their own performance if the teacher employs verbal praise. If the teacher cannot praise the performance, perhaps an outstanding effort is worthy of praise. The teacher may offer these words to a student who had just come in second in a race in the track unit: "You didn't win this race, but you reduced your time and in the last 100 yards you closed the gap between yourself and the winner. I'm pleased with that effort."

Recognize and publicize successful accomplishments. Successful accomplishments may be recognized within the class by announcing them, posting them on the bulletin board and complimenting individuals, teams, or the entire class. The "top ten performers" may be recognized as well as the "top ten improvers." Publicity may also extend to the school newspaper as well as the local city newspaper.

Allow students to perform and demonstrate in public. There are many possibilities available for students to demonstrate their skills in front of an audience. Some of these possibilities are at half time of basketball games, at school assemblies, PTA meetings, open houses, in front of service clubs, as visitors in other schools, and at state conventions. The students will be motivated to work hard in class to prepare for these demonstrations.

Provide Out-of-Class Opportunities

Provide opportunities for participation. Participation that ends with the class time is insufficient. Out of class participation is needed for fitness, skill development, and enjoyment. Specific opportunities could include an intramural program, sports clubs, and simply opening the facilities for recreational play.

Provide opportunities for visitation. Field trips can be arranged to college and professional games of all sorts, so students may observe sport at an advanced level. Trips can also be made to see outstanding facilities, not only of the game and spectator type, but also to human performance laboratories and training rooms.

Use Awards and Rewards for Motivational Purposes

We may borrow a technique used successfully by the interscholastic athletic program. Awards that are given should not be of monetary value, but symbolic of achievement. For example, in an inter-class track meet, a long roll of ribbon may be purchased, and lengths of it awarded for participating in various events. This may be the only award one of the individuals in class ever receives and will be valued as much as a varsity letter by someone else. Certificates or awards may be given for physical fitness test results or sport skill performance.

155

CAUTIONS TO BE OBSERVED

The teacher should be cognizant of the fact that there are aspects of this part of teaching that may lead to negative results. For example, many teachers have attempted to motivate students by threats of punishment, or by actual punishment. This is effective with very few students, and then for only a short while. The same thing is true regarding verbal abuse, or extreme admonishment. Teachers who use these methods regularly may well be building a dislike for activity, or for what is being taught that day — the exact opposite of what they are trying to accomplish.

Another development that is to be guarded against is over-motivation. It may actually cause students to perform at a level less than their capability. It is known that students may be categorized as having different levels of anxiety. There are high-anxious, medium-anxious, and low-anxious students. Students who are in the low-anxious group are difficult to motivate with any technique. Students in the high-anxious group often perform worse when they are urged (whatever the technique used) to do better. It is primarily the medium-anxious student that responds best to motivational techniques. Seagoe (1961) lists six guidelines for the avoidance of over-motivation:

1. Learning increases with increased motivation up to a certain point.
2. Maximum gain in learning occurs at a moderate degree of motivation.
3. The point at which maximum gain in learning will be reached depends on:
   a. complexity of the problem
   b. ability of the learner
   c. degree of concentration of the motivation
   d. the susceptibility of the learner to motivation
4. When tension increases beyond the optimal point, learning is disrupted.
5. An increase in the degree of motivation increases the variability in a group.
6. Altogether, the intermediate degrees of motivation result in the greatest efficiency of learning (Seagoe, 1961, pp. 247-48).

Before we close, a word needs to be said concerning competition. Offering competition in class, and making skill drills competitive, are listed as usable techniques for motivating students. These are often structured so that there is a winner and a loser. While beneficial to some, this mode of competition should not be used at all times. There is a phase of competition called "competition against themselves," which is often more advisable. Many psychologists recommend this type in preference to competition against others. Especially in young students, competition

156

against themselves is preferable to competition against others. There is no winner or loser, only the individual attempting to better a performance in a track or field event, a physical fitness item, or a sports skill. If the improvement is not there, the individual simply tries again. The activity is structured so there is a positive performance in store for the student — even if it comes at a slightly later period of time.

SUMMARY

Teachers cannot be successful unless they can motivate students. To motivate students, teachers must first be able to motivate themselves. If the teacher is motivated, believes in what he or she is doing, and is enthusiastic, much of this outlook will be "caught" by the students.

Although the urge to play is natural, there are many societal influences and individual differences that interfere. The teacher needs to remember that what will motivate certain students will not be effective with others. Basic to the process of motivation is to remember that all individuals possess the need to have fun and feel worthy.

Motivation has been categorized as being either intrinsic or extrinsic in nature, depending on whether it originates within the student or comes from an external source. Integral to successful motivation is feedback, which provides information and reinforcement to the student as to how he or she is performing.

Educators and psychologists have been able to identify successful motivational techniques. All physical education teachers should study these, and employ the ones that best fit the students in their classes. Some of these techniques are related to the use of correct instructional strategies, while others are related to good non-instructional behavior.

In attempting to motivate their students teachers should be careful not to over-motivate. Over-motivation causes students to perform less than their capability, and may be caused by incorrect techniques employed by the teacher.

SELECTED READINGS AND REFERENCES

Alderman, R. B., "Strategies for Motivating Young Athletes," in *Sports Psychology: An Analysis of Athlete Behavior.* Mouvement Publications, Inc., Ithaca, N.Y., 1978.

Crawford, Larry, "All-Star Motivation for Your P.E. Program," *Scholastic Coach,* December, 1981, pp. 36 and 72.

Daughtrey, Greyson, *Effective Teaching in Physical Education for Secondary Schools,* W.B. Saunders, Co., Philadelphia, 1973.

Morris, Arlene, M., "Keys to Successful Motor Skill Performance," *JOPER,* March, 1981, pp. 49-50.

Nideffer, R. M., *The Inner Athlete: Mind Plus Muscle For Winning,* Thomas Crowell, New York, 1976.

Seagoe, May V., *A Teacher's Guide to the Learning Process,* Wm. C. Brown Co., Dubuque, Iowa, 1961.

159

No one would recommend that a physical education program should consist only of activities designed to build physical fitness. The development of skill in life-time sports, and the appropriate time devoted to knowledges and the social-emotional aspects of physical education, are necessary if physical educators are to meet the aim of the discipline, as stated in Chapter 1. At the same time it is a disservice to the students enrolled in classes, to the community, and to the profession itself, if the present effort to develop physical fitness is not improved and enlarged.

Every individual needs to be physically fit. The reasons for this are numerous and have been documented many times. Fitness is necessary for daily work tasks, for successful participation in leisure-time pursuits, and to meet emergency situations. The very basis for a regimen of life-time sports participation, as well as participation in personalized exercise programs, lies in being physically fit.

On the previous pages of this book we have intentionally omitted any specific consideration of the curricular content of physical education programs. This has been done because the techniques, methods, and procedures discussed have been applicable to many different activities and experiences commonly found in school physical education programs. However, when discussing techniques and methodology appropriate for the development of fitness through physical education experiences, it is necessary to deviate from the above policy. It is important for instructors to keep foremost in their thinking the following important principle: In developing physical fitness, there are certain activities that are more appropriate than others.

Examples of the above principle are numerous. Two familiar ones are the singing games done in many elementary programs and the archery class frequently offered on the secondary level. Yet, if we carefully document the individual components of physical fitness — especially the health-related fitness items, it is easily recognized that singing games and archery do not contribute noticeably to cardio-vascular efficiency, muscular strength, muscular endurance, flexibility, or the correct body composition. Furthermore, there does not exist much possibility for the teacher to devise methods that are conducive to reaching the objective of fitness through these two activities.

PHYSICAL FITNESS DEFINED

This discussion of how to develop fitness in one's teaching is predicated on the assumption that the instructor has a clear picture of what physical fitness is. *Physical Fitness* is defined here as the condition enjoyed by an individual whereby he or she can perform efficiently all the daily requirements of their work without undue fatigue, still have enough energy and enthusiasm to participate in some form of physical recreation, and, if such a condition presents itself, react favorably to the physical demands of an emergency.

Although there are numerous publications, as well as personal opinions, about the concept of physical fitness, it is difficult to improve on the approach taken by Corbin (1983). He has divided the component parts of fitness into two categories: (1) those that are important to health, and (2) those that are important to performance. The two divisions are as follows:

Health-Related Physical Fitness Components
Cardio-Respiratory Efficiency
Muscular Strength
Muscular Endurance
Flexibility
Correct Body Composition

Performance Related Physical Fitness Components
Agility
Co-ordination
Balance
Speed
Power
Reaction Time

It would seem to the writers of this text that the first list is more important than the second. This statement is made for two reasons: (1) in a priority of characteristics important to students in our classes, health should rate above performance, and (2) due to the restricted amount of time available to physical educators, it is extremely difficult to be competent in both categories. Hence, the emphasis in the instructional program is placed on the health-related items.

It should be realized that the two categories listed above are not specifically exclusive of each other. Many times they overlap, and frequently one area, developed as a specific objective contributes to a second area. An example of this may be seen where the instructor engages the students in a continuous repetition of an agility drill. If this is done to the extent that the students are challenging their muscular endurance and raising their heart-rate significantly, they are also contributing to their cardio-respiratory fitness.

IMPORTANT FACTORS IN DEVELOPING PHYSICAL FITNESS

The Cognitive Aspect

Physical education classes for years have contained fitness-building activities. Teachers have required calisthenics, had tug-of-war activities, and assigned students to run ten laps around the gymnasium. Unfortunately the students seldom knew why they were doing these activities, and because they were uncomfortable for the student, a distaste for them developed. It seems that the time has come for helping the student to understand what happens to an exercised individual and an unexercised individual. It is time for students to learn about their bodies anatomically, physiologically, and kinesthetically. In relation to cardiac fitness, concepts like intensity, duration, and frequency should be taught. It is time for students to be able to distinguish between strength and endurance, and to understand flexibility and correct body composition.

Certainly this is not a shiney new idea. Herman and Osness (1966) suggested this approach as necessary if we are to build fitness, especially

163

among our secondary school students. Further impetus has been given to this approach by the program at Penny High School in Connecticut, where Meyers (1976) has devised a specific unit on the Physiology of Exercise for their high school physical education program. At exactly what level these concepts should be introduced remains a point of debate. Certainly the instructor does not have to wait until the students are able to handle an upper-level course in a foundation science before introducing the basic knowledge factors about fitness. The key, of course, is the preparation of material appropriate to the student's grade level. The *Basic Stuff Series* (AAHPERD, 1981) and *Physical Fitness for Life* (Corbin, 1983) present two sets of materials for this approach for the secondary school level.

An analysis of the preceding paragraphs suggests one method of developing fitness for students in physical education classes — that of a classroom, or academic approach. This would include discussions, assigned readings, question and answer periods, the use of films, and individual research by students. Both Corbin, and Herman and Osness, are of the belief that an integral part of this approach must be a laboratory, where students are able to observe, participate in, study, and record the phenomena present when students engage in exercise. An important adjunct to this approach is the use of bulletin boards and fitness record boards.

Selecting Appropriate Activities

If singing games for the elementary student and archery for the secondary student are not appropriate for the development of fitness, what activities are? This is a tricky question. Many activities not usually associated with fitness can be recommended if done correctly. Other activities that are usually thought to be high in their contribution to fitness actually rate very low unless desirable methodologies are used. An example of an activity in the former category is badminton, but if the badminton play is competitive singles between highly skilled players, it ranks highly in the development of one of the aspects of health-related fitness — cardio-respiratory endurance. An example of an activity usually thought to be good for developing fitness is basketball. However, the *way* basketball is taught in many physical education classes (with students standing in line, teams taking turns to play, and the teacher talking too long) does not make it a productive class in developing any of the aspects of health-related fitness.

To develop fitness in physical education classes teachers should choose activities that have the potential to contribute positively to one or more of the aspects of fitness. Among these activities are:

Team Sports	Rhythms	Winter Sports
Soccer	Aerobic Dance	Cross Country Skiing
Basketball	Rope Jumping	Ice Skating
Speedball		Snow Shoeing
Field Hockey		
Selected Mass Games		
(e.g., Crab Soccer)		

Outing Activities	Aquatics	Formal Activities
Hiking	Distance	Calisthenics
Backpacking	Swimming	Weight Training
Bicycling		Circuit Training

Running Activities	Gymnastics	Individual Sports (Skilled Singles)
Cross Country Running	Apparatus	Racquetball
Track and Field	Tumbling	Handball
Selected Mass Games	Chinning	Paddleball
Running Relays	Rope Climbing	Competitive Wrestling
Jogging	Peg Boards	Badminton
		Tennis

In addition to specific activities that lend themselves well to the development of fitness, there are specific fitness programs available in the literature. These are designed for certain ages, for various levels of fitness, or for specificity in training. Teachers should select several that best meet the needs of their program and their classes. Some of the better known fitness programs listed by Corbin (1976) are:

President's Council on Physical Fitness and Sports
Royal Canadian Air Force, XBX and 5BX Programs
Speed Play or Fartlek
Interval Training

Additionally, individual programs can be designed using jogging, aerobic dance, weight training, and calisthenics.

Progression in Activities

Since any activity must be participated in vigorously to develop fitness, it is necessary for the teacher to do two things: (1) ascertain each individual's fitness level at the beginning of the program, and (2) gradually increase the intensity in what the individual and the class is doing. Because of individual differences, seldom can the teacher start a whole class in fitness-developing activities at the same level. What would be appropriate for some would be too difficult and demanding for others less fit, and would not challenge those who are most fit. Ascertaining the present fitness level of each student in class necessitates some sort of testing or evaluation. The AAHPERD Health-Related Physical Fitness Test (1980) could be used for this purpose. Students could then plan a program of

165

progression in each of the components of fitness based on their own entry fitness level. This would allow students to participate against themselves instead of against others in the class. It would enable them to see positive results from their own progress, instead of trying to match those who are more fit at the beginning. An example of this would be where the teacher has the class perform the 12-minute run. Regardless of the initial scoring for the students, they now have an accurate measurement of their cardio-respiratory efficiency. The teacher helps the students interpret the score, aids in planning a program of running activities so progression can be observed, and helps to explain to the students what is happening physiologically and why it is important. The same procedure can be followed for activities selected to build muscular strength, muscular endurance, flexibility, and correct body composition. For further information on this type of evaluation, see Chapter 14.

Time Allotment

Many elementary physical education classes meet once or twice a week. Seldom do we find a daily program. Likewise, many secondary school programs meet less than five days a week. In situations like this, the first objective of the physical educator should be to work for an increase in the time allottment. Recent research seems to indicate that an effective exercise pattern must be conducted at least four days a week if positive benefits are to accrue. In school programs where this frequently is not possible, it is incumbent upon the teacher to motivate the students enough so that they are impressed with the fact that they must exercise on their own in out-of-school environments. With elementary school students this most certainly will necessitate the cooperation and assistance of the parents. With secondary school students the teacher will need to acquaint the student with community facilities and programs such as the YMCA and YWCA, community recreation programs, commercial fitness facilities, running tracks, fitness trails, and bicycling routes.

In secondary physical education programs where classes do meet daily, developing fitness is still a difficult assignment. The worst enemy of the student desiring to develop fitness is inactivity. In the traditional class, roll taking, teacher announcements, explanations, demonstrations, assigning teams, changing teaching stations, and taking turns on apparatus and other equipment accounts for too large a portion of the class time being consumed without vigorous participation by the student. The teacher should minimize this "down time" as much as possible by being aware of it and planning for its elimination when constructing the daily lesson plan. Refer back to Chapter 7 for more ways to minimize wasted time.

166

Additional help is available when the teacher has enough equipment and supplies so that students are active at all times, and do not have to wait for their turns. Additional exercise time can be obtained for each student if the teacher will learn to modify the various activities. Many suggestions for maximizing student participation time may be found in Chapter 5. The teacher should remember at all times that no fitness is being developed in any category when the students are standing.

It is also possible to extract additional time from the normal day of the student in which he or she might work on fitness activities. Often the school facilities are not in use just prior to the formal opening of the school day, or just after the final class. Additional times facilities may be available are the lunch period, late evening hours, and Saturday mornings. Students should be acquainted with the possibility of using the facilities at these times. They should also be informed which ones are supervised and what equipment and supplies are available.

Physical fitness has a unique quality. It can be developed, but once developed it must be maintained. A certain amount of each day or week must be devoted to fitness in order to keep it to the degree that it has beneficial outcomes. Even if well taught, the school setting is too limited to maintain fitness components in each student. Physical education teachers must motivate their students through education to continue a maintenance program outside the physical education class time, and yes indeed, throughout their entire life! Teachers should encourage each student to set, reach for, and maintain their personal fitness goals. This can be accomplished only by teaching fitness concepts and values, affording the student opportunities to participate in selected fitness activities, and assisting them in developing life-styles where this participation will be of high priority throughout their life.

METHODS FOR DEVELOPING PHYSICAL FITNESS

To Develop Cardio-Respiratory Fitness

1. Be sure the curriculum contains a unit on aerobic dance. It is vigorous, takes care of any number of students, is an appropriate co-educational activity, and provides for maximum participation at a high level of intensity without any wasted time. In addition it is interesting to the students because of the rhythm involved, requires no specialized equipment, and can be varied in content daily.
2. Use a lot of rope skipping or rope jumping. This activity can be a part of the daily class routine used at the beginning of the period, or a special unit can be scheduled for it. Competition can be held from student-to-student, or the competition can be held with the students competing

against themselves (e.g., How many times can I jump without missing, or how many successful jumps can I do in a specified number of minutes). Jumping can be done individually, in pairs, or in groups. It can be done to music, and there are a variety of skills that can be added for variety.

3. Incorporate a unit on cross-country running. The unit will basically be one where the students are running. The correct style of running should be taught. Times and distances should be individualized, and running schedules devised for each student. Any size class can be accommodated, and very little equipment is needed, although the selection of proper shoes is essential.

4. Schedule a unit on jogging. This is designed for after-class use, and for after-graduation use. It will teach the students the correct equipment to use, acquaint them with routes on which to run in the area and teach the concepts of intensity, duration, and frequency. The unit should also explain the necessity for and the use of stretching routines, how to correctly take one's pulse, acquaint them with the "threshold of training" concept, and warn each student of the potential dangers of jogging. As a motivational technique students may record their mileage on a map to indicate cities that they have run far enough to "visit."

5. Incorporate in the aquatics unit the swimming of lengths of the pool. Too often the swimming class becomes a recreational swimming period, or is devoted solely to stroke development. By devoting an increasingly large amount of the swimming class period to developing the ability to swim longer distances, a valuable fitness element is added. This is true even if kickboards have to be used. To add interest, the class may select cities of various distances, and swim the mileage to match the distance, as in the jogging unit.

6. Devise a circuit training course for the class to use. This entails "stations," arranged in a circular fashion, through which the student must traverse as quickly as possible. As an alternate method, the student may adopt a standard time to run the circuit, but attempt to do "more" of a certain stunt at one or more of the stations than was formerly accomplished. Circuits should be devised so that more than one facet of fitness is developed as the students run through them. A sample circuit is shown in Figure 10.1.

7. Employ running relays and tag games. These activities require no specific equipment, fit all size classes, and can be varied to keep the student's interest. There is relatively little "standing around," and a vigorous period is possible for all students. A good selection of this type of activity can be found in *Active Games and Contests* (Donnelly, Helms and Mitchell, 1958).

8. Plan Sustained Effort Activities. There are a number of activities that

168

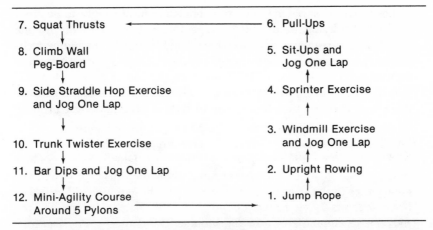

7. Squat Thrusts ←	6. Pull-Ups ↑
8. Climb Wall Peg-Board ↓	5. Sit-Ups and Jog One Lap ↑
9. Side Straddle Hop Exercise and Jog One Lap ↓	4. Sprinter Exercise ↑
10. Trunk Twister Exercise ↓	3. Windmill Exercise and Jog One Lap ↑
11. Bar Dips and Jog One Lap ↓	2. Upright Rowing ↑
12. Mini-Agility Course Around 5 Pylons →	1. Jump Rope

Figure 10.1   A Circuit Training Course for use in a Gymnasium.

develop cardio-respiratory efficiency if they are sustained for most of the class period, repeatedly day after day, at a maximum level. These are the team sports of basketball, soccer, and field hockey, and the individual and dual sports of tennis, badminton, handball, and racquet ball when played as singles. As employed in many programs, especially where large numbers of students are present, these recreational sports are played as doubles. This drastically reduces the fitness component. In both team and individual sports, it is necessary to have a high degree of equal competition, as high skilled against low skilled also defeats the fitness objective. Taking turns playing, long periods of explanations, and initial skill-drills for beginners also do not develop fitness. However, if the above activities are played full-court, for long periods of time, with very even-competition, or as singles, cardio-respiratory efficiency will increase.

9. The Use of Conditioning Skills. Some physical educators make good use of what they call conditioning skills. These are in reality drills, where running is combined with calisthenics and rope jumping. They are usually organized in relay formations, where students run the length of the gymnasium and back, then repeat immediately, but this time a strenuous calisthenic is inserted along the relay route. During the third repetition an additional calisthenic is inserted, and on the fourth repetition a number of rope jumps are added. The relay is continued until the degree of exercise needed to benefit the students in the relay has been reached.

To Develop Muscular Strength and Endurance

1. Offer a class in weight training. For this purpose, either weight ma-

chines or free weights may be used. The amount of weight to be lifted should be individualized, with no attempt to "keep up" with anyone else. Training regimens with weights should be taught, including techniques, progressions, safety procedures, and lifting to benefit specific muscle groups. Willgoose (1979) suggests the use of a One Hundred Ton Club to build interest, wherein the students keep track of their daily lifts, and accumulate totals until they reach one hundred tons.

2. The Use of Mass Games. One of the best examples of a mass game that builds endurance is crab soccer. When running on all fours, with the back to the floor (the crab position), the musculature of the shoulder girdle is vigorously exercised. Repeated frequently this type of activity contributes to the strength and endurance of those muscles. The use of floor scooters have proven popular in the elementary grades for movements emphasizing arm and shoulder development. Physical education teachers at the junior and senior high school level will also find their students receptive to their use, and by being creative in designing more demanding and intricate movements, they may add an additional dimension to strength and endurance development.

3. The Use of Apparatus and Self-Testing Activities. There are a number of activities the teacher can acquaint the student with, and then make the equipment and time available for the student to do on an individual basis. Among these are rope climbing, using the overhead ladder, chinning bar, and climbing peg boards. These activities are challenging and interesting, as well as beneficial for developing muscular strength and endurance.

4. The Use of Isometrics. Because of their limitation in developing endurance, isometric exercises are often neglected. However, their ability to develop pure strength in a muscle is valuable. Their use, in a limited fashion, should definitely be considered.

To Develop Flexibility

The most successful method of developing flexibility is by having the students do specific flexibility exercises. There are numerous references (Anderson 1980, Corbin 1978, Falls, et al., 1980 and Hockey 1981) which contain excellent flexibility exercises. Flexibility exercises may be presented in two ways: (1) schedule them as part of the daily routine, or (2) schedule a unit on flexibility, in which the term is defined, the necessity of flexibility is explained, and means of attaining it are presented. Specific flexibility exercises may be identified for the legs, trunk, and arms.

170

To Teach the Concept of Body Composition

Many students are not acquainted with the "percent body fat" concept, and initially this will have to be taught as a cognitive aspect of fitness. The teacher may begin by taking the body weights of all students, and relating them to the various body builds. Measurements of body-fat can be taken with skin-fold calipers, which can be purchased at a very reasonable price. Conferences between individual students and the teacher are an integral part of using the data collected. Goals for each student should be set, and a progress chart started for every individual. Classroom sessions should be held in which the students are taught the relationships existing between diet, exercise, and body weight.

Miscellaneous Fitness Activities

1. Outdoor Fitness Trails. Schools with outdoor space adjacent to the school may design fitness trails. A course of varied length is designed, with instructions at different points along the trail indicating to the student that a certain physical performance must be done at that point. After completing these intructions, the student continues on until another set is found. Running between the points is an important part of the trail.
2. Give periodic applications of the AAHPERD Health-Related Physical Fitness Test. Individual scores should be kept, goals set for each student, and patches and awards should be distributed.

SUMMARY

Physical fitness has been defined as the condition enjoyed by an individual whereby he or she can perform efficiently all the daily requirements of their work without undue fatigue, still have enough energy and enthusiasm to participate in some form of physical recreation, and, if such a condition presents itself, react favorably to the physical demands of an emergency. To develop such a state in their students, physical education teachers must be discriminating in the selection of curricular experiences, as well as select the correct teaching methodologies.

The component parts of physical fitness have been divided into two main categories: (1) health-related components, and (2) performance-related components. The health-related aspects are the most important, and consist of cardio-respiratory efficiency, muscular strength, muscular endurance, flexibility, and the correct body composition. One of the approaches to teaching this information that has received additional emphasis recently is the cognitive or conceptual approach, involving classroom

171

and laboratory experiences, as well as the traditional activity classes.

Because physical fitness is such an individual condition, it is important for the teacher to ascertain the state of fitness for each member of the class, and then plan a program of progressively more vigorous activities for each student. Testing is an integral part of this process. It is also necessary for the teacher to obtain as much time as is possible for participation, both in class situations and in out-of-class opportunities.

To develop physical fitness in students, physical education teachers need to identify what aspect of fitness is their objective for each unit offered in the curriculum, and then devise specific strategies for bringing it to fruition. Specific strategies are suggested for developing cardio-respiratory fitness, muscular strength, muscular endurance, flexibility, and the correct body composition. These strategies are an integral part of each day's lesson plan.

SELECTED READINGS AND REFERENCES

AAHPERD, *Basic Stuff Series*, AAHPERD, Reston, Virginia, 1981.

Anderson, Bob, *Stretching*, Shelter Publications, Bolinas, California, 1980.

Corbin, Charles and Ruth Lindsey, *Fitness for Life*, Scott, Foresman and Co., Glenview, Illinois, 1983.

Corbin, Charles, et. al., *Concepts in Physical Education*, Wm. C. Brown, Co., Dubuque, Iowa, 1978.

Donnelly, R., Wm. Helms, and Elmer Mitchell, *Active Games and Contests*, Ronald Press, New York, 1958.

Falls, Harold, Ann Baylor, and Rod Dishman, *Essentials of Fitness*, Saunders College Book Publishing, Philadelphia, 1980.

Herman, Don and Wayne Osness, "A Scientific Curriculum Design for High School Physical Education," *JOHPER*, March, 1966, pp. 26-27.

Hockey, Robert V. *Physical Fitness, The Pathway to Healthful Living*, C. V. Mosby Co., St. Louis, 1981.

Myers, Edward J., "Exercise Physiology in Secondary Schools," in *Ideas for Secondary School Physical Education*, AAHPER, Washington, D.C., 1976.

Willgoose, Carl, *The Curriculum in Physical Education*, Prentice-Hall, Inc., Englewood Cliffs, New Jersey, 1979.

PRINCIPLES OF MOTOR LEARNING

What practice factors can I use to get them to the next level?

Physical education methodologies are increasingly being reviewed and adjusted based on scientific research. This trend is most visible in the area concerned with the learning of motor skills. Research can aid the teacher in achieving one of the objectives of physical education; that is to develop each individual to his or her optimum level neuromuscularly. Although research has identified many principles of motor learning, not all of them will equally aid the teacher of physical education. A few principles have been selected for discussion in this chapter that will initially help the teacher. It is suggested that additional reading on the subject is desirable. Several selected references are listed at the end of the chapter.

LEARNING DEFINED

In order that teachers may more completely guide students toward their maximum skill attainment, they must possess a basic understanding of several principles of motor learning. First, however, learning needs to

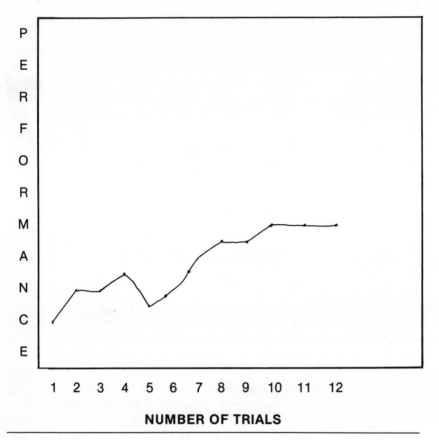

P
E
R
F
O
R
M
A
N
C
E

1 2 3 4 5 6 7 8 9 10 11 12

NUMBER OF TRIALS

Figure 11.1 Learning Curve

be defined. Traditionally it has been stated that three variables are required to determine that learning has occurred: (1) there must be a
change in the student's performance, (2) the students must retain that
changed performance, and (3) the change must be the result of practice or
experiences (Stallings, 1982).

The learning curve in Figure 11.1 shows the typical pattern followed
in skill acquisition. Each trial will either improve, remain the same, or
regress from the previous one. Learning is said to occur when the trials
show a greater number of improvements, as well as improving from the
first to the last trial. Learning would definitely not have occurred if the
students' performance remained the same or declined.

According to our definition, a change in performance must be retained to be considered learning. This would eliminate skills which improve by conditioning alone but are not long lasting. If in Figure 11.1 the
curve indicated an increase in muscular strength, measured by the

number of sit ups performed, it would not be indicative of learning as the level would drop off when practice was discontinued. This condition of learning differentiates between changes which occur because of conditioning or growth and maturation and those that can be learned. This is a difficult area to separate. It requires that during the practice of the skills the teacher emphasize quality rather than quantity. The conditions of practice, not just repetition, is what should concern the teacher.

Learning can not always be measured in overt performance. A student can learn a great deal about a skill or game and yet may not possess the necessary perceptual or motor abilities to perform it. This weakness in defining learning in terms of performance changes alone is noted by Dunham (Stallings, 1982). The authors of this text are assuming that optimal performance at each stage of learning motor skills increases the probability of attaining a higher final level of proficiency.

READINESS TO LEARN

Many of us can recall an instance in which a loving parent wanted to teach a child how to ride a bicycle, only to find that the child simply did not develop the necessary skill. Three months later the child announces a desire to learn to ride the bicycle and subsequently accomplishes the task on the very first attempt. In the first instance the parent was ready for the child to learn, but in the second instance the child was ready to learn. This simple illustration shows the effects of one's readiness to learn.

This may be a psychological, physiological, or maturational readiness. In each instance it is very important for the teacher to understand the principle of readiness. About the only evidence of readiness at this time is the average age at which previous individuals showed interest in, and success at, performing skills. Some longitudinal studies have tried to list developments which are necessary in skill acquisition before the next step may successfully be attempted. Because there exists a wide range of differences among individuals, this has been of little value.

In many fields, but particularly in that of motor learning, research is finding that the individual may be "ready" long before it was previously thought. Important factors in determining readiness are heredity, environmental experiences and the individual's interest. Attempts to force learning on very young children before they have developed the necessary bases for the skills may cause emotional blocks to later learning. Most often, however, the error has been to postpone early exposure to skills rather than to start them too soon. The degree of interest and the attention span are the best cues for determining individual readiness.

Students may be ready for particular types of motor developments but the unit of learning in which they are contained is too complex for their present levels of skill development. For example, individuals are not ready to begin even the simplest of baseball games until they have learned to throw and catch a ball.

Teachers need to be familiar with the average ages at which certain types of skills, movements, and experiences can best be learned, both physically and mentally, by the majority of the students. Teachers must also be aware of the readiness levels of individuals within age groups. Whereas most of the class may be ready to learn a handstand roll, a few students may need to continue working on a less demanding movement. On the other hand, the class may contain certain individuals who possess the desire and ability to attempt challenging skills and movements well in advance of the other students. Innovative teachers will find ways to satisfy all students' needs in this area.

COMMUNICATION WITH THE LEARNER

An important factor that may affect the learning of motor skills during practice is teacher communication. Before and during practice the teacher should communicate to the students exactly what they are expected to do. This can be accomplished in different ways. One is in the form of visual stimuli, generally done in the form of a demonstration. It may be a live demonstration, a film, or another supplementary aid. The model that the students watch should be able to perform the skill as correctly as possible. The demonstration should be done at the same speed and rhythm and under the same conditions that the skill is to be performed by the students. During the demonstration verbal cues could be used to reinforce some of the more important points. It is generally believed that demonstrations are more beneficial than verbal cues during the early learning stages, no matter what the age of the learner. However, this seems to be especially true for younger students.

A second method of communication with the student is verbal, in which the teacher simply explains to the students what they are to do. The less skilled the students are, the less lengthy this explanation should be so they do not become confused or overloaded with stimuli. As the skill proficiency of the students increases, the verbal directions may become more complex and analytical.

In some instances the use of manual guidance may be necessary. Manual guidance involves the teacher physically manipulating the student through a movement. This will enable the student to experience the "feel" of the movement. This type of communication should be viewed as a last resort. There is controversy in the literature dealing with the effectiveness of this type of aid. Manual guidance throughout the entire skill, where the performer is passive, is not an effective technique for the majority of students, and it may be a hindrance. This is not to be confused with spotting in gymnastics where the spotter is sometimes in direct contact with the performer and only intervenes when the safety of the performer is threatened. More typically in this sport an occasional tap to the student at a critical point in the skill aids the student in establishing the timing of the movement.

Each method of communication will have various degrees of success with different students, and each student's responses will vary. Most students need more visual information, while others (usually the older and more skilled student) can understand what is desired simply by listening to a description. Teachers must be aware of these differences, and be ready to alter their form of communication when warranted.

SKILL RETENTION THROUGH OVERLEARNING

Many researchers would indicate that learning has occurred when a person performs a skill correctly one time. Therefore, when a student correctly throws a ball and hits the target, the skill is said to have been learned. Indeed, the student has accomplished a task, and there is great joy in it. However, integrated within education, and a determining factor as to whether or not learning has occurred, is the degree of retention of the skill. The extent to which motor skills, as well as other types of learning, are retained rests principally on the conditions of practice.

Retention is defined as the capacity to remember, whether it be a date in history, rules to follow, or the performance of a motor skill. Often one thinks of verbal or cognitive skills when the discussion centers around memory. Although part of the learning of motor skills is mental, a larger portion is neuromuscular. Experimentally the term retention refers to the degree of proficiency of a skill after a period without practice.

Continued practice of a skill beyond reaching a criterion level of performance is referred to as *overlearning*. If the criterion level for learning a cartwheel on the balance beam is 10 of 10 trials, then the student would be encouraged to practice until 15 of 15 trials are successful. It would then be said that fifty percent overlearning has occurred. Overlearning requires more time than early learning. Therefore, teachers must ask themselves how much extra time they want to spend in achieving higher levels of proficiency. Research has shown that fifty percent overlearning is generally advantageous. Practice beyond this is said to have diminishing returns (Singer, 1980, Stallings, 1982). That is, the increase in time spent in overlearning is much greater than the results received. Therefore, this extra time could be best spent in another area.

Overlearning results in a performance becoming automatic or a

179

habit. Knowing that a habit will be established, it must be determined whether the habit created will be positive or negative. Habits are difficult to break. Can you imagine the problems that would be created if starting tomorrow all drivers of automobiles had to stop for a green light and continue on a red? Overlearning creates a habit or permanence of performance. This does not guarantee that the performance will be correct. If the student practices a skill incorrectly it will create a permanent incorrect performance.

With closed skills, such as archery and golf, the best method for overlearning is repetitive practice. This is generally done in the form of drills. Open skills, such as tennis ground strokes and soccer dribbling, can also profit from the application of overlearning. The extra practice in these skills involves practicing under varying situations which occur during a game. Teachers must realize that extended drills have their own problems. Often boredom or fatigue set in and then the performers may become careless in their practice and use incorrect techniques due to a lack of concentration. This may result in creating an undesired technique. Methods for enhancing motivation become critical during this time. Several motivational techniques that may be helpful in developing motor skills may be found in Chapter 9.

The fact is that most physical education classes seldom bring the students to the point of overlearning. One of the often used excuses is the lack of time. The question becomes, then, how to attain higher proficiency in the given amount of time, since retention depends on the level of proficiency achieved. Increasing the learning rate is one way. The faster the students learn, the more time is available for overlearning. It is impossible to say how much overlearning is most desirable, but it can be shown that overlearning does result in increased retention of the material learned. It also assists the student in obtaining skill mastery. This would make overlearning a desirable point to pursue, and therefore it should be planned for within the physical education class structure.

TRANSFER OF LEARNING

Transfer of learning refers to the influence of a learned task on a second task to be learned. One must understand that the influence may result in zero, positive, or negative transfer from a learned skill to a new skill. *Zero transfer* occurs when former learning has no effect upon the learning of a new skill. Skills learned in tumbling, for example, would have little or no effect upon learning tennis. *Negative transfer* occurs when previous learning has an inhibiting effect upon learning a new skill. One might recall the need for a firm wrist in tennis strokes, which has a negative effect upon learning badminton, since these skills require a very flexible wrist. *Positive transfer* takes place when some previously learned skill can be utilized directly or at least applied to the learning of an immediate task. The example of tennis and badminton provides an example of positive transfer in the sense that they both use a racquet, cover a netted court, and strike an aerial object. Skills developed in one sport may transfer positively to the other sport when similar elements of the skill are present in both.

Before the principle of transfer can be used, it is necessary to have an understanding of its' potential contributions and its' limitations. It is common for one to assume that transfer will aid in learning when similarities exist between two tasks. These similarities can be between the stimulus, the movement responses, or between both stimulus and reponse.

Attempts to determine the effect of transfer between tasks on the basis of their stimulus and response have resulted in several hypotheses. The most popular is that of Osgood (Stallings, 1982). In general these hypotheses state:

1. Negative transfer is more likely to occur when the stimulus is the same but the response is different.
2. Negative transfer is less likely when the stimuli differ but the responses remain the same.
3. If both stimulus and response differ, zero transfer is expected.
4. Positive transfer is predicted when the stimulus and response are identical in the two tasks.

Transfer can be utilized within several situations. The most common is skill-to-skill transfer. An example may be seen in gymnastics. The techniques mastered in performing the forward roll are similar to those in the front sommersault. Therefore, it is felt that the skills learned in the roll will transfer to learning the sommersault.

Another area in which transfer may be used is transfer from practice to performance. During a basketball unit the students may begin dribbling in a stationary position, advance to dribbling while moving, and finally, work against a defensive player. This creates a practice situation that will favorably transfer to a game environment.

Additionally, bilateral or cross transfer (from limb-to-limb) may increase skill learning. The more the students practice kicking a soccer ball with their preferred foot the greater the possibility of transfer when it comes time to kick the ball with their nonpreferred foot.

Transfer of knowledge in one activity to knowledge in another activity should also be considered. A game such as newcomb may be used to prepare students for volleyball due to the similarity of knowledge necessary for the two activities.

Transfer from principle to skill may also have a positive influence upon learning. This aspect of transfer infers that learning a principle may enhance skill learning. An example might be the effect that learning the principles of balance has upon learning to perform a balance movement.

To utilize the above concepts as completely as possible the instructor should keep in mind some selected conditions which tend to allow for positive transfer. These include:

1. The similarity between the practice environment and the final situation in which the skill is to be used should be maximized.
2. As more experience with the original task is provided, the possibility of transfer to the new skill becomes greater.
3. Transfer will occur more completely if the teacher teaches specifically that transfer is possible. In other words the teacher must identify, either verbally or visually, the similarities of the skills.
4. In order to avoid negative transfer the teacher should make the students aware of skills which may appear to be the same but actually are not. The earlier tennis and badminton comparison is an example. The teacher should make sure that the students understand the differences in the wrist action in the two sports.

MENTAL PRACTICE

Mental practice is the "cognitive rehearsal" of a motor task in the absence of overt, physical movements (Sage, 1977). It is important for the student to have a clear mental picture of the skill since much of motor learning is perceptual. There exists a constant communication between the brain and the muscles. Mental practice can add to the final outcome and even to the speed of skill development. Experimental evidence shows that mental practice helps in: (1) learning new skills (skill acquisition), (2) refining performance (skill performance), and (3) reinforcing proper responses (skill retention).

Mental practice in conjunction with physical practice seems to be a positive aid to the learner. In cases where skill acquisition is desired, mental practice between attempts allows the students to sort out what was correct or incorrect about the trial. Thinking through the skill will allow them to determine corrections to be made or successful patterns to repeat. As an example the students may be having difficulty in the hurdle during a track lesson. The teacher may tell them to sit out for a few moments and try to mentally picture themselves going through the skill 15 times perfectly before returning to the physical practice.

In skill retention, mental practice can be used immediately following a correct trial, and before the next attempt, to set the correct response. It can also be used when, by the nature of the activity, it is impossible to physically practice the skill. As an example, during a softball game a batter performs a good swing and gets a hit. Although the swing cannot be repeated immediately, the batter may take a few moments, once play has stopped, to try to mentally recapture the action which led to the successful swing.

During competition mental practice is often seen to increase skill performance. Before diving, the diver will mentally practice the dive from start to finish. After "watching" this correct "mental film" the diver will try to perform the dive as it was pictured.

To be effective mental practice must be specifically described to the students before they attempt to engage in it. The teacher should tell them to imagine doing the skill correctly. Often this is done with the eyes closed to eliminate visual distractions, and perhaps in a specific spot or stance, such as sitting or lying. The students should also be instructed as to the number of "practices" to imagine.

Following are several ways in which teachers may use mental practice in physical education classes:

1. Mental practice may be used to prevent retroactive inhibition. This is accomplished by guiding the student to mentally practice the correct responses following an unsuccessful attempt. The student concentrates on what must be done to perform the task correctly rather than thinking about the mistake and the results. However, care must be taken that the student does not suffer from "paralysis from analysis" due to overconcentration.
2. Through mental practice students may review the procedures, successes, and failures of skill practice. Additionally, they may get new ideas of what to try next.
3. Students may use mental practice to plan precisely what they will do on their next physical practice and which points they should emphasize.
4. Mental practice may aid students in formulating a proper mental set for the next physical practice.
5. Mental practice can supplement learning when physical practice is not possible or unwise due to overfatigue. It is used to accelerate learning at the advanced levels, to aid in retention, and to refine skills.
6. Mental practice helps keep the inactive students occupied, as well as providing them with the opportunity to learn. Inactivity could be a result of lack of equipment or limited space that requires waiting for a turn, a result of being injured, or because they are not at the practice area (outside of class).

While mental practice isn't a cure all and cannot take the place of physical practice, it is a valuable supplement. The use of mental practice will depend on the task complexity, the past experiences and skill level of the students, and whether or not the learner has a clear mental concept of the skill. The best form of practice would be a combination of both physical and mental practice.

THE ROLE OF PRACTICE

By definition, learning is a result of practice. Practice is the means by which new skills are acquired. Practice in itself will not guarantee good performance, but it will insure permanence in performance as discussed earlier in overlearning. For quality skill performance to occur, practice must be carried out with the intent to improve and under favorable conditions.

Variability in Practice

Variability of practice is important in open skills where novel responses must be made. The game of tennis is an example where often a response is needed which is different from any previously practiced skill. It is desirable in this case to practice as many different shots as possible. Shots should be practiced from many positions on the court, from various angles, and with different types and amounts of spin placed on the ball. This will increase the likelihood that there will not be a completely new movement required during a game, but simply an adaptation of another well-learned movement (Magill, 1980).

Even with closed skills, variability in practice has its usefulness. One major advantage is to change some aspect of the skill drill to avoid boredom as a motivational technique. In gymnastics the students may be able to perform the cartwheel successfully but are not yet ready to move ahead. Overlearning is necessary before the next skill is attempted. To keep them on task longer (both mentally and physically) they may be asked to perform the skill with slight variations. If the students tire of the task and are not concentrating on it during practice, they may become injured or begin to practice incorrectly. In the example of the cartwheel, the students could be asked to perform it at various speeds, to combine it with a second or third skill (which may be the same or different) or with other slight variations to the skill. These variations will motivate the student to perform the same basic skill over and over and give them a chance to master the skill before progressing further.

Emphasis on Speed and/or Accuracy

When teaching a skill it must be determined whether speed and/or accuracy is the basic factor. *Speed* is the rate that specific motor skills are performed. *Accuracy* refers to the skill being performed without errors, an error being a deviation from some correct and accepted standard.

Early writings suggested that in skills where speed and accuracy are integral, attention should be placed on accuracy. The basic thought behind this was once the skill was perfected then the speed could be gradually added. This assumes that it is easier to speed up accurate skills than it is to correct inaccurate skills. It was also felt that errors were in part due to increased speed which resulted in a lack of control.

Kinesiologists reported later that slow movements are different in form than identical movements produced rapidly. Timing, coordination, balance and force are a few items that would be changed as a skill is performed slowly as opposed to quickly. Correct performance at the required speed must be emphasized at the start. Therefore, skills where speed is the primary goal should emphasize that aspect during practice.

More recently research has shifted away from this speed-accuracy debate *per se* and is now concentrating on determining the factors that effect speed and accuracy on that skill. Examples of skills where speed is emphasized would be found in track and pitching. In ballistic skills, i.e., throwing or striking, where there exists an accumulation of momentum for success it would be a deterent to skill acquisition to place an early emphasis on accuracy. In the same manner if accuracy is the key point of the skill it should be initially encouraged. Form would be a primary concern in golf and diving, and an emphasis on accuracy is found in archery and riflery. In skills where both speed and accuracy are basic factors early emphasis should be on both, with slightly greater time spent on speed, since accuracy will be specific to the speed practiced (Sage, 1977). For example, basketball players must shoot rapidly in a game situation. If they practice at a slow speed, they will then have to shoot at a faster speed in the game situation which will alter the skill they learned in practice. The result of this will be poor performance. The physical education teacher must decide whether speed, accuracy, or a combination of both will most influence the success in learning the skill.

Practice of Part or Whole

It must be decided whether the skill or skills need to be broken into parts when introduced to the student. The problem comes in deciding what is the whole skill. Is the "whole" the game of soccer and the "parts" the individual skills, i.e., dribbling, heading, or shooting? Is the "whole" the side stroke in swimming and the "parts" the arm and leg action and the breathing? Is the "whole" the coordination of the arms in the side stroke and the "parts" a single arm movement?

For purposes of clarity we will consider the whole as a complete skill such as the tennis serve, the breast stroke, or a volleyball spike. Most re-

185

search has concluded that single skills should be practiced as close to an actual situation as possible. In many skills the sequence of the move is very important. If one part is isolated for practice it may take considerably longer to blend the various segments together. An example may be found in the tennis serve. Breaking the serve into parts could be detrimental to the final learning of the "whole" movement. Once the whole swing is conceptualized by the students they should practice the total movement. Especially with beginners, the learner's first attempts are to grasp and respond to a total idea or the gross-framework of the pattern. Attention is not given to details of movements but rather to a general impression of the skill.

Often, if students are left alone, by a combination of maturation and observation, they pick up general ideas of the various skills and can carry on a game. It is important to remember, however, that under these conditions, they will not learn and master motor skills to their optimum. In fact, they may create incorrect habits if some time is not spent practicing the skills in a controlled learning environment.

Later, when more advanced students are trying to perfect a skill, a single aspect of it can be isolated for practice. For example, once the students are fairly proficient with the tennis serve, they could go back and work on the ball toss. In the higher levels of skill development this part drill is used to smooth and polish the performance. This can be accomplished now that the part is meaningful to the whole skill. An additional thought is that they will now practice with purpose for longer periods of time.

When the desired performance outcome is complex or contains a number of sub skills, it is recommended that it be broken into parts. Most sports are placed in this area, as they usually contain many individual skills within the game. Once the concept of the game is discussed, or the whole game explained, the students will see how the individual parts relate to the whole, and it will then be beneficial to practice the parts separately. In soccer, for example, there are many indpendent skills within the game. These are affected by teammates, opponents, and the rules. Each skill needs to be practiced independently before combining them with others in a formal game for the most desirable outcomes.

Length of Practice Time

The length of practice time will depend on many variables. It would not be possible to lump skills together under an exact "ideal" length of practice time. Each student will vary on the length of practice required. The practice session needs to be long enough for the student to become involved in the task, and not so long that boredom or fatigue sets in. A good guide is to begin with shorter practice sessions for new skills and repeat them often, then gradually increase the length of time spent in one session as the skill proficiency increases. For example, in a beginning volleyball class the teacher may have the class practice the serve for five minutes the first day, ten minutes the second day, and for fifteen minutes on the third and fourth days for a total of forty-five minutes. It would be unwise for the teacher to have the students practice the serve for a full forty-five minutes on the second day of the unit, even though the total amount of time spent is the same in both examples.

An important factor in determining the desired length of practice time is the age of the learner. Generally, the younger the student, the shorter the attention span; therefore, a shorter practice is more advantageous.

The complexity of the skill and amount of output required are also factors. More complex skills require more time. Skills which are very strenuous may demand that practice be interspersed with rest periods to allow the student time to recover between practice sessions.

The specific purpose of the practice will mandate the type of practice necessary. If the skill is being practiced for an impending performance, to polish a weak aspect of the skill, to correct a consistent error, or to develop additional speed or endurance, the practice will be intense. If the skill is for recreation and fun the practice will be much less intense.

Another factor in practice length and frequency is the level of learning that has previously been attained. A beginner with little skill will practice for shorter periods of time than will the advanced performer. This is due to: (1) lack of motivation to stay on task, (2) lack of ability to concentrate for long periods of time, and (3) greater fatigue at the lower skill level.

The environmental conditions also affect the practice. Examples include the temperature of the room, the amount of space, and the time of the day. A class generally has limited time and days for practice, as well as limited space and equipment. All these play an important role in the practice length as well as practice frequency.

FEEDBACK FOR IMPROVED LEARNING

Feedback refers to the learner receiving information regarding the correctness or incorrectness of a movement pattern. The information students receive can be used to correct an error, reinforce a correct response, or motivate them to continue practicing. The importance of feedback, or knowledge of results, has been reported by Bilodeau, Bilodeau, Bilodeau and Schumsky (1959), and more recently by Stelmach (1978). They stated that knowledge of results was the most important variable in learning and the most effective way to influence performance.

Feedback may be either intrinsic (see Figure 11.2) or augmented (see Figure 11.3). *Intrinsic feedback* is that feedback which is derived by the learner as an inherent consequence of the performance. *Augmented feedfack* is that information received by the performer which is not a normal part of the task. This may be verbal information from the teacher or another student, or information received from a machine such as a videotape recorder. When feedback is received while the performer is in the midst of a performance, it is called *concurrent feedback*. When the feedback is received after the completion of the performance it is referred to as being *terminal*. Intrinsic concurrent feedback may be expressed when individuals rely upon their kinesthetic sense to feel the exactness of a movement. *Kinesthetic sense* refers to the ability of the body to provide

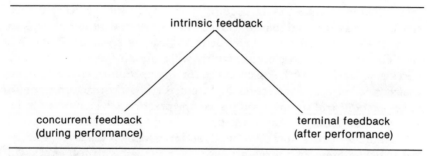

Figure 11.2   Forms of intrinsic feedback.

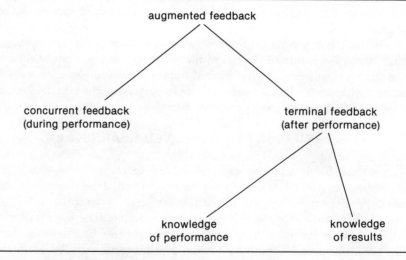

Figure 11.3   Forms of augmented feedback.

information concerning its' position in space and the relationship of its' parts. The student who engages in a golf game may indicate that the swing did not "feel good." Indeed, the swing may not have been of good quality and the resulting flight of the ball ended in disaster. This ability to feel the movement may be used by the student to improve skill learning.

Intrinsic terminal feedback is expressed as the students' observation of the results of the task performance. Watching the basketball bounce off the backboard and miss the goal provides graphic evidence to the student that the basketball was shot too hard. Adjustments may now be made to shoot the ball more accurately. Augmented concurrent feedback is that information which is provided by the teacher during the performance by the student. This type of feedback is only feasible for those tasks which are performed at a speed slow enough to allow time for the feedback to be given. Augmented terminal feedback is supplied by the teacher, a student, or a mechanical device at the completion of the performance. Sage (1977) points out the importance of both concurrent and terminal augmented feedback. He suggests that even if intrinsic feedback is present, supplemental information frequently enhances learning. If the feedback is information concerning the learner's movement patterns it is referred to as *knowledge of performance.* If the feeback refers to the results of the performance or changes in the environment, it is called *knowledge of results.* Gentile (1972) suggests that knowledge of performance is the most powerful form of augmented feedback for closed skills, and knowledge of results is most effective for open skills.

Perhaps the teacher's role in feedback can be viewed as a three-part cycle as can be seen in Figure 11.4. First, the teacher must observe the student's motor performance. Second, this observation needs to be interpreted. Thirdly, the teacher decides whether or not intervention (augmented terminal feedback) would be beneficial at that time, and if so what form it will take. From here the cycle is repeated. The teacher again watches the student to observe the effects of the intervention, or lack of it, on the motor performance and so on.

The importance of the observation and interpretation levels cannot be over-emphasized. It is necessary to practice observing various levels of skill performance, and in fact to understand the various developmental stages of all the basic motor skills. If this is not done it will be difficult, if not impossible, to develop the criteria necessary upon which to base the type of intervention that should be used.

There exists an "ideal," mature pattern or "book form" of each motor skill. In actuality there is a continuum of performance levels starting with the most beginning or immature performance, and gradually developing through to the most advanced or mature performance. It may

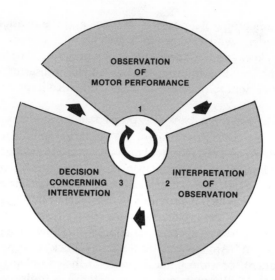

Figure 11.4   The teacher's role in feedback: the three-part cycle.

be noted that the student's skills may match various points along the continuum, and progress is measured by moving toward the mature pattern rather than reaching it.

The decision to interact or not interact during skill practice depends upon several factors. Is the student ready to go on? Does the student possess the desired strength, flexibility, or other necessary physiological skills to advance? Has the student maintained a pattern of performance whereby incorrect segments are consistent and can be identified? Is the student capable of understanding what is necessary to progress? Are the student's basic skills mastered to the point that they provide a strong base upon which to build further skills? Is the student motivated to continue?

Once the teacher decides to intervene during the student's practice, augmented feedback will be provided to the student. For the feedback to be usable it must answer one important question. What does the student need to do to improve the next performance? All too often the feedback answers the questions, "How did the student do?" and "What did the student do wrong?" If the students can see the ball miss the target they know how they did. However, they do not always know why it missed the mark and what adjustments need to be made in the next attempt to improve.

The time feedback is given is also important. The longer the delay in giving feedback, the less effect it has. Therefore, it is important to give feedback as soon after the performance as possible. It is also important for the feedback to relate to the most recent attempt made by the student and not an earlier one.

The feedback needs to be precise enough to benefit the students without confusing them. For example, a student attempts to perform a back somersault and the instructor says, "You were not high enough." In this case the student was not given sufficient feedback to aid in the next trial. The student would be confused by too much feedback if the teacher says, "You didn't snap your feet down fast enough on the roundoff, you over blocked, your arm lift wasn't sufficient, you dropped your head back, and you did not tuck enough." In the first instance the student was given no information on how to improve. Therefore, the feedback was ineffective. In the second example, too much information was given, resulting in "paralysis from analysis." The student is faced with so many adjustments that the focus on the intended task is lost. The teacher should determine the error that has the most impact on the skill, and work to correct that error before going on to others. In the case of the back somersault the teacher should say to the student, "Jane, try snapping your feet down faster on the roundoff this time. That will give you a better angle of take off and you will be able to get higher."

How the teacher interacts, and the type of feedback given, will depend on the observation of the skill as well as each individual student. The teacher may give a verbal cue to the student as was shown before. The interaction could be visual in an attempt to help the student mentally picture the movement. This could be accomplished by returning to a picture, film, or other visual aid, and watch the skill being performed correctly. Physically touching the student to encourage the correct movement is another way the teacher may choose to interact. It must be remembered that the choice not to interact is also there, and at times may be in the students' best interest. The students must be given the opportunity to develop some consistency before adjustments need to be attempted.

THE QUESTION OF FORM

There is a hypothetical "correct form" which exists for each motor skill. Teachers must constantly decide whether or not the students should be guided towards this ideal form or if their skill is sufficient at its present level. Students need to be allowed to make mistakes. These mistakes or errors often are corrected by the student without outside help if there is sufficient visualization of the correct form. However, if the same error is repeated over and over it will result in erroneous behavior. These errors should be corrected before a great amount of practice is spent on incorrect form.

191

For the average learner failure to correct *major* errors early will slow learning. Violation of basic principles of mechanics, such as throwing only with the arm, or stepping with the incorrect foot when throwing, are *major* errors. This is because they deviate from the gross framework of the skill. In the early stages of learning these gross errors must be corrected. Later when the skill advances, the errors become more subtle and require closer analysis. At this point teachers need to ascertain how the error is effecting the skill and what it is the student wishes to accomplish.

If the error is greatly affecting the efficiency of the skill an attempt to correct it should be made. If, however, the basic skill efficiency is satisfactory to the student perhaps no attempt needs to be made to correct it. Small errors that do not greatly effect the efficiency of the performance will not need to be changed. This will be determined in part by what the skill will be used for and the age of the student. If the student plans to use the skill as a basic stepping stone for further skills, or wants to become highly competitive in that area, then any errors should be corrected if possible. If the students are highly successful with the way they perform, even though it is not correct book form, there may not be a need to change. The younger the students the easier it is to change errors before they become too ingrained. Their maturation, however, may not allow them to advance to the next level until a later date. Once the older student has performed a skill incorrectly over a period of time it will be very difficult to change.

SUMMARY

Learning is said to have occurred when there is a change in the student's performance which is retained and is the result of practice. Before learning will occur there must be a level of readiness. Teachers need to understand the average age at which individuals show interest in, and adaptability for, specific motor skills. At the same time teachers must be sensitive to the individual readiness within each class.

Teacher communication with the learner is an important factor in determining successful skill acquisition. Teachers may communicate visually, verbally or through manual guidance. Skill acquisition is also influenced by the quality and quantity of practice. Variability in practice aids the learner in avoiding boredom in both closed and open skills and in increasing skill levels of open skills. Skill retention can be enhanced through overlearning, positive transfer of learning, and mental practice.

When determining how skills are to be taught teachers must consider such concepts as speed versus accuracy and whole versus part. In order to determine if the practice should emphasize speed or accuracy the teacher should decide whether speed, accuracy, or a combination of both will most influence the success of learning the skills. Skills in which accuracy is a prime concern should highlight that aspect. Practice should emphasize speed when working with skills where speed is the main concern. Speed and accuracy should be emphasized early in the practice of skills in which both are basic factors.

Teachers must also decide if the skill should be taught as a whole or if it should be broken into parts. Complex skills may be divided into parts after the whole concept is presented. Less complex skills should be practiced as a whole to establish a general idea of the skill and to work within the correct sequence and timing of the movement. Once this is established the teacher may work with a student on a part of the skill which is causing difficulty.

The length and frequency of practice is an area of concern and is dependent upon several factors. The factors include the age and skill of the student, the complexity of the skill, the purpose of the practice, and the environmental conditions.

For maximum learning to take place the learner needs to receive feedback. Feedback can help to correct an error, reinforce a correct response, or motivate students to continue. All three types of feedback, intrinsic, kinesthetic, and augmented should be utilized. The teacher's role in feedback is seen as a three part cycle which includes observing the performance, interpreting the observation, and deciding on the type of intervention to use. Feedback can be verbal, visual or tactile and should be precise and clear.

Deviation from the ideal form needs to be considered as to its affect on the final performance. Major errors must be corrected early in the learning process. Later, subtle errors, which do not significantly effect the skill, may need to be corrected. This will be determined by the age of the student and the purpose for which the skill will be used.

SELECTED READINGS AND REFERENCES

Adler, J., "Stages of Skill Acquisition: A Guide For Teachers," *Motor Skills: Theory into Practice*, 1981, pp. 75-81.

Austin, J.S. and D. Pargman, "The Inner Game Approach to Performance and Skill Acquisition," *Motor Skills: Theory into Practice*, 1981, pp. 3-13.

Bilodeau, E.A. and I. Bilodeau, "Variable Frequency of Knowledge of Results and the Learning of a Single Skill," *Journal of Experimental Psychology*, 55, 1958, pp. 379-383.

Bilodeau, E.A. and I. Bilodeau, "Motor Skills Learning," *Annual Review of Psychology*, 12, 1961, pp. 243-280.

Bilodeau, E.A., I Bilodeau and D.A. Schumsky, "Some Effects of Introducing and Withdrawing Knowledge of Results Early and Late in Practice," *Journal of Experimental Psychology*, 58, 1959, pp. 142-144.

Bloom, B.S., et al. *Taxonomy of Educational Objectives, Handbook I: Cognitive Domain*, David McKay Co., New York, 1956.

Corbin, C.B., "Mental Practice," in W. P. Morgan (ed.) *Ergogenic and Muscular Performance*, Academic Press, New York, 1972.

Cratty, B.J., *Teaching Motor Skills*, Prentice-Hall, Englewood Cliffs, NJ, 1973.

Darst, P.W., "Analyzing Coaching Behavior and Practice Time," *Motor Skills: Theory into Practice*, 5, 1981, pp. 13-23.

Drowatzky, J.N., *Motor Learning: Principles and Practices*, Burgess Publishing Company, Minneapolis, 1975.

Ellis, H.C., *The Transfer of Training*, MacMillan, New York, 1965.

Gentile, A.M., "A Working Model of Skill Acquisition with Application to Teaching," *Quest*, January, 1972, pp. 3-23.

Lawther, J.D., *The Learning and Performance of Physical Skills*, Prentice-Hall, Inc., 1977.

LeBato, L.T., "Overloading and Overlearning: Principles of Physical Education," *The Physical Educator*, Vol. 29, May, 1972, p. 95.

Magill, R.A., *Motor Learning Concepts and Applications*, Wm. C. Brown Co., Iowa, 1980.

Morris, A.M., "Keys to Successful Motor Skill Performance," *Journal of Physical Education and Recreation*, March, 1981, pp. 49-50.

Sage, George H., *Introduction to Motor Behavior: A Neuropsychological Approach*, Addison-Wesley Publishing Company, Reading, Massachusetts, 1977.

Schmidt, R.A., "Schema Theory: Implications for Movement Education," *Motor Skills: Theory into Practice*, 21, 1977, pp. 36-48.

Singer, R.N., *Motor Learning and Human Peformance*, MacMillan, New York, 1980.

Singer, R.N. and C. Milne, et al., *Laboratory and Field Experiments in Motor Learning*. Charles C. Thomas, Springfield, Ill. 1975.

Stallings, L.M., *Motor Learning from Theory to Practice*, C. V. Mosby Co., St. Louis, 1982.

Stelmach, G.E. (ed.), *Information Processing in Motor Control and Learning*, Academic Press, New York, 1978.

Photo by David Brittain

THE USE OF SUPPLEMENTARY MATERIALS
IN INSTRUCTION

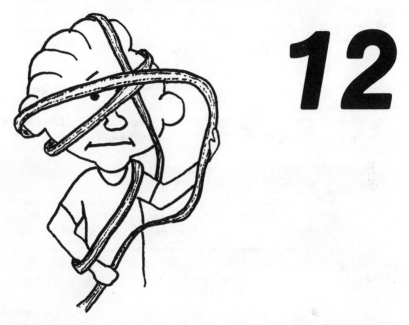

12

Supplementary materials are any materials the instructor uses to expand the lesson to all its possible parameters. They may be visual, audio, or tactile in nature, and are only limited by imagination. Each of the five developmental objectives from Chapter 1 should be studied to determine how supplementary materials can be included to assist in the student's learning.

THE VALUE OF SUPPLEMENTARY MATERIALS

There are several ways that supplementary materials can be valuable to the program, teacher and/or students. They can provide a clearer visualization for the students, and make abstract materials more concrete. They aid in the retention of factual knowledge, as students tend to remember more when they have a clear mental picture. Additionally, the materials can be used to create a more exciting and interesting lesson that serves to motivate the students and increase or recapture their attention. If the physical education teacher follows the lead of the entertainment business of radio, television, and illustrated publications, the same type of devices can be effectively used within the physical education class. This will enable teachers to create variety in their teaching, and allow for differences in individual rates and patterns of learning.

Interrelationships between complex wholes can be effectively shown through the use of supplementary materials. For example, each of the players' movements throughout a sequence of plays during a soccer game can be examined through the use of a film or diagram. This would be an overwhelming task to verbally discuss without the use of some form of visual aid.

Supplementary materials can extend the class beyond the limits of the building and even the community. By including sports from other countries or other parts of the United States, the students can travel without leaving the class. A historical reference can be added to give a better understanding of the important effect physical education and sport has on society.

These aids can also be used to permit students to come in contact with expert teachers and specialists. A small number of students have a chance to see a championship match, game or meet, in person. Even fewer students have the opportunity to take a lesson from a champion. Yet a film showing a series of lessons by an expert of this caliber could make this experience possible for everyone. Additionally, one could follow top athletes through regular intervals of their training, the stages of their progress, and the steps used in learning new skills and perfecting others.

Instructional materials can also provide feedback for students. This is particularly true of video replays where the students can actually see how they have performed. Computers are becoming recognized as excellent means of providing immediate feedback to students. In addition, the traditional type of equipment used in physical education may also be designed to provide feedback. An example that may be used in the elementary grades is a clown bean bag target where the nose lights up when the student hits the target.

PRINCIPLES OF USE

Supplementary teaching aids must be used properly if they are to enhance the lesson. The materials, in and of themselves, will have little effect upon learning. However, skillful teachers can guide students through the proper use of the materials so that maximum learning effectiveness will occur. There is a wide variety of teaching aids available and all of them tend to create an initial interest just from their presence. Since they do increase interest and perception in the students, they may make a major contribution toward motor, cognitive, and affective learning. By adhering to the following principles of use the teacher may enhance learning.

1. The teacher should carefully select and screen all materials that are to be used. The selection of any teaching aid should be made on the basis of its potential contribution to the objectives of the lesson. The aid must be appropriate to the age and skill level of the students as well as relevant to the specific lesson. Materials that are secured from an outside source should be screened by the teacher prior to their use with the students. By doing this the teacher may insure the content is appropriate for the class, and also have a basis for preparing discussion content to be used prior to the use of the materials.
2. All supplementary teaching materials should be presented properly and in an interesting manner. Keeping in mind that instructional aids have a positive impact upon learning only if they are used correctly, it can be seen that preplanning must take place before their use. Prior to the arrival of the students the teacher should strive to have all equipment, such as the projector and screen, in place. Other preparation tasks, such as writing an outline on the chalkboard or preparing a transparency, should be completed so that neither class time nor teacher attention is taken away from the class. When the material is used it should be done in as interesting a manner as possible. It is the responsibility of the teacher to create interest in the teaching aid so that its contribution to learning will be maximized.
3. Supplementary teaching aids should be used at the proper time in the learning unit. Very few instructional aids are effective if they are used at a particular time simply because they are available. Rather, the aid must properly fit into the context of the lesson for it to have the desired impact. This guideline is most concerned with materials such as films which have to be ordered from an outside source. To insure the availability of these materials at the proper time, the teacher should plan the units to be covered and the desired teaching aids prior to the beginning of the academic year.
4. Follow-up procedures should be utilized after the use of supplementary teaching aids. All students do not perceive the same thing from a film, recording, or other teaching aid. Because of this the teacher may want to insure that all students have a correct impression of what was seen or heard. This may best be accomplished through a review, asking questions of the students or entertaining questions or comments from the students. As a part of the follow-up, the use of the material should be evaluated by the teacher to determine its effectiveness. This can be done by listening to students' comments and questions and by observing their behavior. The teacher should observe if the use of the material changed an attitude, created an interest, improved a skill, or increased student knowledge.
5. A variety of supplementary teaching materials should be used. This

variety will stimulate interest. Using only a few types fails to take full advantage of the diversity of materials at the teacher's disposal. While a variety of materials should be used, the teacher should use caution to not overuse them. Placing a reasonable time limit on the use of extra materials will provide a balance between their use and the regular instruction. There are times when it may be stimulating and profitable for the students to see an expert on film. In another situation it may be more advantageous for the class to see a demonstration by the teacher or a peer. Instructional materials should be considered as aids in learning and not ends in themselves.

6. An accurate inventory of supplementary teaching materials should be maintained. It is important for the teacher to keep an accurate record of instructional materials that are available. Those materials that are part of the teacher's own inventory should be recorded and stored in such a way that they are safe and easily accessible. Those materials that must be secured from other sources must be accounted for as well. Records should be kept of what is available, where it can be secured, and how and when it should be ordered to be available at the appropriate time. The quality and usefulness of each aid is important information to be kept. Keeping good inventory records of all materials available will help the teacher avoid duplication of materials. Also the teacher will be able to identify materials which are of poor quality, inaccurate, or out of date.

7. All supplementary teaching aids which belong to the school or teacher should be kept in good repair. The teacher should do everything possible to insure that all materials remain in good condition. Posters and other perishable materials must be handled carefully and stored in a safe place where they will not be damaged. Equipment such as projectors and recorders must be stored and used properly. If students are to operate the equipment, they should be properly trained. Any damage to equipment should be repaired immediately or reported to the person who will attend to their repair.

TYPES OF MATERIALS WITH SELECTED METHODS FOR IMPLEMENTATION

A variety of supplementary materials should be used to broaden the scope of the class. There are many commercial aids available to the teacher who takes time to search for them. An excellent time to begin collecting addresses and sources from which different aids may be secured is during the college years. Clinics and workshops offer opportunities for teachers to see what is new on the market in terms of books, teaching aids, and films. Physical education or sports journals are additional sources from which information about supplementary materials may be gathered.

Other extremely beneficial aids are those that are made by the teacher to fit a specific situation or topic within the unit. These personally made materials are well worth the time invested in their creation, as they are more relevant to individual programs. The following section includes some specific devices which may be used. These suggestions are not all inclusive, but are given to demonstrate some examples.

Films

The type of teaching aids most frequently used in physical education are films. Motion pictures and loop films are excellent forms that may be utilized.

Motion pictures. Next to live demonstrations, moving pictures are the most effective means of teaching motor skills. Their advantage over live demonstrations is that a more ideal model can be used. Research shows films to be especially helpful early in the learning process. The projection speed of films can be slowed down when viewing motor skills. This greatly enhances the learner's mental image and understanding of the skill. Once the mental image is established it can be transferred to a kinesthetic pattern through practice. Films also have a positive motivational effect upon the learning of motor skills. At the beginning of the lesson a specific skill may be viewed, the students can then practice the skill, and part way through the practice view the skill again to re-establish the mental image.

Films may benefit the student to a higher degree if they are shown more than once. During a second showing the sound may be turned down so the teacher may add comments or further explain a pertinent idea or concept. Another alternative is to review specific parts of the film for emphasis. When using films it is advisable to preceed the film by an explanation and follow it with a discussion.

Motion pictures of sport events can be used to create interest in the next unit to be studied. They may also be used to give some historical background to the lesson. This is especially profitable for an activity such as gymnastics. Health and fitness related films can be used to demonstrate their impact on human movement. The basic mechanical principles of action/reaction, law of inertia, and similar concepts, along with their effects on motor skills, can be clearly illustrated in films.

Loop films. In addition to full length films, loop films are excellent tools to aid in the introduction of specific skills. They can be very helpful in individualizing instruction. The simplicity of operation permits use by students with minimal instruction and in most cases without supervision.

Loop films can be set up anywhere in the gymnasium or other teaching stations and can be used by large groups, small groups, or individuals.

Frequently there are different skill levels of the same activity available on loop films. The students, once divided into groups of similar skills, can work with a loop film which corresponds to their skill level, freeing the instructor to work with another group.

35 MM Slides

The use of *35 MM Slides* is an effective means of motivating students while at the same time presenting information. Slides may be shown to the class as a whole or to smaller groups in the same fashion as mentioned above for loop films. They can be presented to the entire class for general comments and then left in view to serve as a model for later reference. Students may advance the slides as they are viewing them, or the projector may be prepared to automatically advance the slides. Used in this fashion the slide projector may serve as a complete teaching station.

Slides taken of the class during activities at various stages in the year can give a quick overview of the physical education program. These can be of great help in improving public relations. The slides can become a slide presentation for the PTA, open house, school board, and other school functions. Action shots of the communities' students engaged in active, enjoyable, and educational physical education classes helps the public see the benefits of the program. A few key words included in the presentation can help explain the goals and values of physical education to the community and its students.

Prints

The use of a *print* or *picture* is, as the saying goes, "worth a thousand words." Retention seems to be greater when a narration is accompanied by the use of pictures. Pictures taken of a skill and put in sequence can assist the students in achieving a proper mental picture before attempting a new skill. Pictures which are discussed and explained can direct the student's attention to a certain aspect of a skill.

The primary difficulty with using prints as an instructional medium is that, due to their small size, a limited number of students can view them at one time. Passing pictures around the class is usually not very effective, because it is distracting and it encourages visitation between students. An effective means of using prints is to project them onto a screen with an opaque projector. This allows the entire class to view the same print, but it does require that the room be dark and, therefore, communication is not as effective. Prints may have their greatest value when used on bulletin boards or in show cases. Displayed in this manner, they may be viewed and studied by students.

Overhead Projector

The *overhead projector* has the potential for being an effective instructional medium. For this to occur teachers must learn how to use the overhead projector properly. The effective use of the overhead projector depends upon the proper preparation of the instructional site, the preparation or selection of good transparencies, and the use of good instructional techniques (DeChenne, 1982).

The proper preparation of the instructional site is primarily concerned with having the students the proper distance from the screen. The size of the screen determines how close the projector must be located to the screen, which determines the size of the information being projected. It is recommended that students should not be seated closer than two times the width of the screen, and they should not be further away than six times the width of the screen. For example, if the screen is 6 feet wide, the students should not be closer than 12 feet nor further than 36 feet from the screen. In addition to the distance from the screen, attention should be given to the seating of students so their viewing is not blocked by someone else. Additionally, the teacher needs to eliminate the effect whereby the projected image is wider on one side of the screen than the other or wider at the top than at the bottom. The wider image at the top may be eliminated by slightly tilting the screen forward. The wide image on one side of the screen may be eliminated by slightly turning the projector sideways.

The use of good quality transparencies is the second important factor in the effective use of the overhead projector. The transparency should depict one general idea and should include a maximum of six words per line and six lines per transparency. To have the words on the transparency large enough, the teacher may consider the use of a typewriter with primary size type.

Good instructional technique is necessary for the overhead projector to be an effective teaching aid. The following suggestions may be used to enhance its effectiveness (DeChenne, 1982):
1. The attention of the students may be controlled by turning the projector on and off at appropriate times. In this way the attention may be focused upon the teacher or screen as desired.
2. The overhead projector may be used as a chalkboard. During a discussion key points may be written on the transparency, and the teacher maintains eye contact with the students.

3. Reveal each part of a transparency as it is being discussed. This will maintain student attention on the point being discussed by the teacher. This may be accomplished by simply covering portions of the transparency with a piece of paper and revealing parts as desired.
4. Use a pointer to focus attention on specific parts of the transparency. The teacher may touch the pointer to the transparency rather than the screen and maintain eye contact with the students.
5. Use the silhouette technique directly on the projector platform. Objects placed upon the platform will be projected as silhouettes upon the screen. Small objects may be used to represent players and their movements may be graphically demonstrated. This may be especially useful if a transparency outlining a playing court, floor, or field is first placed on the projector.

Videotape Recorder

The use of the *videotape recorder* is becoming increasingly widespread. Many schools have videotape machines, and teachers are encouraged by their administrators to utilize them in their classes. The videotape recorder is commonly used to provide feedback to students, serve as a teacher in the class, and assist teachers in self-evaluation.

The main purpose for which teachers and coaches use the videotape is providing feedback to students. The effectiveness of this type of feedback is not completely understood at this time. Rothstein and Arnold (1976) reviewed 52 studies which used some form of videotaping to provide feedback to learners. They found that in 33 out of the 52 studies no significant difference was found between the feedback by videotaping means and other control factors. This would seem to indicate that there is still some question as to the effectiveness of videotaping as a means of providing feedback.

Rothstein (1980) further synthesized the findings of the 52 studies to find the critical factors which determined the observed outcomes. From her analysis the following conclusions were drawn: (1) advanced beginners benefit more from the use of videotape replay than beginners, (2) repetitive use of the videotape replay is necessary for improvement to be significantly greater than control conditions, and (3) cues must be given to direct the learner's attention to specific parts of the replay for improved performance to occur.

Rothstein (1980) makes the following suggestions for the use of the videotape recorder for providing feedback to students:
1. The teacher should provide verbal cues to the student prior to viewing the videotape, indicating where to look and what to look for. Statements such as, "Notice the position of your racquet when you contact

the ball," or "Can you tell me what is wrong with the position of your left arm?" should be used.

2. The videotape replay should be used frequently. The replay should be used on at least five separate occasions with several replays each time. This will allow the learner to focus upon the important aspects of the replay.

3. The videotape should be used with advanced beginners and intermediate performers. Some knowledge of the skill is necessary for the performer to benefit from the feedback provided. Therefore, it is not very effective with beginner performers.

4. Opportunities for practice should be provided following the videotape replay. It is important that the performer has an opportunity to practice after the feedback so errors in performance can be corrected immediately.

5. The camera operator should zoom in on particular aspects of the performance. In this way the teacher can be sure attention is focused upon the important details. It is suggested that the use of the zoom lens may focus attention in enough detail to be useful for the advanced performer.

6. The angle at which the performance is taped should be changed from time to time. This allows the performer to view aspects of the performance that would otherwise go unnoticed.

7. The use of the videotape should be consistent with the goals of the activity. That is, in an activity such as gymnastics where form is the goal, the focus of the camera and verbal cues given by the teacher should emphasize the form of the movement. However, in an activity such as badminton, the focus of the camera and the verbal cues should relate to how the performer reacts to the environment (move to the shuttle and use the proper stroke).

Another way this instructional aid may be used is to actually teach a lesson. Teachers can videotape themselves or other demonstrators to teach a lesson, or they may use a professionally prepared tape for this purpose. The tape can lead the students in individual or mass activities, freeing the teacher to move around and provide individual attention. For example, the tape may be of a warm-up sequence or aerobic routine. The students may follow the videotape, and the teacher is free to circulate and correct improper form. The videotape may be even a greater help for the teacher than the student. In the example above it allows the teacher to teach the lesson repeatedly for several classes. If the teacher had to "lead" each aerobic routine, his or her energy level would surely suffer as the day progressed.

Teachers may also use the videotape to record their teaching style. This self-evaluation procedure can add greatly to the effectiveness of the teacher. Distracting mannerisms and behaviors by the teacher may be seen which would otherwise go unnoticed. Many aspects of class organization may be seen by the teacher while viewing the videotape which cannot be obseved by a teacher during the lesson. Other instructional behaviors such as the frequency of interactions with students and teacher movement may be observed and recorded. These observations will prove to be very useful data for teachers desiring to improve their abilities.

Television

Television can be an additional resource for learning. A television show can be used for a single period in the same way as the motion picture. On the other hand, it can be used for whole units extending over several weeks. For physical education it is more likely to be used as a supplement rather than a basic teaching method.

Television can be used to increase appreciation of sports and other forms of human movement. With some effort to guide its viewing, it can improve the students' understanding of games. Sports programs can be used as an assigned viewing to be discussed in class. If the program is assigned, it should be relevant to what is currently being studied in class. The students can be expected to look for skills they are studying and discuss what they observed. In some instances a study guide may be prepared by the teacher to focus the viewing by the students.

Some sports programs have expert commentators and can increase the students' knowledge and appreciation of sports. Through television, students may be exposed to sports they would not be able to cover in class.

In addition to the sports contests shown on television, there are often specials which highlight skills or individuals in non-competitive situations. Examples of such specials are some of those that deal with ice skating, physical fitness, home fitness programs (where the viewer is to join in the class), and human interest shows involving sports figures.

Computers

Although *computers* are new to the physical education class, their uses are growing by leaps and bounds. Information dealing with game rules, strategies, and physical fitness components can be retrieved by the students. There are many commerical programs that ask questions dealing with the above mentioned material that the students are asked to answer. The computer may be programmed to simulate games by showing a situation on the screen and asking the user to describe what should be done.

Teachers may use the computer to aid in work to be done outside the classroom, such as assigning students to classes or teams and compiling tournament standings. The teacher may use the computer to determine grades, do inventory checks of equipment and supplies, and chart student progress for comparison at a later date. Individual skill check lists can be designed and printed by using the computer. Tests and handouts may be constructed and printed with the computer. In addition, the computer can be used to randomly select test questions and thus change their order for each class over the years. Also, individual student contracts can be written and progress checked by use of the computer.

Records and Magnetic Tapes

Records and *magnetic tapes* are absolutely necessary in the units on rhythms, gymnastics, aerobics, and synchronized swimming. In selecting recordings for any part of the physical education program, several general criteria should be considered. These criteria are as follows:
1. The quality of the sound is very important, so old, scratchy records should be replaced.
2. The selections should be made according to what will contribute to the growth of students. Songs with objectionable words or ideas should be avoided.
3. The recordings should be appropriate to the activity. In recordings for rhythms or marching the rhythm should be discernible.
4. The selections of music should be somewhat varied.

Other forms of activity, not traditionally done to music, could be incorporated into the program. One activity easily put to music is rope jumping. Music can be used as a cue for changing stations in the form of a march or with a less structured selection. Music can also be used in combination with activity when involved in a lesson on creative movement. Each motor skill seems to have an internal rhythm of its own. Music can be used to help develop fluid movements in motor performances in much the same manner that the metronome aids the pianist. Although music may aid learning some motor skills, it is not appropriate in all class situations, so its use should be well planned.

Bulletin Boards

The use of *bulletin boards* is highly desirable in physical education. With the large number of students, and the diversity of activities and programs, a consistent medium of communication is necessary. This communication can easily be provided by a bulletin board.

Bulletin boards can be used to dissiminate general information such as: (1) records of achievement, (2) announcements of coming events, (3) promotions of sports events, (4) the introduction of new activities, (5) announcements of new books or magazines, (6) reminders of due dates or special required items, (7) schedules of the days activities, or (8) the daily assignments for students, student assistants, and squads.

Bulletin boards may also be used to highlight a special theme when the principal interest is motivation or the stimulation of thoughts about a concept. An example may be when the bulletin board displays the advantages of becoming physically fit. Often the success of the unit depends on the students repeatedly applying certain concepts or following rules. Bulletin boards serve as a constant reminder of these often used concepts or procedures.

Bulletin boards must be well-designed and carefully planned for the entire year. When designing the board, it is important to determine what idea the teacher wants to project or emphasize. Bulletin boards are teaching aids as well as decorations, so it is especially important to know exactly what point is to be made by its use. The way this point is presented must be planned. Headlines in newspapers and advertisements in magazines are designed to attract the attention of the reader. The title, slogan, or headline used on the bulletin board should serve the same purpose.

The bulletin board should be attractive and appealing. It is in essence a work of instructional art. Bright colors and clear bold lettering, with a vocabulary that fits the age of the students, will draw their attention. The concept should be simply displayed since lengthy or complicated exhibits tend to lose their effectiveness. To have the greatest impact, the contents of bulletin boards should be changed periodically.

Bulletin boards can be designed and assembled by either the teacher or one or more students. Those who learn the most from the use of bulletin boards are the ones who create them. Getting the student involved can change an "educational display" into a valuable hands-on "learning experience." This could be a voluntary student project or part of a class assignment.

Because bulletin boards need to be located in areas where students congregate, and still allow for traffic to continue, their physical placement should be considered carefully. They can easily be torn by balls, brushed by players, or subjected to vandalism, so they should be protected. A recommended place for their location is where students enter or exit from class. The purpose of bulletin boards is to display information or relay a message to the students. All efforts should be made to communicate this information effectively.

Charts

Charts are another form of supplementary materials that can help increase students' understanding of physical education. As is true with other aids, charts are designed to be time savers for the teacher. If they require extensive explanation, little has been accomplished, and their value is questionable. Teachers may develop their own charts, or they may purchase them from commercial sources. Professionally prepared charts are available for many sports and can often be purchased from sports equipment and supply companies. Examples of sports for which charts can be easily purchased are gymnastics, weight training, swimming, and diving. Additionally, publishing companies are a source of charts on such topics as physical fitness and anatomical and physiological studies.

Charts which are designed and constructed should follow the same basic guidelines as applied to designing bulletin boards. They should be neat, colorful, attractive, easy to read, and should contain a vocabulary appropriate to the ability range of the students. The construction materials should be durable so that the chart may be used for several years. Charts need not be designed only by the physical education teacher. They may also be designed and/or constructed by paraprofessionals, interested parents, and physical education students. Also, students in other classes, such as art and science, may assist the physical education teacher by designing bulletin boards as a project.

Task Cards and Task Posters

Task cards and *task posters* are supplemental aids that are designed specifically for use with the task style of teaching. They contain a listing of practice steps that can be followed by the students independent of the teacher's direction. The card or poster may be designed so that all students follow the same range of practice steps, or it may contain different levels of practice steps. If there are different levels represented on the card or poster, the student must determine the appropriate level to pursue. The various levels may be designated by colors so they are easily distinguished. This procedure allows students to work at their own individual level.

The use of task cards usually involves the teacher making available a number of identical cards for each specific skill in a series of lessons. These cards may be stored in a file box. Individual students then select the card for a particular skill and practice independently. If the card is divided into levels, the student will select the appropriate level. Upon completion of that task the card is returned to the file and a card for another skill is selected. In this instance various students in class may be working on different skills at the same time. Over a period of days all of the students will have practiced most of the skills for which task cards were prepared.

For use by groups of students, the task card information may be put on a large poster. The poster is most often attached to a wall or fence. If several posters, each covering a different skill, are located in different parts of the gymnasium, various groups of students will be working on different skills at the same time. Rotating the groups will accomplish the objective of working on all of the essential skills of a unit.

Books and Magazines

Books are used in all other disciplines, and their use should not be overlooked in physical education. Their increased availability and variety allows for many possible uses. Many teachers have reported great success with having sufficient copies of selected books in the school library for assigned reading by the students. In this way the expense of buying books is not great, and they are always available to the students. Outside reading may be assigned dealing with such topics as the rules of sports, history of various sports, biographies of sport figures, and physiological components of fitness. Written reports prepared by the students will greatly increase their knowledge in the area of physical education.

Sports *magazines* and journals can also be sources for supplementing the lessons. They may be used in a manner similar to that suggested for using books. Students should be encouraged to share with the rest of the class what they read on a topic that interests them. The topic could be presented in the form of an oral report or a class discussion.

Miscellaneous Materials

Chalkboards have traditionally been the supplemental material most used at all levels of education. There is usually one available in each classroom, and they are convenient to use. Physical education classes that have access to classrooms will find many excellent ways to use the chalkboard. The board may be used in such diverse ways as outlining a presentation on golf rules, explaining the forces operating on a gymnast while doing a movement or sketching a basketball play.

Physical education teachers have a unique problem in that most of their classes are taught in the gymnasium, on the softball field, and other locations where they do not have access to a chalkboard. For these instances the teacher may secure a small portable chalkboard that may be carried to the remote teaching stations. Another excellent way to accomplish some of the same tasks is with a *portable magnetic board.* These are especially helpful in designing plays for various sports and activities.

Another type of teaching aid is a *model.* Models range from a total body model, with movable limbs, to the more traditional models such as a heart, lung, or muscle. The use of models not only assists the teacher in explaining a concept, but they also hold the interest of students.

SUMMARY

Supplementary materials are used to expand the lesson to its full potential. They may be visual, audio, or tactile. They can: (1) provide a clearer visualization of materials, (2) motivate students, (3) add variety to the lesson, (4) extend the class beyond its physical limits, and (5) provide feedback to the students.

Supplementary materials need to be handled and used in specific ways to receive the full impact of their value. Therefore, several principles of use should be followed to insure that the desired effect upon the student's learning occurs. A variety of supplementary materials should be used.

Commercial, as well as teacher-made, materials can be utilized. The most frequently used are films which include motion pictures and loop films. Other forms of supplementary materials are: (1) 35 MM slides; (2) prints; (3) overhead projectors; (4) television; (5) computers; (6) records and magnetic tapes; (7) bulletin boards; (8) charts; (9) task cards and posters; (10) books and magazines; (11) chalkboards; and (12) models. Each should be examined to determine their most valuable uses to the program, teacher, and students.

SELECTED READINGS AND REFERENCES

DeChenne, James, "Effective Utilization of Overhead Projectors," *Media and Methods,* January, 1982, pp. 6-7 +.

Ehrgood, Allen H., "The Camera and the Self," *JOPER,* November/December, 1979, p. 70.

Hinderholtz, G.F., "Helpful Hints: Let Students Do It," *Science and Child,* January, 1982, p. 11.

McConnell, Ann and Shelia Fages, "Videotaped Feedback in Physical Education Methods Class," *JOPER,* May, 1980, pp. 64-65.

Pulmley, Barry, "Video Sport for All," *Sport and Recreation,* Winter, 1978, pp. 41-42.

Rothstein, A.L., "Effective Use of Videotape Replay in Learning Motor Skills," *JOPER,* February, 1980, pp. 59-60.

Rothstein, A.L. and R.K. Arnold, "Bridging the Gap: Application of Research on Videotape Feedback and Bowling," *Motor Skills: Theory Into Practice,* Fall, 1976, pp. 35-62.

Schafer, L.E., "Making Bulletin Boards and Instructional Art," *Science and Child,* October, 1981, pp. 32-40.

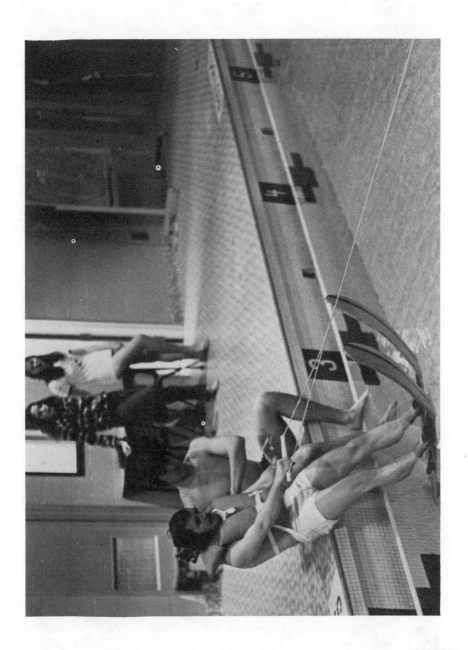

213

Photo by David Brittain

AVOIDING LIABILITY THROUGH SAFE TEACHING PRACTICES

During the past few years there has been an alarming increase in the number of lawsuits related to physical education and sport. According to Arnold (1980), this is not necessarily a direct attack on the profession of physical education. Rather, it is a result of the increasing availability of legal services, some well-publicized suits awarding enormous damage awards, and an increased emphasis on individual rights. These developments have resulted in an increased anxiety among physical educators, along with public embarrassment and financial losses of astronomical amounts. To the above factors must be added the ending of sovereign immunity in most states, which in the past has kept many school boards, administrators, and teachers from being sued.

There is a danger that this state of affairs will affect the effectiveness of the individual physical educator, and cause many schools to eliminate some of their curricular offerings. This does not need to happen if the teacher is aware of some of the basic facts about liability, knows how to prevent being accused of unsafe practices, and is cognizant of some of the dangers involved in the teaching of physical education.

DEFINITION OF TERMS

Basic to the understanding of the problem of legal liability is the knowledge of what some specific legal terms mean. Physical educators do not need to be legal experts, or even know a long list of legal terms. However, there are four that they should fully understand if they wish to avoid legal liability.

Tort Liability is a concept that is based on the premise that someone is at fault, and through this fault, injury has been caused to another party.

Negligence, according to Harry Rosenfield, an expert in school law, is ". . . the failure to act as a reasonable prudent person would act under the particular circumstance "(Appenzeller 1978)." A reasonable prudent person is a creation of the mind, an ideal, with whom the jury measures the defendant. Just because an accident occurs does not mean someone is negligent. The courts realize the system cannot "child-proof" the school, and the courts are as much a shield to protect the defendant as a weapon for the plaintiff. Negligence is something that must be shown. Before there can be negligence the following four elements must be present: (1) there must be a legal duty on the part of the defendant, (2) damage, or injury, must have occurred against the health, property, or character of the plaintiff, (3) it has to be shown that the defendant failed to perform his or her duties; exercise due care in carrying out that duty or provide a safe environment, and (4) a connection must be established between the conduct or behavior and the injury.

An *attractive nuisance* is a piece of equipment, a specific facility, or individual supplies that, by their nature, are interesting to students and their "just being there" tempts the student to try them or experiment with their use. Examples include a swimming pool, trampoline, weight machine, or a pair of boxing gloves. These items must never be left unattended or unsupervised, for if they are used and an injury results, the individual responsible will be classified as negligent. Such items are attractive to the normal, inquisitive, and active boy or girl, and adult physical education personnel should expect students to be attracted to them. Therefore an important aspect of preventing negligence is to either keep the attractive nuisance locked at all times, or provide trained supervision when it is available for use.

Malpractice may be defined as negligent behavior, or improper or unethical conduct by a professional, resulting in damage or injury. Lawsuits have been filed charging school districts and individual teachers with negligence for failing to provide their children with a minimum level of basic skills for survival in present day society. Examples of malpractice suits have included charges that students have been allowed to graduate from high school without competency in basic skills. Thus, parents are attempting to hold schools and teachers accountable for the academic accomplishments of their children. Social promotions have been the norms in some schools. In physical education classes students have received passing grades, and in some cases A's, just for dressing and attending class. These, and similar practices, leave the schools open for accusations of malpractice.

CONDITIONS THAT CAUSE LIABILITY SUITS

A close examination of physical education curricula and of practices of individual physical education teachers, enable us to identify conditions that give birth to charges of being negligent and generate liability suits. Among those most commonly charged are the following:
1. Failure by the teacher to provide proper supervision.
2. The use of equipment that is unsafe and defective.
3. Failure by the teacher to give adequate instruction on how to perform a movement, or the teacher giving improper instruction.
4. Allowing students to participate on dangerous equipment, on improper surfaces, or under hazardous conditions.
5. Having students participate in activities that are dangerous or improper for the age, skill level, and background of the students.
6. Incorporating an activity or experience in the curriculum that has not had official approval of the schools curriculum authority.
7. Treating injured students improperly, or failing to apply the appropriate treatment commensurate with the training of the teacher and the injury to the student.
8. Forcing a student to perform an activity that is hazardous and involves the possibility of personal injury.
9. Slandering students through verbal comments.
10. Administering corporal punishment.
11. Giving academic punishment (lowering grade) for non-academic acts (undesirable behavior).

METHODOLOGY FOR PREVENTING LIABILITY

Once the physical education teacher understands that tort liability is a condition that causes injury for which someone is responsible, it is possible for him or her to adopt methodologies that will prevent teacher liability. Most tort liability cases in the field of physical education are caused by negligence. The following suggestions are made to help teachers prevent this.

Use Good Instructional Strategies

Of all the practices the individual teacher may employ to prevent liability and being accused of negligence, the most important is to use appropriate instructional strategies. Among these are the following:

1. Engage in proper planning. Proper planning is best exemplified by the presentation of a written, daily lesson plan. A properly prepared lesson plan, such as is described in Chapter 4, with the day's objectives, activities, needed equipment, and instructional strategies to be used, is proof that the teacher has planned each segment of the lesson in advance. The absence of such a plan could be an indication that the teacher is negligent.
2. Plan for progression in the presentation of the day's and the unit's activities. Each movement experience that is above the beginning level should be based on the fact that the students have mastered the preceding step. Failure to do so indicates an omission of a basic concept of good instruction. Teachers should keep written records of student skill accomplishments to verify readiness to move to higher level skills.
3. Use correct teaching procedures. Good teaching procedures for physical education activities have been identified, and failure to employ them indicates improper teaching. Among them are choosing activities appropriate for the skill level of the students and taking into consideration their physical abilities. Also important are providing practice sessions, using the equipment and supplies correctly, helping the students who are having difficulty, and using a variety of teaching techniques.
4. Place the correct emphasis on the safety aspect of all student activities. The teacher must use safe practices in presenting the activity, and must insist that students follow safe practices. In addition, the teacher must be sure that all equipment and supplies used are proper for the activity and are in good condition.

Employ Proper Supervision

Even if physical educators use proper instructional methodologies when conducting an activity class, they are leaving themselves open for a suit charging negligence if they are not present and on the scene when they should be. Due to the nature of physical education classes, the adult teacher needs to be present if correct supervision is to be supplied. Physical education classes involve a lot of movement, and are often conducted in confined spaces. Some of the physical education activities involve some "risk" in their performance, such as swimming, contact sports, and movements on apparatus. Even though the students have been told what practices are safe and what practices are not safe, it is foolhardy to assume that these practices will then be followed by all of the students at all times. Proper supervision of them will require the teacher to be there.

It must also be remembered that students are young, immature, and in most cases not safety conscious. To them accidents are something that happens to someone else. In addition, because they are often new to the activity, they do not realize the hazards inherent in some movement experiences. Teachers, because they are older, more mature, and professionally trained in movement and human performance, have a better grasp of these things. Therefore, it is their responsibility to supervise the class properly.

The aspect of supervision discussed above deals with safety. There are two other aspects of proper supervision that also need to be mentioned. One of these is concerned with supervising the class so that the teacher is present to assist the students in skill development. One of the roles of supervision is concerned with the quality of the class, and with the degree of excellence of the teaching and of the students' performance. Without supervising the drills, games, and fitness activities, this excellence is not possible.

A final concern of supervision is that of class control and correct student behavior. It is a well known fact among educators that students behave better, waste less time, and are less apt to engage in deviant behavior when they are properly supervised.

Plan For The Safe Use Of The Locker Room and Shower Area

Since much of the whole subject of legal liability depends on the safe conduct of the various aspects of physical education, and safe conduct is concerned with the prevention of accidents, the locker and shower rooms deserve special consideration. Physical education teachers need to be aware of the potential hazards existing in the shower and locker room area, and then devise strategies that will not put them into the position of being negligent.

Locker rooms and shower areas are potential hazards for the following reasons: (1) they are traditionally small areas, with the entire class using them at the same time, and usually under some kind of time limit, (2) there is often water on the floor, making the potential high for slipping and falling on a hard surface, (3) students perceive the locker room as an informal, non-teaching environment, in which they may laugh, joke, and engage in friendly scuffling or "horseplay," (4) because of the presence of hot water, the possibility of burns exists, and (5) students are wet, or standing in water, while electric fixtures and switches are within their reach.

Accidents occurring from any one of the situations mentioned above are often accompanied by the charge that the teacher did not do something they should have, and are therefore liable. To prevent the occurrence of this charge, the following suggestions are given:

1. The teacher should devise a system for showering and dressing that allows students enough time so that it is not necessary for them to rush.
2. Traffic patterns should be established for the shower area and locker room.
3. Time limits should be set for the shower and for the dressing period.
4. Students should not be allowed to run in the shower or locker room under any circumstances. The danger of this should be explained to the various classes, and severe penalities established for violating rules prohibiting running.
5. Students should not be allowed to behave in a rough, unstructured manner that might result in injury in the shower or locker room.
6. Students are not to adjust the shower controls of other students' showers, or if the controls are operated by the teacher, they are not to touch any control. This will prevent students from being exposed to a dangerously hot shower when they are least expecting it.
7. Periodic inspections should be made of the locker and shower area to ascertain if any hazards exist that may cause injury to students.

To put the above suggestions into effect and see that they are carried out, the physical education teacher needs to use a three-pronged approach: (1) cover all the above points with the students during the orientation period, identifying dangers, elaborating on rules established, and answering any student questions, (2) post rules and guidelines in prominent places, and identify the penalties for their violation, and (3) periodically review the safety procedures and guidelines with the class, and make frequent checks on the environmental safety aspects of the locker and shower area.

Require Physical Examinations

A large portion of many physical education curricular experiences are vigorous in nature. To expose students to them without any prior knowledge of their physical condition is perilous indeed, and teachers might well be found negligent for doing so. Schools should see that the physical education teacher has a copy of the results of each student's physical examination, physical limitations, and medication currently being taken, plus their general health history. Ideally, each student will be required to take a complete medical examination as a prerequisite to enrolling in physical education classes. To say this is an impossibility is not being realistic, for most interscholastic athletes benefit from such a requirement. The teacher and the school administration should join hands in implementing this procedure. The examination may be performed either by the school physician or the family doctor. In situations where this is not yet implemented, the physical education teacher should consult closely with the school nurse in identifying students that need special consideration. The very least that should be done is for the teacher to have each student in class complete a personal health history, indicating physical limitations, health problems, medication being taken, and any recent illness. An additional protection for the teacher may be implemented by having each student that is absent from class for any injury or sickness present permission from their family physician stating they are once again cleared for vigorous activity.

Lawsuits have been initiated a number of years after an injury had occurred. Therefore, the suggestion is made that all records dealing with physical examinations, plus health and medical histories of students, be kept for at least five years. They may become vital information in establishing that the physical education teacher was not negligent. The records kept on file should also include a copy of the accident report. This report, which explains all the circumstances and the extent of the injury, are vital to the teacher's protection.

Heed Excuses

Every physical educator is faced with the problem of how to handle students who wish to be excused from the activity class. Sometimes the excuses are valid, and sometimes they are not. The teacher needs to make individual decisions about each one.

There are two areas, though, in which the teacher must heed excuses without exception. These are medical excuses signed by physicians and religious-based excuses. To ignore them is to invite legal action.

Medical excuses, of course, may at times be contrived and not really valid. They must still be honored. If bona fide medical personnel, such as nurses and physicians, affix their signature to an excuse for a student, the teacher is not in a legal position to dispute it. Granted, sometimes family physicians will sign such an excuse at the request of the student's parents, even though the teacher is convinced the student is able to participate. Still, the excuse must be honored. The teacher's role then is to talk to the student, and the parents if possible, and ascertain what the motive is behind requesting the excuse. Even while this process if going on, the excuse must be honored.

In the case of the request for an excuse based on religious reasons, the teacher must honor each one. Tradition has decreed that one's religion is his or her personal choice, and if certain beliefs dictate that a student not dance, dress in a gang shower environment, or participate in co-education activities, the teacher should accept this. In practically all previous court cases regarding religious beliefs, they have been honored. To force a student to perform against these beliefs, leaves one open for legal action.

Be Aware of Areas Requiring Special Consideration

Recent legislation, much of it on the national level, have given birth to procedures the individual teacher must comply with, or be legally liable. Four of the most visible of these are listed below:

1. *Title IX.* The Educational Amendments Act of 1972 prevents any discrimination between students based on sex. In physical education this has many implications. Most of the accusations of discrimination have charged that the female student was not being given the same opportunity to participate as the male students. If, in fact, a physical educator is guilty of employing an instructional strategy, offering any curricular experience, or providing an opportunity for participation that is not equal for both sexes, they are open to legal action. One does not have to guess as to what correct practices are. The American Association for Health, Physical Education and Recreation has printed a pamphlet (AAHPER 1978), outlining the procedures professionals in the field of physical education and sport must adhere to in order to avoid sexual discrimination. To conduct programs otherwise leaves a teacher liable for legal action.

2. *Public Law 92-142, The Education for All Handicapped Children Act of 1975.* This law requires that all handicapped students receive instruction in physical education, as well as a free education which emphasizes special education and related services designed to meet their unique needs. If free programs have not been established; if special students are not periodically assessed; if they do not receive the services they need; if appropriate objectives have not been established; and if their progress toward these goals have not been monitored, then the teacher is guilty of violating this piece of legislation.

3. *Section 504 of the Rehabilitation Act of 1973 (Non Discrimination on the Basis of Handicap).* This act provides that a person who is qualified otherwise, may not be denied benefits, kept from participation, or subjected to any discrimination if the program or activity is receiving financial assistance from the federal government. All schools that fall under the scope of regulations covered in Title IX are

also required to abide by the provisions of Section 504.

4. *Individual Student Rights.* For many years students in school, minors, and other youth of various status, did not have the protection of the courts regarding protection of their individual rights, as did the average adult. During recent years this has radically changed. Now "students rights" are a highly visible concern of school administrators, and of course individual teachers. In cases where teachers have abrogated what the courts have determined are the rights of students, litigation has held the teachers liable. It is not the purpose of this discussion to examine the effect this action has on the discipline of the school, or to get into a philosophical discussion as to where the rights of the student end and the rights of the school administration and faculty begin. The point is that to avoid liability the teacher should be cognizant of this development. Cases where students rights have been involved has covered a wide spectrum, and have been concerned with items such as: length of hair; wearing of beards; wearing certain clothing; exhibiting specific badges; buttons, or armbands; ridicule in public; invasion of privacy; being denied their due process; or being the victim of unauthorized corporal punishment.

Provide a Safe Environment

As in every other facet of school, students are deserving of a safe environment in the conduct of their physical education activities. In the field of human movement, the provision of a safe environment becomes a more complicated assignment. This does not, however, exempt the physical education teacher from being responsible in this area. To ask students to perform and participate in unsafe surroundings not only leaves the teacher open to accusations of negligence, but is educationally unsound, and morally indefensible. Some specific areas that the physical educator must consider to have a safe environment are listed below:

1. *Safe facilities.* This aspect includes turfed areas free from hazardous articles lying on the ground; sound construction of elevated structures such as bleachers; diving boards and gymnasium apparatus that is without flaws; pools and gymnasiums that are well-lighted; and inside teaching stations where glass and metal and wood protrusions are protected.

2. *Safe equipment and supplies.* Physical education teachers employ a lot of supplies to teach the various activities offered in the modern curriculum. It is easy to overlook the deterioration that occurs through normal wear and tear. The teacher needs to be alert to bats that are splintered, masks where the wire is broken, ropes that are frayed, support poles that are no longer strong, and dozens of similar

223

examples of equipment and supplies that may no longer be service-able. To use them when they are not safe creates a situation where a charge of negligence may occur.

3. *Professional conduct of the teacher.* An integral part of the instructional scene, of course, is the individual instructor. The environment in which the student is asked to learn, practice, and perform is not safe if teachers are not doing their job. The professional goes to class prepared, uses correct instructional techniques, is present to supervise hazardous activities, makes sure the students are in proper physical condition to handle what is being taught, and maintains proper student control.

4. *Choose safe activities.* What is proper to teach in physical education at the various grade levels is usually determined by the school's curriculum committee. In some school systems curricular offerings must be approved by the board of education. When planned programs are thus approved, the teacher is mandated to follow them. To deviate from what the school has authorized the teacher to offer leaves the teacher open to legal action. This is especially true if what the teacher selects has an additional element of danger. This is not to say that all activities with an element of danger are to be eliminated from the curriculum. This would deny students some experiences that are desirable, such as swimming or combatives. The point is made here that the teacher should not offer dangerous activities that are unapproved, or selected on a whim. Pyramid building, with some students perched high on top of other students; boxing; and endurance activities carried to the point of exhaustion have no sound educational basis and should be avoided.

Notify the Administration of Unsafe Situations

Since the teacher is actively involved with students who are participating in the physical education class, they often see practices or environmental conditions that are unsafe. Too many times these are reported verbally to the administrtion and nothing is done about them. Accidents or injuries that then occur put the teachers in a position where they seem to be negligent. Therefore, the suggestion is made that when a condition that needs correcting is identified by the teacher, it should be brought to the attention of the administration through a written communication. This is especially true when the dangerous situation is one that teachers cannot correct by themselves. Copies should be kept of all such written communication, along with the action that was taken by the administration.

Be Sure There Is Adequate Insurance Protection

In spite of all the precautions that a good physical education teacher may pursue, occasional accidents and injuries occur. As was noted at the beginning of the chapter, the number of lawsuits stemming from injuries in physical education classes is increasing. Therefore, it is wise for physical education teachers to see that they are adequately insured. Many states have a well-defined plan of insurance coverage for all teachers. Other states put the responsibility on the local school district. Most educational associations provide insurance coverage of almost all activities included in the contract. In addition, professional associations, such as the *American Alliance for Health, Physical Education, Recreation and Dance,* have provisions for their members to take out policies to protect them in case of being sued. And finally, almost all commercial insurance companies have policies that may be purchased to specifically cover physical education teachers. Teachers should investigate the conditions of employment under which they work, and make sure their own insurance coverage is adequate.

If the school system has an insurance plan to cover students that are injured in classes, the problem is somewhat alleviated. Policies that adequately cover the student's doctor fees, hospital expenses, x-ray examinations, and dental fees often prevent the institution of any lawsuits to collect damages.

SUMMARY

Because of the large increase in the number of lawsuits involving physical education teachers, it is necessary to employ as many practices as possible to avoid being put into a position whereby one is accused of being liable. The teacher needs to employ safe practices without narrowing the physical education program and eliminating activities from the physical education program.

To avoid liability, the teacher needs to understand the terms tort liability, negligence, attractive nuisance, and malpractice. Most litigation involving physical education teachers are based on the claim that the teacher was, in some fashion, negligent. Claims that the physical education teacher was negligent are most often based on some aspect of supervision, defective equipment, poor teaching strategies, improper curricular offerings, improper treatment of the injured, or the use of improper disciplinary techniques. Recently the question of violating students' rights has been added to this list.

To avoid liability, it is suggested that the physical education teacher should: (1) use good teaching strategies, (2) employ proper supervision,

(3) plan for the safe use of lockers and showers, (4) require physical examinations, (5) heed excuses, and (6) be aware of special requirements that are mandated by state or national legislation.

Because accidents happen even in the best-planned programs, physical education teachers should carry adequate insurance to protect themselves against financial loss.

SELECTED READINGS AND REFERENCES

American Alliance for Health, Physical Education, Recreation and Dance, *Complying with Title IX of the Education Amendments of 1972 in Physical Education and High School Sports Programs*, American Alliance for Health, Physical Education, Recreation and Dance, Washington, D.C.

Appenzeller, Herb, *Physical Education and The Law*, The Michie Company, Charlottesville, Virginia, 1978.

Appenzeller, Herb, *Athletics and The Law*, The Michie Company, Charlottesville, Virginia, 1975.

Arnold, Don E., "Positive Outcomes of Recent Legislative and Case Law Developments which have Implications for HPER Programs," *The Physical Educator*, March, 1980, pp. 24-29.

Dougherty, Neil J., "Liability," *JOPER*, June, 1983, pp. 52-54.

Loft, Bernard I., "Safety Problems in Physical Education and Athletics," *JOPER*, January, 1981, pp. 60 and 76.

Marcum, C. Everett, "Risk Acceptance Among Physical Educators," *JOPER*, January, 1981, pp. 73-75.

Martin, Cecilia, "Beginning Teachers and School Law," *The Physical Educator*, May, 1982, pp. 95-97.

Moskowitz, Michael, "Safety Hints for the Administrator," *JOPER*, January, 1981, p. 62.

Shroyer, George, "Legal Implications of Requiring Pupils to Enroll in Physical Education," *The Physical Educator*, October, 1982, pp. 159-162.

Thomas, Stephen B. and Carol L. Alberts, "Negligence and the Physical Education Teacher: Legal Procedures and Guidelines," *The Physical Educator*, December, 1982, pp. 199-203.

van der Smissen, Betty, "Where is Legal Liability Heading?" *Parks and Recreation*, May, 1980, pp. 50-53.

Photo by David Brittain

EVALUATION OF STUDENT PROGRESS

Physical education purports to enhance the development of students in five broad areas, which are labeled the objectives of physical education. The only way one can determine if development is actually occurring is to use measurement instruments designed to assess abilities in specific attributes. Comparing the results obtained from measurement to standards allows the teacher to make an evaluation.

Evaluation is an essential step in the total instructional model. Only through evaluation can the teacher make intelligent decisions regarding students, programs, and instruction.

UNDERSTANDING THE TERMS

The overall concept of evaluation is confusing to many students, and this need not be so. An explanation of a few terms will enhance the reader's understanding and application of the topic of evaluation. In this section there is presented a concise discussion of measurement and evaluation, formative and summative evaluation, criterion-referenced and norm-referenced standards, and objective and subjective evaluation.

Measurement and Evaluation

Mistakenly, teachers often use the terms measurement and evaluation interchangeably. Although they are interdependent terms, they have

229

very different meanings. *Measurement* is the application of a test to a group of individuals for the purpose of gathering data. *Evaluation,* on the other hand, is the comparison of data to some standard for the purpose of making a value judgement. The interdependency of the two concepts is an important consideration. Data produced from measurement has little meaning in and of itself. For example, a score of 14.3 seconds on a basketball dribbling test probably means little. However, when the 14.3 seconds is compared to a standard (evaluation) which shows that only 20 percent of a defined group performs the same test in 14.3 seconds or better, the score now takes on significant meaning.

Formative and Summative Evaluation

For the best learning to occur, evaluation must be a continuous process. Various types of evaluation are conducted at different times during a learning unit for a variety of purposes. *Formative evaluation* is the evaluation that is conducted throughout the unit. It is often of a self-testing nature, and it has as its purpose, the provision of feedback to the students. Typically, data gathered from formative evaluation does not contribute to the assignment of a student's grade.

Summative evaluation is the evaluation that occurs at the termination of a unit of study. The primary purpose of summative evaluation is for the assignment of a grade for students. Therefore, summative evaluation data should be gathered from teacher constructed and administered tests and instruments, or carefully selected standardized tests.

A complete evaluation plan will include both formative and summative evaluation. It is important for the teacher to understand that most formative evaluation techniques are learning experiences in themselves, so they are not detracting from time alloted for learning or teaching.

Criterion and Norm-Referenced Standards

Evaluation is the process of comparing a measurement against some standard to give it meaning. The two types of standards that measurements are most often compared against are criterion-referenced and norm-referenced. *Criterion-referenced standards* are those which have a specific level of performance against which students are compared. A performance by a student either will or will not meet the stated criterion. The criterion is usually determined by the teacher or a group of teachers. Baumgartner and Jackson (1982) recommend that criterion-referenced standards should be equal to the performance that an average student could meet after adequate instruction. Criterion-referenced standards tend to be used extensively in formative evaluation.

Norm-referenced standards are used when students are to be compared to other members of a well defined group of students. Norm-referenced standards are developed by statistical procedures. The norms, of course, are developed for a defined group (e.g., seventh grade girls) on a specific test. A student's performance on the same test may now be compared to the norms. Norms are often available for published tests, but where they are not the teacher can develop a set of norms without undue effort. Norm-referenced standards are usually used in summative evaluation where the goal is the assignment of a grade.

Objective and Subjective Evaluation

Evaluation is *objective* when it is based upon defined standards. With the presence of such standards there is no judgement necessary by the evaluator. Common examples of objective evaluation include: (1) a true-false type of question on a written test concerning a factual piece of information, (2) a standard of three allowed absences, and (3) a time of 12.5 seconds for credit on the 100-yard dash. Objective evaluation is obviously easy to determine and very defensible to students and parents. For these reasons teachers tend to use considerable amounts of objective type evaluations.

Subjective evaluations are those which require the evaluator to make judgements about the performance, whether it be in the affective, cognitive, or psychomotor domain. Some examples of subjective evaluations might include: (1) an essay question on a written test, (2) an evaluation of a student's display of sportsmanship, and (3) a judgement of the quality of a dive. These evaluations require an "opinion" by the teacher concerning the quality of the performance. It is our belief that subjective evaluations become more objective as the evaluator becomes more qualified. The professional training that a physical education teacher receives and the experience one derives as a practicing teacher should prepare that individual to make rather accurate subjective evaluations. If the teacher knows what kind of behavior is expected of students in each domain, he or she should be able to judge how close students come to meeting those desired behaviors.

Many teachers have found such instruments as rating scales, behavior scales, and check lists very useful in making their subjective evaluations more productive and accurate. These instruments guide the teacher in making a subjective evaluation by focusing attention upon the major aspects of the behavior under consideration. These instruments are discussed further in later sections of this chapter.

The teacher is encouraged to use both objective and subjective evaluation techniques. There are many excellent objective tests available for measuring performance in sport skills and physical fitness components. Written tests may be constructed which measure knowledge and other intellectual abilities by using both objective and subjective forms of questions. Subjective evaluation should be conducted by the teacher in those areas such as form in skill performance, and affective and social behaviors for which objective tests are difficult to find or are not available.

PURPOSES OF MEASUREMENT AND EVALUATION

There is tremendous variation among physical educators and schools relative to the use of measurements. Some teachers do not measure at all, and this is inexcusable. Others administer a lot of tests and gather considerable data which is filed away and never used. This practice represents a tremendous waste of time and effort for both teachers and students. Most students, and many teachers, feel that the assignment of grades is the only purpose of measurement and evaluation. This represents a very limited and wasteful view of measurement. There are nine useful purposes of measurement and evaluation presented in this text.

Placement of Students

Teachers may wish to group students according to some known quality. Height and weight measures, physical fitness scores, and skill test scores are often used for placement of students in groups. Having students of similar abilities together may result in better student achievement, since the teacher can come closer to personalizing the instruction. Objectives and learning experiences are developed for specific groups in this situation. Placement of students requires pre-assessment by the teacher using criterion-referenced standards.

Diagnosis of Weaknesses

Diagnostic measurement is done to determine student weaknesses and learning difficulties. It is not used to simply determine a level, but to discover the underlying causes of the weakness. Diagnostic measurement can become quite involved and should only be used if remedial work is to follow. The remedial work, based upon diagnostic measurements, should lead toward the correction of the weakness.

Determination of Achievement

Having a record of achievement is important to both the student and the teacher. Formative evaluation informs the teacher of the daily progress made by students and it provides regular feedback to the students. Summative evaluation provides a measure of how close students have come to meeting instructional objectives. Both criterion-referenced and norm-referenced standards may be used in measuring student achievement.

Prediction of Future Achievement

Measurements taken on students may be used to predict the possibility of future success in a similar skill or area of endeavor. Students may be counseled into activities in which they have the greatest chance to be successful. However, due to the many extraneous variables associated with performance in any endeavor, the teacher should use this function of measurement carefully.

Motivation of Students

Students are motivated through receiving feedback. Measurement results are a form of feedback and therefore can be a source of motivation. Successful achievement in the form of improvement can be an incentive for the student to achieve at a higher level. The most effective motivation probably comes from some type of formative evaluation which provides immediate feedback relative to the students' performance.

Assignment of Grades

The most obvious purpose of measurement is the assignment of grades at the end of a period of instruction. Students' grades should be based upon their ability to achieve the objectives stated for the instructional period. This achievement is normally based upon summative evaluation methods using norm-referenced standards. This task should be taken very seriously by the teacher. Well planned measurement procedures should be used since the grade assigned will become a part of the student's permanent record.

Evaluation of Program

Program evaluation is a complex procedure involving several different aspects. It may involve adding or deleting activities from the curriculum. It may involve studying the performance of students over a period of years as they are compared to the standards in use. It may involve comparing local student performances with student performances from other schools, state norms, or national norms. No matter what aspect of a program is being studied, student performance is a valuable contribution to the process.

Evaluation of Teaching

The ultimate measure of teaching effectiveness is the performance of students in the class. Learning is not an automatic phenomenon. The degree to which students learn is attributable, to a great extent, to the teaching methods employed. If students continually fail to learn, the teacher should examine and perhaps alter the teaching methods being employed. Teacher evaluation has always been, and continues to be, a complex task. The lack of objective data has made dealing with the topic difficult. Student performance represents one type of objective measure which can be utilized in teacher evaluation.

Research

Research is the means by which educational practices are tested, improved, or discarded. Physical education abounds with research opportunities due to the vast amount of quantifiable characteristics associated with the field. Measurement provides the data about which conclusions may be drawn. Research allows the professional to make intelligent decisions regarding the usefulness of specific instructional techniques, the worth of measuring instruments, and the value of various activities to be included in the school program.

MEASURING INSTRUMENTS

Evaluation must be based upon data gathered on students through the use of valid and reliable instruments or tests. A *valid* test is one which measures what it purports to measure. A *reliable* test is one which gives consistent results. Only valid and reliable tests can produce accurate scores. Evaluations which are based upon accurate scores will truly represent achievements by students. It might also be mentioned here that test administration procedures can have an impact upon the accuracy of the scores attained.

Paper and Pencil Tests

Paper and pencil tests are most often used to measure students' intellectual abilities. We say they are most often used because these same abilities may be measured through verbal testing and demonstration by the student in some cases. Very seldom can one find published paper and pencil tests to satisfactorily measure knowledge. The teacher usually must construct a test which reflects the content of the unit.

There are a variety of types of questions that may be included in a paper and pencil test. In this chapter we will present an example and a limited number of guidelines for the construction of true-false, matching, multiple choice, and completion questions.

True-false test items. True-false items are the most common form of alternate choice questions. Other alternate choice items are yes-no and right-wrong questions. Slightly different wording is necessary for these forms, but they are useful in adding variety to tests. A true-false item is a statement which is either completely true or it is false. The student responds to the statement by marking the item as either true or false. The use of these items is limited to testing low-level knowledge, usually of a factual nature. An example of a true-false test item is:

T F 21. The badminton smash is a defensive stroke.

A few guidelines to be followed in constructing true-false items are:
1. Include only one concept in the statement.
2. Do not use such terms as generally, sometimes, always, and never.
3. Keep the statements short.
4. Keep the vocabulary simple.

Matching test items. Matching test items are effective in testing recognition knowledge such as definitions of terms and rules interpretations. A small set of matching items are presented in Figure 14.1.

A few guidelines to be followed in constructing matching items are:
1. The statements should be numbered and the potential answers identified with letters.

Directions: Select the statement from column "B" which best describes a term in column "A" and mark the letter representing the statement in the blank located to the left of the term.

Column A	Column B
_____Divot	A. Long grass bordering the fairway.
_____Apron	B. Another name for a golf course.
_____Rough	C. Bunkers, water, and such that require special rules of play.
_____Links	D. Turf that is dug up by the clubhead.
_____Green	E. The putting surface.
	F. The direction the grass grows on the green.
	G. The short grass surrounding the putting surface.

Figure 14.1 Sample matching test items.

2. Keep both statements and potential answers short.
3. Provide more potential answers than statements. Make sure there is more than one potential answer for each statement.
4. Group similar content. Construct more than one set of matching questions if needed.

Multiple-choice test items. A multiple-choice question consists of a statement or question followed by several potential answers. Most often it is recommended that there be from three to five potential answers. Students are to read the statement or question and select the correct answer from those presented. A sample multiple-choice question is:

22. The height of the net in men's volleyball is

   A. 7'0"   B. 7'6"   C. 7'8"   D. 8'0"

Some guidelines to follow in constructing multiple-choice test items are:
1. Make both the statements and the answers short.
2. Include from three to five answers for each statement. Use the same number of answers for each question.
3. Number the statements and use letters to identify the answers.
4. If the statement is an incomplete sentence, each answer should complete the statement in correct grammatical form.

Completion test items. Completion test items are those in which one or more words are left out of a sentence, and the student is asked to provide the missing information. Completion items are of questionable value due to the fact they can easily be misunderstood and the information tested can be better tested with other types of questions. A sample completion test item is:

23. If a football team scores a_____it receives six points.

In the construction of completion test items the teacher should adhere to the following suggestions:
1. Each test item should contain only one blank.
2. Use a uniform length blank in all questions so the length of line does not give a hint about the answer.
3. The missing information must be very specific and the information provided clear enough to lead the student to the intended answer.

Physical Fitness Tests

There are many physical fitness tests available for use. A primary question that has continually plagued the measurement of physical fitness has been a lack of agreement as to exactly what constitutes physical fitness. A recent committee appointed by the American Alliance for Health, Physical Education, Recreation and Dance approached the problem by differentiating between physical *fitness* related primarily to functional health, and physical *performance* related primarily to athletic ability. They pursued the development of a test which measured the components of physical fitness that are related to health. Items to be included in the test battery were selected on the basis of the following criteria: "(1) a physical fitness test should measure a range which extends from severely limited dysfunction to high levels of functional capacity, (2) it should measure capacities that can be improved with appropriate physical activity, and (3) it should accurately reflect an individual's physical fitness status as well as changes in functional capacity by corresponding test scores and changes in these scores." (AAHPERD, 1980, pp. 3-4).

Three areas of physiological functioning were selected to be measured as components of physical fitness. The components are cardio-respiratory function, body composition, and abdominal and low back-hamstring musculo-skeletal function. A brief description of the tests which were selected to measure these components of physical fitness is presented in this section of the chapter. The reader is encouraged to purchase the complete *AAHPERD Health Related Physical Fitness Test Manual* (1980). The manual contains a description of each test, required facilities and equipment, administration suggestions, and norms which were developed after testing several thousand children.

Distance runs. The purpose of the distance runs is to measure maximal functional capacity and endurance of the cardio-respiratory system. Students up to 13 years of age are to take either the 1-mile run for time or the 9-minute run for distance. Students who are 13 years of age or older may be given the 1.5-mile run for time or the 12-minute run for distance.

Triceps and subscapular skinfolds. The purpose of the skinfolds is to measure the level of fatness in the body. The two skinfold fat sites were chosen for this test because they are easily measured and are highly correlated with total body fat. The triceps measure is taken over the triceps muscle of the right arm at a point halfway between the elbow and the acromion process. The subscapular measure is taken just below the inferior angle of the scapula. The sum of these two measures is the measure of fatness.

Modified sit-ups. The purpose of the sit-ups is to evaluate abdominal muscle strength and endurance. The starting position is with the knees raised so the feet are between 12 and 18 inches from the buttocks, and the arms are crossed on the chest with the hands on the opposite shoulders. The student sits up, keeping the arms in contact with the chest, until the elbows touch the thighs.

Sit and reach. The purpose of the sit and reach is to evaluate the flexibility (extensibility) of the low back and posterior thighs. While sitting on the floor with the knees fully extended, the student reaches forward as far as possible along a measuring scale which is mounted on a specially constructed box.

Skill Tests

The development of skills is a major objective of physical education. An examination of most physical education programs would reveal that the majority of instructional time is devoted to this endeavor. To determine if skill development is actually occurring the teacher must employ appropriate tests. There are many skill tests available in the literature, so it is very seldom that the teacher cannot find a test to meet particular needs. However, if an appropriate test cannot be found, teachers should consider constructing their own. More often the concern is in selecting the best test from an array of possible choices. In selecting a skills test the teacher may find the following guidelines useful.

1. Select a test that is specific to the skill you are interested in measuring.
2. Select a test that has good reported validity and reliability.
3. Select a test that does not have more requirements for equipment and facilities than you have available.
4. Select a test that is not too time consuming.

As was stated earlier, there are many tests available for most skills the teacher wishes to measure. Excellent sources of skill tests are various issues of *The Research Quarterly*, as well as many tests and measurement books. The reader may find the following list of books especially valuable in locating appropriate skills tests.

1. *Application of Measurement to Health and Physical Education*, H. Harrison Clarke.
2. *A Practical Approach to Measurement in Physical Education*, Harold Barrow and Rosemary McGee.
3. *Measurement in Physical Education*, Donald K. Mathews.
4. *Measurement Concepts in Physical Education*, Frank M. Verducci.
5. *Measurement and Evaluation in Physical Education*, D. Allen Phillips and James E. Hornak.
6. *Measurement and Statistics in Physical Education*, N. P. Neilson and Clayne R. Jensen.
7. *Practical Measurements for Evaluation in Physical Education*, Barry L. Johnson and Jack K. Nelson.

Subjective Evaluation Instruments

Subjective evaluations are quite often necessary and desirable. In the psychomotor domain it is often necessary to make subjective evaluations of the form displayed in such movements as the golf swing, gymnastics stunt, or dive. Measurements in the affective domain are difficult to attain. They are, at best, estimates of the behavior being evaluated. This should not stop the teacher from conducting evaluations in this domain, because there are several types of instruments which may aid the teacher.

Checklists. A checklist is a simple sheet with the names of students listed down the side and a series of skills listed across the top of the sheet. As students complete the skills in compliance with the criterion established by the teacher (which is the subjective evaluation), they are checked off. This serves as a record for both the student and teacher of the progress of each student. The checklist is especially useful in units where a progression of skills is necessary for the safety of the performer. Such activities as swimming and gymnastics exemplify this point. The checklist may be established to indicate that certain skills must be completed satisfactorily before other skills may be attempted. Figure 14.2 shows an example of a checklist for a tumbling unit. A checklist may be used to inform and evaluate, or it may be used as an aid in assigning a grade. Some teachers base a portion of a student's grade upon the number of skills that can be mastered.

Rating scales. Rating scales can be developed for many purposes. Rating behavior, form in the performance of a movement, and game performance are three common uses. A rating scale consists of a selected set of traits to be observed and a scale for indicating the extent to which each trait is present. Phillips and Hornak (1979) identify three functions that rating scales serve: (1) they direct the observations of the teacher toward specific aspects of the behavior being rated, (2) they provide a common frame of reference for comparing all students, and (3) they provide a method for recording the teachers' judgements.

Figure 14.3 contains an example of a rating scale for judging the form displayed in the golf swing. In the example there are 3 rating positions available. It is generally felt that there should be from 3 to 7 ratings possible, with the teacher making the choice of how many will serve the specific purpose best.

Student response scales. Student response scales includes all instruments which require students to respond to questions or statements regarding their own feelings, attitudes, or manner of behavior. For obvious reasons students should never be graded on the basis of their responses to these instruments. The results may be used to ascertain how students feel

239

CHECKLIST FOR TUMBLING

Students	RED				BLUE				GOLD			
	Forward roll	Backward roll	Tripod	Cartwheel	Handstand roll	Bridge	Headstand	Roundoff	Layout dive roll	Back extension	Handstand	Handstand arch over

*Red skills must be mastered before blue skills are attempted.
*Blue skills must be mastered before gold skills are attempted.

Figure 14.2   Sample checklist for tumbling.

about the teacher, class or program. In addition, a valuable outcome may be the initiation of discussions relative to such topics as getting

Student _____Class_____

Component	Rating Criteria	Rating
Address Position		
Grip	Proper hand position	3 2 1
Stance	Proper position of feet	3 2 1
	Proper weight distribution	
Body position	Alignment with target	3 2 1
	Proper arm position	
	Proper head position	
Club position	Proper club alignment	3 2 1
	Proper position relative to body	
Takeaway	Club path straight and low	3 2 1
	Weight shift to rear foot	
	Proper shoulder turn	
Backswing	Full backswing	3 2 1
	Club position parallel to ground	
Downswing	Weight shift	3 2 1
	Pull with target arm	
Hitting area	Head steady	3 2 1
	Hand action	
Follow through	Body facing target	3 2 1
	Club high over shoulder	
	Weight on target foot	

Comments:

Figure 14.3   Sample rating scale for the golf swing.

along with others, sportsmanship, and how to handle winning and losing.

A popular type of instrument of this type is a scale in which students indicate their degree of agreement or disagreement to a series of statements concerning a topic. These are normally used to determine the students' attitude toward a specific concept such as a particular sport, physical education in general, or a concept such as physical activity. Another useful instrument is one in which students are asked to identify how they would react to a situation by selecting one response from several alternatives. A third type of instrument to be used as a springboard for discussion is the open-ended statement. The teacher formulates the topic in the beginning of a statement, and the student is asked to complete the statement.

TEST ADMINISTRATION PROCEDURES

Tests should be administered in an efficient manner which will produce accurate scores. The procedures used should not require an excessive amount of time, should give all students an equal opportunity to perform the test to the best of their ability, and should provide for safety for the students. This can be accomplished if the teacher follows a few suggestions:

1. The teacher should select a test which is conducive to measuring large numbers of students in a relatively short period of time.
   a. The test may be one that can be administered to several students at one time, such as a distance run, where the teacher stands at the finish line and calls out the time for each student.
   b. The test may be one that uses partners to test each other, such as the sit-up test, where one partner holds the performer's legs and counts the number of sit-ups.
   c. The test may be one in which duplicate test stations can be employed, such as the badminton short serve test or a soccer dribble course through cones.
2. The teacher should carefully plan all of the test procedures in advance of the testing period.
   a. Plan the design and arrangement of test stations.
   b. Determine who will supervise each test station.
   c. Plan and prepare score sheets for each test being administered.
   d. Plan the pre-test warm-up and practice.
   e. Determine how the students will rotate among the test stations.
   f. Plan activiites for the students as they finish the tests.
3. The teacher should select and train student assistants prior to the test period.
4. The teacher should make sure all equipment and supplies are in place before the test period begins.
5. The teacher should make sure all students understand all of the test procedures prior to beginning any testing. Some teachers explain these procedures at the end of the previous day's lesson to save time for actual testing on the test day.
6. The teacher should motivate all students to their best performance on the tests.
7. The teacher should remain free to supervise the entire testing organization, handle problems, and encourage students. Student assistants assigned to the class, and reliable class members, should record scores and assist with other duties of test administration.

The administration of tests should not be viewed as a loss of instructional time if a good quality test is selected and good administration procedures are used. Although the primary purpose of testing is to gather data for evaluation, the students are also active and performing the skill or other behaviors.

The Assignment of Grades

Although the assignment of grades is only one of the nine purposes of measurement and evaluation, it is a very important one. The remainder of this chapter will focus upon the concept of the assignment of grades.

Develop a Philosophy of Grading

A grading system should be based upon a philosophy that is formulated and agreed upon by all teachers involved with the physical education program. Consistency of philosophy among all teachers helps student performance to receive the same grade regardless of who the teacher might be.

The development of a philosophy should include a determination of the purposes of the grading system, as well as an agreement upon what items will be included. In addition, the teaching staff should consider what type of data will be gathered and what measuring instruments will be used. If the teacher or teachers give serious thought to a sound philosophy, they will have a much improved chance of developing an effective grading system.

Be Consistent with Other School Subjects

Physical education should be thought of as just one of many separate but equal disciplines within the total school program. With this position comes the sharing in the requirements and responsibilities of all school disciplines. Students are entitled to receive a fair, accurate, and understandable estimate of their abilities and achievements in physical education, as well as in their other school subjects. Teachers of physical education should employ a system of grade reporting that is consistent with the rest of the school subjects. In some schools a variety of reporting systems are used, depending upon the subject. The goal is to utilize the reporting system most appropriate for each specific subject. In this situation the physical education staff is justified in using a marking system which is most appropriate for reporting student progress. Teachers of physical education should never be guilty of using a separate grading system from the rest of the school simply for convenience or because it is "too hard" to grade students in physical education.

Attributes of a Good Grading System

It should be the desire of every teacher to have a marking system that is consistent with other aspects of good instructional methodology. The most important attribute of a marking system is that it should accurately report the progress of each student. Verducci (1980) believes that a good grading system is necessary to: (1) inform the parent or guardian of the student's progress, (2) inform the student of his or her own progress, and (3) inform the teacher of the progress being made by each student. To accomplish these goals the marking system must be clear and understandable. Any technique that is used (letter grade, points, percentiles, standard scores) must be explained to the students and parents in an understandable way.

A good grading system is one that is fair to all students. Students come to physical education in all sizes, shapes, and abilities. Again, let us be reminded that physical education operates under the umbrella of five developmental objectives. Therefore, all of the objectives should contribute to the grade received by the student. One of the best ways that teachers have found to accomplish this is to have several items upon which to base a grade. Most successful grading systems observed have contained from four to six components for which students received a mark. Each component of the marking system must be measured with instruments of good quality. The quality of the measurement instrument is determined by its validity (truthfulness) and reliability (consistency). One final attribute of a good grading system is that it should be useable. That is, it should meet the criteria mentioned above without being unduly burdensome. It must be one that can be applied to a rather large number of students without being too time consuming.

Components of a Grading System

Probably no topic about teaching physical education is more emotional and confusing than on what specific items a student's grade should be based. Other teachers in the school seem to have rather defined parameters for grading — results on achievement tests. Teachers of physical education do not seem to have such a clear answer to the grading dilemma. Over the years students have been given a grade for skill ability, physical fitness levels, participation, sportsmanship, cleanliness of clothing, showering, and a plethora of other items. Each item is important in itself to some teachers. There is no simple and clearcut answer to the problem, but some guidelines may be offered. An important step toward determining on what students should be graded can be derived from the following model of instruction:

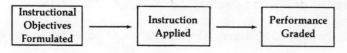

Admittedly, this is a simplified model of instruction. It serves the purpose to show that instructional objectives must be formulated by the teacher. Instruction will then be based upon the stated objectives. Grading must then be based upon what was taught, with the criterion being how close the student came to meeting the objectives. Therefore, the students are graded on the elements which best represent the stated objectives. Baumgartner and Jackson (1982) give three criteria against which any potential item for grading should be judged. The criteria are: (1) Does the item represent a major objective of the physical education program? (2) Do all students have equal opportunities to demonstrate their ability relative to the item? and (3) Can the item be reliably and validly measured?

GRADING SYSTEMS

There are many grading systems that teachers have used in physical education. Each system has both strengths and weaknesses. If a school staff has developed a philosophy of evaluation and grading, as has been strongly suggested earlier in this chapter, a specific grading system should be selected which most accurately represents that philosophy. There are two stages to a grading system: the assignment of grades for individual test items, and the assignment of final grades.

Assignment of Individual Test Grades

Needless to say, the method selected for assigning a grade for individual items must remain consistent. These individual grades will be combined to assign a final grade. In this section we have presented five methods of assigning grades to individual tests.

Percentage method. The percentage method has also been referred to as a form of teacher standard grading. In this method specific percentages of the total possible points are required for specific grades. As an example:

$$90 - 100\% = A$$
$$80 - 89\% = B$$
$$70 - 79\% = C$$
$$60 - 69\% = D$$
$$\text{Below } 60\% = E \text{ or } F$$

A specific example of grading by the percentage method for a class of students on a 70 point test is shown in Figure 14.4 The final outcome of this method is a letter grade assigned to the test.

The biggest weakness in the percentage method is that the required percentage for each grade is an arbitrary figure based largely on tradi-

Knowledge Test Scores
(70 points possible)

90% X 70 points = 63 points for a grade of A

80% X 70 points = 56 points for a grade of B

70% X 70 points = 49 points for a grade of C

60% X 70 points = 42 points for a grade of D

Figure 14.4   Grading by the percentage method.

tion. This method is most effective when used by the experienced teacher who is quite familiar with the ability of specific age level students, the subject matter, and the level of difficulty of the test. The major advantage of this method is that all students have the same opportunity to receive a specific grade, and it is consistent from class to class as well as year to year.

Natural breaks method. The natural breaks method of assigning a grade is the simplest method available. It simply requires the teacher to place the scores in a frequency distribution so that the scores can be examined. Breaks in the distribution are identified and grades are applied accordingly. For example, in Figure 14.5 it can be observed that there is a

Knowledge Test Scores
(100 Points Possible)

Column A First Semester Scores		Column B Second Semester Scores	
95		94	
94	A	93	
93		92	A
		91	
90		90	
89			
87		88	
86	B	87	
85		86	B
83		84	
82		83	
81		82	
80			
79		80	
		79	C
77		78	
76	C	77	

Figure 14.5 Grading by the natural breaks method.

break in the score column A between 93 and 90. Therefore, the score of 93 would receive an A and the score of 90 would receive a B. As was true of the percentage method, the natural breaks method results in a letter grade being assigned to the test score. The weakness of this method can be seen if one compares the second semester scores (column B) with the first semester scores (column A) for the same test. A score of 90 during the first semester received a grade of B, whereas the same score received a grade of A in the second semester. This illustrates that in the natural breaks method an individual's grade is not only based upon his or her own performance, but also upon the performance of the other students and the semester the student happens to take the test. The natural breaks method is seldom used by itself as a means of assigning grades.

Combined percentage and natural breaks method. Some teachers have found success with combining qualities of the percentage and natural breaks methods. This is illustrated in Figure 14.6. Using the percentage method a score of 90 would be necessary to receive an A. However, since there is a two point break between the scores of 89 and 87, the teacher may reason that since the score of 89 is closer to 90 than to 87 the student should receive a grade of A. Normally, the break is considered if it is located no more than one point from the standard. It is important to note that giving the student with the score of 89 an A does not change the standard for future tests. As was true in the two previous methods, this method results in the assignment of a letter grade to each test.

Score	Frequency	
96	1	
95	2	
94	1	
93	3	**A**
92	2	
91	4	
90	1	
89	1	
87	2	
86	3	**B**
85	2	

A = 90% = 90 – 100
B = 80% = 80 – 89
C = 70% = 70 – 79
D = 60% = 60 – 69

Figure 14.6 Combined percentage and natural breaks methods of grading.

Standard score method. There are several types of standard scores that may be used. The reader is referred to one of the many tests and measurements books for the computation procedures of various standard scores. In brief, the assignment of a standard score for a test involves the following steps:
1. Administer the test and record a score for each individual.
2. Compute the mean and standard deviation for the distribution of scores.
3. Compute a standard score for each individual using the student's score, distribution mean and standard deviation.
4. Record the standard score in the grade book for later computation of a final grade.

Point method. As the name implies, in this method each test is assigned a point value. These points are entered into the grade book and will be totaled for a final grade. This method will be explained in more detail in the next section regarding the assignment of final grades.

Assignment of Final Grades

At the end of a grading period the teacher usually must combine all of the individual test grades into a final grade. In this section there are three grading systems which may be used to derive a final grade.

Average of letter grades. This system may be applied when letter grades are assigned to individual tests. It involves averaging the grades received for the various items upon which the final grade is to be based.

Figure 14.7 shows some sample grades and point values for four items which were used to evaluate students. The assignment of a final grade involves the following four steps:
1. A letter grade is assigned for each marking attribute which represents the average of all measurements of that attribute.

Marking Item	Grade	Point Value
Skills Tests*	C −	4
Knowledge Tests*	B +	9
Physical Fitness Tests*	C −	4
Participation, Effort, etc.	A −	10
	Total	= 27
	Total ÷ 4	= 6.75
Final Grade	= B −	

*Grade represents an average of each item.

Figure 14.7 Assignment of a final grade by averaging letter grades.

2. Each letter grade is converted to a point value using a scale where an A+ = 12 points, A = 11 points, and so forth until E = 0 points.
3. The point values are totaled and divided by the number of attributes on which the grade is based.
4. This figure is converted back to a letter grade using the same scale as in number 2 above.

Teachers often want certain components of the grading system to have more effect upon the students' grade than some other components. This may be accomplished by a system called weighting. Each grading attribute contributes its own weight toward the computation of the final grade. Figure 14.8 shows the effects of weighting upon the same grades which were previously used in averaging letter grades. It will be observed that the unweighted grade was a B— whereas the weighted grade was a C+ due to the percentage of contribution of each attribute. The steps in computing an average of letter grades with weighting are as follows:
1. Determine the percentage (weight) that each marking attribute will contribute to the final grade.
2. A letter grade is assigned for each marking attribute which represents the average of all measurements of that attribute.
3. Each letter grade is converted to a point value.
4. The percentage of each attribute is converted to a decimal and multiplied times the point value of each grade.
5. These resulting figures are totaled.
6. The total score is converted back to a letter grade by comparing it to the scale where an A+ = 12, A = 11, and so on down to where an E = 0.

Average of standard scores. This system of grading is used when each test score has been converted into a standard score. The computation of a final grade now involves two steps:
1. The standard scores are added together and divided by the number of scores to obtain an average.

Marking Item	Weight	Grade	Weight X Grade
Skills Tests*	40% (.4)	C— (4)	.4 X 4 = 1.6
Knowledge Tests*	30% (.3)	B+ (9)	.3 X 9 = 2.7
Physical Fitness Tests*	20% (.2)	C— (4)	.2 X 4 = .8
Participation, Effort, etc.	10% (.1)	A— (10)	.1 X 10 = 1.0
		total	= 6.1
		Final Grade	= C+

*Represents an average for each item.

Figure 14.8   Averageing of letter grades with weighting.

2. The standard score average is then compared to a set of norms which the teacher must construct.

The reader may think this is a very simple method of grading since it seems to involve only two steps. However, referral back to how the standard scores are computed for each test score reveals that it involves considerable effort on the part of the teacher. Some teachers go in the other direction and believe that standard scores require too much work and time. Baumgartner and Jackson (1982) estimate that approximately the same time commitment is necessary whether the teacher is using the standard score system or the average of letter grades system.

Point total. A point system is one in which students receive a number of points for each item on which their grades will be based. The distribution of points for each time should be carefully planned to represent the philosophy of the school staff and the emphasis you want each item to have upon the final grade. Figure 14.9 is a sample of a point system for a grading period. The point allotment in this sample shows that 50% of the grade will be based upon skill ability, 30% on knowledge, and 20% on the subjective area of participation, effort and whatever else the teacher decides to include. In addition to assigning points to each grading item as shown in this example the teacher will need to do the following:

1. Norms will need to be developed for each skill test. That is, the score necessary on a particular short serve test to earn 10 points, 9 points, and so forth must be determined. The same must be done for the clear and the two volleyball tests.
2. A scale for earning the 5 subjective points for playing ability in each sport must be developed.

I. Skill ability			50
A.	Badminton	25	
	Short serve	10	
	Clear	10	
	Playing ability (subjective)	5	
B.	Volleyball	25	
	Serve	10	
	Wall volley	10	
	Playing ability (subjective)	5	
II. Knowledge			30
A.	Badminton test	15	
B.	Volleyball test	15	
III. Teacher assessment of participation			20
effort, etc.			
			100

Figure 14.9 Point system for a grading period.

250

3. A method by which the 15 points may be earned on the badminton knowledge test must be developed. As an example, a 30 question test might be given with each question earning ½ point. The same must be done for volleyball.
4. Standards for earning the teacher assessment points must be developed.
5. The number of points necessary for each letter grade must be determined. For example, 90 points equals an A.

The point system requires considerable work at the beginning to develop all of the necessary norms and standards. Once these are developed it tends to be a very quick, simple, and efficient grading system.

Other Means of Grading

In all of the previously presented grading systems, students received a single letter grade as a symbol of their achievement. The reader should be aware that there are other methods of grading in use. Many elementary schools use a marking system whereby each trait to be evaluated is marked "excellent," "satisfactory," or "unsatisfactory." Other words may be used to convey the same basic meaning to the student and parents.

In junior and senior high schools, students sometimes receive marks consisting of "pass - fail," "pass - no credit," or "credit - no credit." These alternate forms of grading have been met with varying degrees of success at the secondary level.

THE STUDENT PROGRESS REPORT

Many teachers believe a single letter grade is inadequate as a symbol of achievement and supplement the letter grade with a progress report. The student progress report is a description of the specific areas where the student is making satisfactory and unsatisfactory progress. It allows the student and parents to better understand where the student has strengths and weaknesses.

The general format of the progress report may include a listing of the important objectives of the grading period, and each is evaluated by a scale similar to the following:

  + The student is making good to excellent progress.
  ✔ The student is making satisfactory progress.
  − The student needs to improve.

A sample of some objectives and their ratings which might be included in a student progress report are shown in Figure 14.10. There is no minimum or maximum number of objectives that should be included in

---

Student Progress Report

Name _____Date_____

Grading Period 1 2 3 4

   + The student is making excellent progress.
   ✓ The student is making satisfactory progress.
   − The student needs to improve.

Objective	**Progress**
1. Learn *(Basketball)* skills taught in class.	_____
2. Learn *(Volleyball)* skills taught in class.	_____
3. Show improvement in physical fitness items tested.	_____
4. Relate well with the other students.	_____
5.}	
6.}The teacher may include as many objectives as desired.	
7.}	

Figure 14.10   Sample student progress report.

the progess report. The only guideline for the teacher is that the extensiveness of the report should be feasible for the time available to the teacher and the number of students to be evaluated.

SUMMARY

Evaluation of student progress is important if teachers are to determine the amount of development that has taken place in students. To utilize evaluation the teacher must be familiar with specific terms. Terms such as measurement and evaluation, formative and summative evaluation, criterion and norm-referenced standards, and objective and subjective evaluation must be understood so student evaluation may proceed in an orderly fashion.

Measurement and evaluation may be used for several purposes. Teachers may selectively use measurement data for: (1) placement of students, (2) diagnosis of student weaknesses, (3) determining the achievement of students, (4) prediction of future achievement, (5) motivation of students, (6) assignment of grades, (7) evaluation of the program, (8) evaluation of teaching methodology, and (9) research. Teachers should not only be aware of the various uses of measurement data, but they should also utilize them for the benefit of the students and themselves.

Data may be gathered through the use of a variety of instruments. These instruments include paper and pencil tests, physical fitness tests, skill tests and subjective evaluation instruments. Excellent skill tests and physical fitness tests can be found in the literature. They should be selected because they have good validity and reliability, and because they are appropriate for the teacher's specific needs. Most written tests, and some skill and affective measuring instruments, will need to be constructed by the teacher. When this is the case, care should be taken to properly develop the measuring instrument. Once the test has been selected or constructed, the teacher should plan good administration procedures which will produce accurate test scores, save time, and be safe for the students.

An important purpose of measurement and evaluation is the assignment of grades. All physical education teachers in the same school should collectively develop a philosophy of grading. The grading system that emerges should be consistent with the other school subjects. The grading system must be fair to all students and should: (1) inform the parent or guardian of the student's progress, (2) inform the student of his or her own progress, and (3) inform the teacher of the progress being made by each student. The components of the grading system should be those that best represent the stated objectives.

There are two stages to a grading system: the assignment of grades for individual test items; and the assignment of final grades. Individual test items may be graded by the percentage method, natural breaks method, combined percentage and natural breaks method, standard score method, and point method. The methods by which final grades may be assigned are average of letter grades, average of standard scores, and point total.

Elementary schools often use a grading system whereby each trait to be evaluated is marked "excellent," "satisfactory," or "unsatisfactory." In junior and senior high schools, students sometimes receive grades consisting of "pass-fail," "pass-no credit," or "credit-no credit."

SELECTED READINGS AND REFERENCES

AAHPERD, *Health Related Physical Fitness Test Manual, AAHPERD,* Reston, Virginia, 1980.

Barrow, Harold and Rosemary McGee, *A Practical Approach to Measurement in Physical Education,* Lea and Febiger, Philadelphia, 1971.

Baumgartner, Ted and Andrew Jackson, *Measurement for Evaluation in Physical Education,* Wm. C. Brown Company, Dubuque, 1982.

Clarke, Harrison, *Application of Measurement to Health and Physical Education,* Prentice-Hall, Inc., Englewood Cliffs, N.J., 1976.

Johnson, Barry and Jack Nelson, *Physical Measurements for Evaluation in Physical Education,* Burgess Publishing Company, Minneapolis, 1979.

Mathews, Donald, *Measurement in Physical Education,* W.B. Saunders, Philadelphia, 1978.

Neilson, N.P. and Clayne Jensen, *Measurement and Statistics in Physical Education,* Wadsworth Publishing Co., Inc., Belmont, Calif., 1972.

Phillips, D. Allen and James Hornak, *Measurement and Evaluation in Physical Education,* John Wiley and Sons, New York, 1979.

Safrit, Margaret, *Evaluation in Physical Education,* Prentice-Hall, Inc., Englewood Cliffs, New Jersey, 1981.

Verducci, Frank, *Measurement Concepts in Physical Education,* The C.V. Mosby Company, St. Louis, 1980.

Photo by Robert Barclay

IN PURSUIT OF THE FIRST TEACHING POSITION

Job Opportunities

15

As the future physical education teacher nears the end of the under-graduate professional preparation years, the need arises to begin the search for the first teaching position. In the past this procedure consisted mainly of registering with the placement office, interviewing prospective employers who came to the campus to recruit teachers, and then selecting the position that best suited the candidate from the list of two or three dozen positions available. This scenario is no longer enacted for those who desire to enter the teaching profession. Two factors have come into play that have changed all this: (1) the overall decline in the number of students enrolled in the public schools due to the declining birthrate in the nation, and (2) economic troubles experienced by the majority of school districts in the nation. Now the prospective teacher must actively pursue the available teaching vacancies, and after locating them, present positive proof to the employer as to why they should receive the position instead of another candidate. Placement officials and professionals in the field of physical education have been able to identify procedures and practices that are extremely helpful in aiding candidates to successfully obtain teaching and coaching positions. It is the purpose of the following pages to share these procedures and practices with the reader.

257

THE UNDERGRADUATE YEARS

The active pursuit of a teaching and coaching position begins while the future physical education teacher is still an undergraduate. The candidate who begins to think of all the facets involved in job-hunting after the bachelors degree is completed is already far behind. While the courses and experience required of the student in physical education are prescribed by the university or college the student is attending, there are other areas with which the candidate must be concerned.

Academic Record

While the old adage "grades aren't everything" is still true, it remains a truism of job-hunting that they will always be an important factor. It is true that grades accumulated while in the undergraduate years only indicate the ability to succeed in the classroom, yet when candidates are relatively equal in their credentials for out-of-class accomplishments, the student with the best academic record has a definite edge. They show the potential employer that the candidate has the intellectual ability to handle the content of college courses, and they also indicate the possession of good work habits, regular class attendance, and the ability to successfully complete assigned work. These are all important when the teacher is actually on the job. It is also true that the discipline of physical education is more "academic" now than it was in former years. There is a greater concentration on the foundation sciences, such as physiology, anatomy, biomechanics, growth and development, and kinesiology. There is also a greater influx into physical education of subject-matter areas such as sociology, history, and psychology.

When examining the grades of the candidate, employers will invariably assign more weight to the grade received in the student-teaching experience than to any other single mark. This represents an on-the-job experience, and is an indicator to the employer as to how well the prospect is able to apply the skills and knowledges acquired during the undergraduate years. It also indicates how well the student-teacher works with colleagues, follows school policies, controls student behavior, and achieves the overall objectives of physical education. It is important for physical education undergraduates to make student-teaching one of their most successful experiences.

Placement For The Student-Teaching Experience

While most colleges and universities have contractual agreements with designated school systems for handling that institution's student

258

teachers, there still remains a degree of freedom for the individual candidate in the selection of a student-teaching site. The plea made here is for each potential student-teacher to attempt to be assigned where the experence will be the most beneficial. The authors of this text have too often seen student-teaching sites selected so that the student might live at home to reduce the living expenses during student teaching. In other cases married students have asked to be assigned close to the campus so married housing can be utilized. In a like manner student/athletes wish to remain close to the university so that varsity athletic competition can be continued. Some select schools because they have been promised a junior-varsity coaching position. Or worse yet, students ask to be assigned back in their hometown, where the school personnel "knows them." All of these reasons should be eliminated from the student's thinking when selecting a student-teaching location. Rather, they should select a locale based on the quality of the program and the expertise of the supervising teacher. Other positive factors to consider are areas similar to those in which they hope to be employed, or areas in which they feel inexperienced, such as a small rural school, an inner-city school, or a system with a large minority enrollment. These kinds of experiences make the candidate more employable, and in pursuit of the first teaching position they are a definite plus.

Type and Variety of General Education Courses

Prospective physical education teachers must keep in mind that before they are physical educators, they are educators in the broadest sense of the term. They must speak and write well, be knowledgeable in world affairs, and present themselves as educated individuals to the entire school and to the community. To arrive at this state, the prospective teacher needs to have a broad general education. A single incident of using poor grammar at an interview, for example, can cause a candidate to be declined. Poorly written sentences on one's resume is reason for them to not be seriously considered. Additionally, teachers are expected to be community leaders, as well as leaders within their profession. Without a sound general education this remains extremely difficult. Students who are unsure as to what general education courses are advisable should seek either general institutional or departmental counseling.

Preparation For an Additional Teaching Credential

Some prospective physical education teachers are fortunate enough to live in states where all teachers are required to have a teaching minor, as well as a teaching major. In other instances this is not so. The suggestion is made here that *all* undergraduate students in physical education should acquire certification in a second subject, so that they are able to teach a subject in addition to physical education. There are a number of positions available in school systems where the teacher is on a split assignment, such as teaching three classes in physical education and two classes in biology or mathematics. Even though the undergraduate wishes to teach only physical education after they graduate, there is no assurance that such a position will be available. A careful analysis of one's abilities, aptitudes, and interests should enable the candidate to make an intelligent selection of a second teaching subject in which to be certified. There are roughly thirty different subject matter areas from which to choose, and either general institutional or departmental counseling is recommended to assist with the choice. It will increase the possibility of being employed.

Wise Use of Physical Education Electives

The physical education professional preparation program varies among institutions and states. However, one condition that almost all professional preparation programs have in common is the privilege for students to elect a portion of their hours. It is this election process with which we are concerned, for we have seen many courses elected for weak and nefarious reasons. We have observed basketball players electing all the basketball classes possible because they like basketball. We have seen students take courses in areas where they already possessed a number of strengths so they might receive a high grade. Courses that students know they need have been avoided because they were "hard" or because the students didn't "like" the instructor. It is the opinion of the authors of this text that the student should select courses within the major that will make him or her a better teaching prospect. An example of wise selection is the student who chooses senior life saving and Water Safety Instructor courses in addition to the required swimming classes. Schools have been known to select one candidate over another simply because the candidate possessed the Water Safety Instructor certificate. Additional examples of good selection may be found among majors who take additional courses in special physical education, athletic training, emergency medical care, or cardio-pulmonary resuscitation. Also worthy of mention are additional courses in coaching, officiating, or biomechanics. The point is, of course, that all candidates become more employable if they have additional competencies, and if they supplement areas in which they are weak.

Participation in Out-Of-Class Experiences

Employers take it for granted that all candidates have successfully completed the course work required for graduation. Therefore, of special interest to the hiring authorities, is that set of supplemental experiences that each candidate can bring to the interview process. Physical education students who have participated in a number of areas, in addition to the required course work, are able to present these experiences as an additional reason why they should be hired over other candidates. In addition, it shows the employer that they are concerned; that they are willing to share their time and talents with others and that they have a variety of interests. And most important of all, a variety of out-of-class experiences of working with boys and girls of various ages will show that the candidate enjoys working with young people. Cases have been recorded where prospective teachers had no experience of this type prior to student-teaching, and then much to their chagrin, it was discovered that they did not enjoy certain age groups!

The possibilities for participation in out-of-class experiences in the field of physical education and sport are almost limitless. On the campus there are major and minor clubs, professional sororities and fraternities in physical education, volunteer opportunities with the Special Olympics, and other groups, intramural and extramural activities, and intercollegiate athletics. In the community there are recreational positions which need assistance, youth teams requiring coaches, and senior citizen groups that need activity planners. Other groups needing volunteers are scouts, church organizations, and local clubs. Statewide and nationally, opportunities exist to participate in student branches of the American Alliance for Health, Physical Education, Recreation and Dance. It is the responsibility of all individuals in our profession to participate in the types of opportunities mentioned above. Additionally, it is the responsibility of those with the ability to do so to assume leadership roles in those activities. It is important for the future employer to know a candidate has been a member of an organization; it is even more significant if that candidate has been an officer, or the chairperson of an important committee.

PREPARING THE RESUME

During the senior year in college the teaching candidate must be concerned with the correct preparation of the personal resume. This is a written summary that describes who you are and what you can offer the employer. It should be carefully prepared. The initial steps to preparing the resume should be taken during the first semester of the senior year, and it should be ready for mailing early in the final semester. Some basic guidelines that will aid in the correct preparation of a resume are listed below:

1. *It should be clear.* The employer will not know you as a person, so the resume must communicate a clear and accurate impression. Aspects on one's education, experience, background, and employment history are important. In regards to the latter, it is recommended that part-time and full-time work experience be kept separate, and gaps should be avoided. Relevant professional activities should be clearly outlined.

2. *It should be concise.* The resume should be kept simple, brief, and to the point. It is not meant to be a comprehensive biography, but rather the emphasis should be on the inclusion of information that is vital to the placement of the teacher, and will spark an interest in the employing authority that reads it. Many good resumes are only one page in length, and in no instances should they be longer than two pages. The candidate preparing the resume should remember that a complete record of all personal data will be present in the credential file, and no attempt should be made to have the resume serve the same purpose.

3. *It should be consistent.* If the applicant submits a resume that is consistent, the employer will know he or she is a good organizer. The chronological order of educational and employment qualifications should not be intermixed. In addition, the style of writing should be consistent throughout.

It has been suggested (Presson, 1977) that the resume should be a Positive Resume, and that it should contain your positive image, positive contribution, and positive appeal.

Some additional points to consider are: (1) use your birth date and not your age, since your age changes, (2) use "would consider" instead of the phrase "prefer to," (3) refrain from mentioning religion, political or fraternal organizations, race, sex, or national origin, (4) use action words to start a sentence, such as developed, directed, or established, and (5) include the names of individuals who have agreed to write letters of reference when requested. A last thought: If your resume includes typing errors, contains improper grammar and is copied poorly, it will receive very little consideration. A sample of an approved format for a resume may be seen in Figure 15.1.

LOCATING JOB VACANCIES

Before teaching candidates can apply for a specific position, it must be ascertained as to where the job openings are. No longer are they just around the corner, or in sufficient quantities in the candidate's home state. The search for available positions is just that — a search. It must be

Name:	
Address:	
Phone:	Use present telephone number and a second number to be used after a specific date if needed.
Personal:	Date of birth, marital status, health, military status, etc.
Objectives:	This section is not absolutely necessary and, if not handled with care, can cause trouble. Just make sure that your objectives are broad enough to cover employment that you are suited for.
Education:	Start with your highest level. It is generally not desirable to show high school if you are a college graduate. Include high school only if there is something special about it or unusual honors were earned. Do not show every incidental or special course you have taken, as you may dilute the image of the degree.
Experience:	Start with the present (or last) position and work backwards to your first jobs using years only! Give the name of the firms, company, or school systems and a BRIEF description of your responsibilities and accomplishments.
Honors:	Include membership in national honorary fraternities or sororities, outstanding professional organizations, scholarships received, graduation honors, etc.
Interests	Include hobbies, especially if related to physical education and sport, interests and skills in music, outdoor education, and handicrafts.
Comments:	Say something about yourself, a sort of positive self-analysis. Factual statements are better than personal self-evaluations.
References:	Include at least three people who are willing to write personal references if requested. Preferred is one from your home town, and one outside the field of education.

Figure 15-1. Guidelines for writing a resume. These guidelines were adapted from an article titled "Writing Your Resume," by W.D. Presson, and published in **THE PHYSICAL EDUCATOR.**

an extremely active search, and more than one avenue must be pursued. Sources for locating job openings that have been used successfully by teaching candidates are listed below.
1. *College Placement Offices.* Although it is true that the number of positions that the university or college placement office has available is no longer sufficient, it is still the recommended place to start. Place-

ment offices have highly trained personnel who work full-time to place graduates in open positions. They have a full set of all candidates' credentials on hand. And most important, they know where the vacancies exist. Many hiring authorities will not offer contracts to applicants unless they have the recommendation of the placement office as part of the candidate's credentials. Placement offices in some universities and colleges offer seminars and workshops relative to locating and applying for positions. Not only should candidates register with their local placement office, but they should keep their credentials up-to-date, and they should keep in frequent contact with the placement personnel. An added benefit is the fact that almost all of these services are performed without charge!

2. *Vacancies Posted.* As the prospective graduate nears the end of their undergraduate professional preparation, they should make frequent visits to the location where job vacancies are posted. This location varies with the institution attended, but most often it is in the placement office, the departmental office, on a professional bulletin board, or in a central location such as the student union or the main library. A regular campus routine should be followed by the candidate that takes them past these posted vacancies often during the hiring season.

3. *Word of Mouth from Colleagues.* During the period that prospective teachers are trying to locate job openings, many of their colleagues are engaged in a similar search. Their travels and conversations may identify vacancies that have been investigated, and found not to include the type of assignment they prefer. All individuals hunting for job openings should keep track of these, and seriously consider pursuing that opening themselves. It could be appropriate for you even though the first candidate did not approve of it.

   Colleagues also include professionals in the field, and the student's major and minor professors on campus. There are certain hiring authorities that prefer to ask experienced faculty members who their top candidates are. Physical education teachers and coaches from the prospects home high school, and those from his or her student-teaching school fall into the category of colleagues who might know of open positions. The reader is urged to explore these fully.

4. *Commercial Agencies.* Commercial teacher placement agencies are private business enterprises whose objective is to search for open positions and match them with available candidates. For this service they charge a fee. If the position is accepted, it is quite common for the fee to be a certain percentage of the first year's salary. Many prospects are willing to pay this in order to acquire permanent employment. The advantage of using a commercial agency is that the agency will work hard to find each applicant a position. The disadvantage, of

course, is the fee they extract for this service.

5. *Professional Organizations.* It has become quite common during the past few years for professional education associations to offer a placement service as part of the enticement to get more members to join their ranks. This source should be followed extensively, for it has been a fruitful avenue for many applicants. The organization may be a general education organization, or it may be a professional organization that contains members of one academic area only. Of the latter type, the American Alliance for Health, Physical Education, Recreation and Dance should be mentioned. The placement service that they maintain during their national conventions is quite extensive. Some state affiliates of the AAHPERD also have a placement service.

6. *Professional Education Publications.* The types of publications in this category include journals, newsletters, newspapers, and special placement booklets. *The Journal of Physical Education and Recreation,* and the newspaper *Update,* from the American Alliance of Health, Physical Education, Recreation and Dance, are two examples. Two others of note, although mostly concerned with positions in higher education, are the newspaper *The Chronicle of Higher Education,* and the *NCAA Newsletter.* Each prospective job-seeker is urged to be alert for other professional publications that exist in their specific locale, and in their respective fields.

APPLYING FOR THE POSITION

In applying for a position, the candidate needs to be aware of procedures that have been successful in the past. The more attention that is paid to these steps, the more successful the job hunt will be.

Identifying the Locale Where Employment is Desired

The recommendation is made that teaching candidates identify where they want to locate, what they want to do in a specific position if hired, and the cities or school districts they are interested in, at least four or five weeks prior to their graduation. This process necessitates that the candidate know the map of this area, and then compiles a definite list of school districts in which they are interested. In this regard it is extremely important to have what placement offices refer to as "geographic flexibility," meaning a willingness, within limits, to pursue jobs in a wide area, and not just in their home state. Traditionally, job markets are regional, meaning that from year to year a larger number of vacancies will appear in one section of the nation than in other sections. The candidate needs to be aware of this phenomena.

Letters of Inquiry

Once the above procedure has been completed, applicants may send letters of inquiry to school systems in which they would like to teach. It is not necessary at this point to have a specific vacancy for which to apply. The letter is to ask if there is a vacancy, or if one might occur in the near future. It should contain a very brief outline of your qualifications, and indicate where a complete file of your credentials might be obtained. It is also proper to ask for an application form. A sample letter of inquiry may be found in Figure 15-2.

I-E Bellows Apartment
Mt. Pleasant, Michigan 48858
March 24, 1983

Dr. Louis Jones
Assistant Director of Personnel
Maywood Public Schools
807 North Bradley
Maywood, Indiana 50277

Dear Dr. Jones:

I am writing to inquire if there will be fall teaching openings in the Maywood Public Schools for which I might be considered. I will receive my B.A. degree from the State University in May with a double major in physical education (K-12) and special education.

As you will note from the enclosed resume, I have had experience with trainable mentally retarded children as well as physically handicapped students at the University School. Later this month, I will begin another eight-week full day student teaching experience in physical education at Harwood Elementary, Midland, Michigan.

My credentials, including references, are on file at the State University Placement Office. If you anticipate vacancies in either special education or physical education I would appreciate receiving an application form and information regarding your interviewing procedures. Thank you for your consideration.

Sincerely yours,

Jane M. Doe

Enclosure

Figure 15-2. Sample Letter of Inquiry.

Letter of Application

When the teaching prospect has identifed a specific job opening, the letter of application is sent. It should state the reason for the letter, the specific position for which the applicant is applying, and indicate the source from which the opening was made known. Candidates should write why they are interested in that position, and what they have to offer. Work experience and educational qualifications that make the writer a qualified candidate should be included. The letter should include a copy of the resume, and reference may be made to it. The letter of application should indicate a desire for an interview, and mention the candidate's flexibility as to the time and place. The phone number should be included. In closing, the writer should also encourage a response, such as asking if a certain date is appropriate, or asking if additional information is required. A statement saying the candidate plans to be in the employer's area on a certain date, and would like to speak with someone about a position at that time, is recommended. Some authorities recommend that the letter of application include a return postcard to facilitate communication with the school system.

This procedure should be followed with a phone call about a week before visitation to the site is made, reminding them that you wrote concerning a meeting with them. It is suggested that this visitation is made, even if there is no return acknowledgement from the school district. This is important for two reasons: (1) it is important for candidates to take the initiative and remain as visible as possible, and (2) candidates need to see the locale of the desired position because they may come upon an undesirable situation for them as far as the facilities, program, or school philosophy is concerned. Additionally, even if the procedure does not end in acquiring a position, the candidate has established a visibility that may be important in acquiring a job at a later date. It is also possible that through contact with alumni in that area other vacancies may be identified. It is also important for the applicant to follow-up the visit after the return home, either with a phone call or by letter, approximately every two or three weeks. The emphasis here is for the candidate to take the initiative, and pursue the position aggressively. A sample letter of application may be seen in Figure 15-3.

The Interview

Many positions have been won or lost at the interview table. There are positive interview techniques that will assist the candidate in getting the position, and there are negative techniques that do just the opposite. Some of these are very simple, such as using a firm, but not crushing,

202 Crapo Street
Mt. Pleasant, Michigan 48858
March 1, 1983

Dr. Wayne Smith, Superintendent
North City School District
49 Colby Drive
Alma, Minnesota 46952

Dear Dr. Smith:

The Placement Office at State University has notified me of a provisional one year opening in the Physical Education Department of the North City School District for the coming school year. Please consider me as an applicant for this position.

I received a Bachelor of Arts degree from State University with a major in Physical Education and a minor in mathematics. My current teaching assignment includes teaching both elective and required physical education courses in grades 10-12. In addition, I assist with the coaching of the boys and girls interscholastic swimming teams, an interest I have pursued throughout high school and college.

The enclosed resume will give you more detailed information concerning my educational preparation and qualifications. My credentials are on file at the Placement Office and are being forwarded today.

I would welcome the opportunity to discuss this position in detail with you. I will be vacationing in the area over spring break, March 20-28, and could conveniently arrange a time to visit with you. Thank you for your consideration.

Sincerely,

John R. Doe

Enclosure

Figure 15-3. Sample Letter of Application

handclasp when shaking hands with the interviewer. Others are more complicated, such as giving a clear view of your educational philosophy when asked. Some are very subtle, such as the standing and sitting posture of the applicant. The "body language" used by the candidate often tips the employer as to the candidate's self-concept and degree of maturity.

The candidate must arrive at a happy medium between being too aggressive and too passive, as leaning too far in either direction will work against the image they desire to project. Also important is the dress and style of clothing worn by the applicant. While no standardized list of what to wear is available, attire that is conservative, well-pressed, and business-like is always acceptable. Other suggestions for making the interview successful is for the candidate to maintain eye contact with the interviewer, and not talk too much.

The suggestion has been made that the student preparing for an upcoming interview might practice the entire procedure with another individual. The rehearsal would cover such items as to why the candidate chose the teaching profession, how the student-teaching experience benefited them, how their undergraduate professional preparation prepared them, courses they enjoyed, how they feel about student control, how they believe they can motivate students, and their basic philosophy concerning physical education.

While much of the interview will consist of the employer asking questions of the candidate, the candidate should also feel free to ask questions of the employer. These types of questions might include asking about the basic educational philosophy of the school district, why the predecessor left, the socio-economic status of the school district, opportunities for graduate study in the area, the possibilities for professional advancement, etc. If mentioned at all, questions about salary and benefits should remain until last, and then be minimized.

The Follow-Up

It is mandatory that after the interview has been completed, the candidate engage in some "follow-up" practices. The most often used technique is to write the employer a letter of thanks. But because this is the most often used technique, the really alert prospect will do additional things such as phoning as a reminder of their availability, visiting again to retain visibility, and mailing any other materials that the interviewer indicated might be important in filling the position. The reader is reminded, once again, that a good candidate is aggressive, and that it is the aggressive applicant that gets hired!

One additional recommendation is made for the job hunter, and that is to keep an organized file or notebook regarding all contacts made. It is not uncommon for applicants to be working on a number of positions simultaneously. For each one there needs to be a record of such items as letters sent and received, the results of each letter, phone calls made, materials sent to each, and future dates that need to be met. One should not trust the memory alone to keep all this information correct.

TEACHING CREDENTIALS

It is important for the prospective teacher to understand the importance of having the correct teaching credentials. The nucleus of the teaching credential is the college degree, with a major or minor in physical education and at least a minor that will provide teaching certification in a second subject. These two credentials are usually given by the candidate's undergraduate institution, and is called institutional certification. It assures the hiring authority that the student has fulfilled what the institution requires for the major and minor, that the candidate has completed the prescribed courses in education, and has satisfactorily completed the student-teaching experience.

The next type of certification needed is that of the department of education of the state in which the institution is located. Many colleges and universities have a certification office on their campus, where an official sees that both the institutional requirements and the state department of education requirements for certification have been met.

A third area of certification of importance to the prospective teacher is that required by those states having a state teacher certification examination. While not being used by all states at present, in a few states (Florida, Texas, and New York for example) successful passing of this examination is a prerequisite to acquiring a teaching position.

A final aspect of acquiring the correct credentials may involve taking the National Teaching Education test. All states do not require this examination, but each candidate should explore the requirements in the states in which they hope to become employed. A booklet of information relative to the NTE is published by Educational Testing Service (Educational Testing Service, 1982).

UNDERSTANDING CONTRACTS

While it is not necessary for the physical education teaching prospect to be knowledgeable in all areas of the law, it is highly beneficial to know about the contents of contracts. This section does not deal with the specific points of law involved, because they vary by state and according to what the contract pertains. However, five areas with which the applicant should be familiar are: (1) description of the position, (2) provisions for tenure, (3) salary, (4) legal terms, and (5) negotiated faculty contracts.

Description of the Position

A candidate does not receive employment simply as a teacher, with only classroom responsibilities. This is more evident with the physical education teacher than with other faculty members. There are invariably duties for which teachers are responsible that are held after classes, at night, away from the school environment, on Saturdays, or prior to the formal opening of the school day. When positions are discussed, and duties are verbally agreed on, these conditions should then be written into the contract. The wording should be specific. Words like "coach," or phrases like "help with the intramurals" should be avoided. Instead, wording such as "assistant coach, boys track and field," or "director of the junior high school intramural program" should be used. Not only does this give specificity to the duties of the teaching candidate, but it establishes a line of authority and prevents disagreements regarding areas of responsibility. The contract, in addition to containing the terms or phrases defining the position, should be accompanied by a special document that is entitled, for example, "Job Description for Assistant Track and Field Coach, Junior High School Level." This is not only a desirable method for the school district to indicate to the candidate what the position entails in its entirety, but is an assist to the prospect in deciding whether or not the position is desirable. In addition, if the position is accepted, it outlines for the new faculty member specifically what the duties of the position are. A sample of a job description is given in Figure 15-4.

Tenure

Tenure may be defined as the terms under which the faculty person is guaranteed continued employment. Also involved in the consideration of tenure are the conditions under which the provisions of tenure are set aside. Usually this involves the two conditions of moral turpitude and incompetency. The number of probationary years required before new faculty are granted tenure status range from two to seven years. Occasionally, work toward an advanced degree, or specified hours of post graduate work are indicated. Teachers who also coach interscholastic athletic teams occasionally have different provisions for tenure than those who only teach. The prospect for any new position should discuss all of the above provisions of tenure with the hiring authorities, be certain they are in the written contract, and ask for explanations regarding any section of the contract that is not clear.

Salary

The salary accompanying any teaching and coaching position should be written in the contract. This includes the base salary for the first-year teacher, plus increments that are added for coaching, directing cheer-

POSITION ANALYSIS

TITLE: Senior High School Physical Education Teacher

SALARY: Commensurate with position on salary schedule. Range is from $14,000 to $26,000 depending on qualifications. Increments for out-of-class assignments as stated on salary schedule.

General Description: Teach five classes of high school physical education, three required classes from 9-11, and two elective classes from grade 12.

Examples of Work: A. General Work. Develop students in cognitive, affective, and psychomotor domains through human movement.

B. Specific Work. Develop all students in a repertoire of motor skills, knowledges regarding activity covered, and good citizenship, character, and sportsmanship through participation in games and sport. Evaluate and improve physical fitness of all students to their potential.

Supervision Received: Supervision is received from the head of the Physical Education department, the high school principal, and the city supervisor of physical education.

Suggested Qualifications for Successful Performance:

A. Educational. Bachelors Degree in Teaching, Physical Education
Major or Minor, major preferred.

B. Experience. Minimum of highly successful student teaching experience.

C. Personal. Physically fit, sound character, genuine liking of high school students, and desire to help them.

Hours Involved:
1. Teach five classes per day.
2. Spend one period per day in preparation.
3. Saturday responsibilities only when the school hosts the state basketball tournament.
4. Be present in the building thirty minutes before classes begin and thirty minutes after classes end.

Number of Students: Classes range from 25 to 35 students.

Public Relations: Establish desirable relationships with parents of students, colleagues, and the administration. Direct one exhibition, open house, or PTA program yearly to display program to public.

Figure 15-4.   Example of a Job Description.

leaders, administering intramural programs, or the sponsorship of student groups, such as a ski club. The candidate should not take it for granted that these duties will be financially rewarded unless they are specified in writing. It is within the accepted parameters of good protocol to question the hiring authority about these items, and insist that they be in writing. In addition to the above, salaries in most school systems are based on years of experience, and additional hours of post-graduate study. If an official salary schedule structure does not accompany the signed contract, these facts also must be included in the contract itself.

Legal Terms

Since the training of the prospective physical education teacher often contains no course work of a legal nature, it is possible that there may be legal terms in the contract with which he or she is not familiar. If such are identified, it behooves the candidate to find out what they mean. Terms such as negligence, tort liability, responsibility, in loco parentis, etc., may be included when teachers of physical education discuss employment. Before signing a contract for employment, the new teacher is encouraged to be familiar with all terms included thereon.

Faculty Association Contracts

The vast majority of school systems now have some form of faculty association, or education association, that "bargains" with the school administration regarding conditions of employment. The prospective teacher, of course, will have nothing to say about the contract that is in force when they arrive on the scene. Such contracts contain provisions for promotion, salary adjustments, lay-offs, out-of-class assignments, tenure, re-assignments, and terminations. The prospect for a teaching and coaching position should obtain a copy of the negotiated contract, read it, and be sure it is understood prior to signing the teaching contract offered. While this is usually a good recommendation simply so the new faculty person will understand how things are done in that particular school system, it is possible that some provisions will be unacceptable, and employment will have to be pursued elsewhere.

CAREER ALTERNATIVES FOR PHYSICAL EDUCATORS

A phenomena that descended upon the physical education profession within the last decade is that of professionally prepared physical educators seeking and accepting employment in positions dealing with human movement and sport that do not include teaching in schools. For lack of an appropriate term to describe all of these possibilities, they have been lumped under the umbrella term "alternative careers." The alternative has come to mean any career in the field that does not include teaching physical education in a public or private school.

The spectrum of professional opportunities for individuals in the field who do not wish to teach is wide indeed. Some are closely allied with the school teaching position, such as serving as an athletic trainer or an athletic coach. Formerly these types of assignments were fulfilled by faculty who were teachers and coaches, or teachers and trainers. However, due to the conditions previously mentioned (declining enrollments and economic problems), the teaching part of these assignments has disappeared.

There has evolved another type of teaching position that is not in a school environment, and that is the private sport or activities school. These individuals have combined the establishment of a private business with teaching.

One of the wider uses made of physical education graduates is that of the fitness consultant, exercise physiologist, or serving as an employee of a health spa or a commercial sports complex. The military also have employed physical education professionals to direct their fitness programs and administer their sports programs.

It is not the purpose of these pages to describe all the professional opportunities that alternative careers present. Each reader is urged to investigate the possibilities that are of the most interest.

One final thought is presented. The type of individual traditionally attracted to physical education is one who is vigorous, people-oriented, competitive-minded, and knows what it is to work as a member of a team. They are often goal-oriented, and have experience in working over obstacles and initial set-backs. The private sector of our society values these traits highly; therefore, the physical education graduate may be attractive to employers from the world of government, business, industry, and other areas of private enterprise.

SUMMARY

Physical education teaching positions are difficult to obtain due to the decreased birth rate and economic difficulties. Therefore, candidates need to pursue an orderly progression of moves that have proven helpful in the past, and are suggested by placement officials. This procedure should start while the student is still an undergraduate, and begins with a successful undergraduate experience in the classroom. Factors determining the value of the undergraduate years include grades accumulated, general and professional courses taken, experiences in out-of-class activities, and the success of the student-teaching experience.

Documents that must be prepared accurately, and used according to specific guidelines include the resume, letters of inquiry, and letters of application. A personalized campaign needs to be designed to locate where the vacancies are. All of the above must be capped by a successful interview if the candidate is to find employment.

Additional areas with which the prospective teacher should be concerned include knowledge of the teaching credential, and the understanding of contracts. If the candidate is unsuccessful in obtaining a teaching position, there remains the option of seeking employment in some area of human movement and sport outside of the teaching profession.

SUGGESTED READINGS AND REFERENCES

Anthony, Rebecca, and Gerald Roe, *Contact to Contract, A Teachers Employment Guide,* The Carroll Press, Cranston, R. I.

Central Michigan University, *1982-83 Annual Report, Placement and Career Information,* Central Michigan University, Mount Pleasant, Michigan.

Educational Testing Service, *1982-83 Bulletin of Information, NTE Programs,* Educational Testing Service, Princeton, N.J.

Florida State Department of Education, *Excerpts from Florida Teacher Certification Examination Bulletins,* Florida State Department of Education, Tallahassee, Florida.

Grebner, Florence, and others, *Physical Education Teacher Education, Education Curriculum, Pedagogy, Certification . . . History, Issues, Trends,* ERIC, Washington, D.C., February, 1982.

Presson, W.O., "Writing Your Resume," *The Physical Educator,* March, 1977, p. 24.

Shroyer, George, "Getting The First Position," *The Physical Educator,* March, 1978, pp. 15-16.

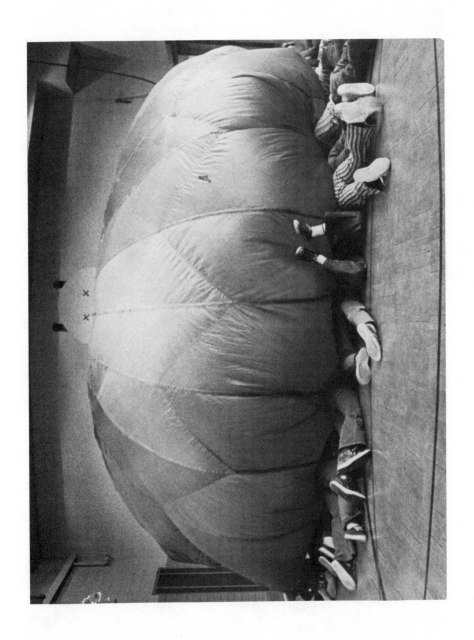

Photo by David Brittain

AS YOU ENTER THE TEACHING PROFESSION

Even the most confident and well-prepared new graduate will face challenges in the first teaching position. There are many difficulties and pitfalls that will face new teachers for which they seem ill prepared to handle. This chapter is written to offer tips and suggestions to ease some of the difficulties that all new teachers will encounter.

Queen and Gretes (1982) reported in a study of first year teachers that the majority (60 percent) of these teachers agreed that their preservice program had adequately prepared them for the first year of teaching. Other researchers (Hoy and Rees, 1977 and Borg, 1975) have reported less positive comments regarding the ability of professional preparation programs to adequately train teachers for the school setting. Crase (1979) states: "It appears that the impact of teacher education in the subsequent performance of teachers is quite limited. The school environment (students, faculty, administrators and resources) seems to be a stronger agent that ultimately assumes the responsibility for inculcating behaviors commensurate with the purpose and mission of the school" (Crase, 1979, p. 11).

Although the undergraduate professional preparation program and student teaching obviously makes a great contribution to the preparation of teachers, it would seem that the first year of teaching has a significant affect upon how the teacher will perform in the remainder of his or her real world teaching career. It should be understood that we believe the college or university preparation program is very important and useful. Guidelines and techniques have been presented in previous chapters which we believe will enable the student to enter the job market as a first year teacher. However, the impact that the first year has upon a teacher calls for careful attention to this first year teaching experience.

AS AN AGENT OF CHANGE

All that is old is not bad. All that is new is not good. Schools need to be in a constant state of evaluation which may better enable them to serve the needs of the students presently enrolled. The changes that may occur should most often be in gradual doses and should reflect a real need for change. Change that occurs simply to accomplish change is usually cyclical and ultimately progresses nowhere.

The teacher can effectively become an agent of change in the school. However, new teachers should not be too quick to attempt to bring about change. It is often wise on the part of the new teacher to be a "student" of the new position for the greater part of the first year. Being new to the school district, as well as new to teaching, the teacher should give the present structure a chance and attempt to learn and understand why things are done the way they are. During this period of learning the teacher may earn a position of respect from other staff members which will enable him or her to become an agent of change in the near future. The new teacher should initially attempt to institute small changes and plan them well so they have a good chance of being successful.

Caution must be practiced by the new teacher so that he or she does not become too complacent during their initiation into the school setting. It is easy to become socialized into the formalized routine and bureaucratic structure of the school to the point that minimum expectations become the guidelines and change does not occur. Crase (1979) states "It is comfortable for teachers to perform minimally, to maintain the status quo and to survive from day to day and year to year without any significant evidence of professional growth." The new teacher, although not out to change the departmental operating procedures the first year, should be as creative and innovative in teaching classes as possible. Care must be taken to not imitate those who have "retired" on the job or those who have decided to meet only the minimum expectations.

280

INVOLVEMENT WITH SCHOOL AND COMMUNITY

A teacher is typically hired by a school to teach physical education and coach one or more sports. The most important concept here is that you were hired as a teacher in the school. Your specific assignment was in physical education and coaching. This means that your responsibilities are to the total school as well as to your specific students.

The new teacher of physical education should become involved with the activities and responsibilities of the school. Attendance at faculty meetings, open houses, and such other faculty endeavors as may be required of teachers is important. It is desirable for the physical education teacher to use these opportunities to acquaint colleagues, parents, and the community of the importance of physical education within the total educational structure. Isolation of physical education teachers from the remainder of the faculty is both common and unfortunate. Participation in the activities of the school can become a habit just as easily as not participating.

The first year teacher has a special reason for becoming actively involved with other faculty. It is very possible that the only other new teachers in the school are located in other departments. It is important for new teachers to have contact with other new teachers to share successes and to offer encouragement to one another. More will be said pertaining to this need under the topic of "preventing teacher burnout."

Teachers should become active members of their community as well as their schools. It may prove very important for the teacher to be seen as someone vitally interested in the entire community and not just his or her specific job. Excellent opportunities for community involvement may be found in such groups as service and youth clubs. Seeing and working with parents outside of the classroom setting can help to establish a rapport between the school and the community. This rapport may be influential when a millage election or bond issue is to be decided.

Teachers have an obligation to become familiar with the community in which they teach. A knowledge of the beliefs and standards common to the community may enable the teacher to be more effective. Being aware of the socio-economic levels within the community will help the teacher to better understand some of the students and the difficulties they bring to school.

PROFESSIONAL ENDEAVORS

Once teachers have left the college or university and taken their first teaching position, their continued growth as a professional becomes an independent matter. There are several viable alternatives open to the teacher whereby he or she may continue to actively pursue professional development. Some alternatives include membership and participation in professional organizations, attendance at conventions, and participation in clinics and inservice workshops.

The primary professional organization available for physical education teachers is the American Alliance for Health, Physical Education, Recreation and Dance. Membership in AAHPERD and its accompanying associations allows teachers to receive such publications as the *Journal of Physical Education, Recreation and Dance* as well as *The Research Quarterly.* The JOPERD contains many articles pertaining to current concerns and problems in the field, as well as practical ideas for teaching specific activities and subject matter concepts. *The Research Quarterly* is the channel through which research in physical education and sport is communicated to the professional in the field. The AAHPERD also publishes a large amount of pamphlets and books on specific topics concerning physical education which may be purchased by practitioners. In addition, AAHPERD produces films which may be rented or purchased.

Professional conventions are another excellent means of professional development. Generally, conventions offer formal presentations in the form of lectures, slide presentations, panels, and discussion groups, as well as demonstrations of various teaching techniques using audience participation or students from a local school district. In addition there may be exhibits by various book and record publishing companies, equipment outlets, and athletic clothing firms. It should also be kept in mind that in addition to the benefits already mentioned, conventions are a wonderful opportunity to renew acquaintances and share ideas with old and new friends in informal conversation. The AAHPERD sponsors a national level convention each year which is rotated among various geographic areas of the country. When the convention is located in your general area it might be very beneficial to attend. Conventions are also sponsored by each state on a yearly basis. This provides for a convention for every individual on a local basis.

Inservice workshops may be one of the most satisfying means of practical professional development for teachers of physical education. These are locally sponsored workshops which cover specific topics that are of need and interest to the participant. Kohlmaier (1981) suggests that those workshops are most effective when teachers help plan, conduct, and evaluate inservice education. Therefore, teachers should make their wishes known of the kind of inservice education that would be most beneficial toward meeting their particular needs and then help make the workshop a success.

PREVENTING TEACHER BURNOUT

Teacher burnout may seem to be an unlikely topic with which the new teacher needs to be concerned. It is true that the new teacher is not likely to encounter burnout in the first year of teaching. However, teacher burnout does not occur at any specific point in a career, and it does not appear all of a sudden. Most often, teacher burnout is a phenomenon that develops over several years and simply reaches a level of consciousness at some point (Penny, 1982). When the teacher recognizes the symptoms of burnout it is too late to avoid its destructive effects. Teachers can certainly recover from burnout, but it is much more sensible to take steps to prevent it from ever occurring. With this thought in mind this section of the chapter contains some steps, procedures, and activities that are recommended to prevent the onset of teacher burnout. These positive steps need to be instituted at the very beginning of a teaching career so that they become habitual and, therefore, a common part of the teacher's behavior.

Teacher stress and burnout are terms which have become closely associated with education in recent years. Austin (1981) states "Habitual chronic stress that accumulates without compensatory relaxation results in burnout. Although burnout is an occupational hazard for physical educators, the effects will vary from one person to another. As a result of burnout, some leave teaching permanently while others reluctantly stay on the job, counting the days each week, turning themselves off when they enter school, and waiting for retirement." This last comment reflects a rather serious situation. Farber and Miller (1982) hypothesize that teacher burnout is the result of factors within the school which lead to a lack of a "psychological sense of community." These factors result in feelings of isolation by teachers. Feelings of isolation make teachers believe they are the only ones who have particular problems. They are unable to share their frustration and problems with other teachers who might be understanding and supportive.

Earls (1981) surveyed, with open-ended interviews, a group of distinctive physical education teachers. A distinctive teacher was defined as a "teacher with at least five years experience who consistently demonstrates sincere interest and enthusiasm in teaching, genuine concern for students, and self-study and continued striving to improve as a teacher." These teachers have not allowed their teaching to suffer from the same things that caused others to lose their enthusiasm. These teachers recommended certain activities which may enhance teacher development and help maintain purposeful productivity as a teacher. Some of their recommendations were:

1. Learn from the students so that you may gain understanding of the

dynamics of student-teacher relationships.

2. Request time to observe other quality teachers and programs which can be inspirational to yourself, as well as an opportunity to contribute to improvements.
3. Participate in regular seminars and support groups which promote sharing among professionals to avoid feelings of isolation.
4. Vary instructional activities and curricula to reduce repetition and boredom.
5. Learn from student teachers and student-teacher supervisors who may introduce something new to try.
6. Participate in summer activities, especially summer employment, which are totally different from teaching and coaching. Without question, teacher burnout is a very real problem.

The repetitiveness of physical education teaching can bring on boredom. Lack of appreciation from the community and dwindling financial and vocal support for education leads to a loss of enthusiasm. The role conflict experienced by the teacher/coach can result in discouragement. Teachers should take specific precautions upon their entrance into the teaching world to counteract these negative influences. Efforts must be made to not only meet the responsibilities of teaching, but also to maintain enthusiasm and commitment to being a productive and happy teacher. Following are some suggestions that may be helpful in maintaining that enthusiasm and pushing back the effects and forces that lead to teacher burnout.

1. Don't take yourself too seriously. An individual is capable of only so much. Do your job well by proper planning and good management, and then don't worry about whether or not you have done enough.
2. Manage your time well. Plan the appropriate amount of time for each of your responsibilities and stay within the time structure. Plan time for yourself for a break during the day and time to eat lunch without interruptions from students.
3. Maintain an enthusiastic and positive attitude toward your teaching career. Don't let the bitterness and complaints of other teachers become your standard. Simply avoid those conversations if they are leading in a negative direction.
4. Try something new and exciting each semester or year. Change your teaching style periodically to give you a change of pace. Introduce a new activity each year, or at least occasionally teach some different activities. Not only will you benefit from these changes, but so will your students.
5. Seek advice from an enthusiastic and effective teacher in your school. Meet on a regular basis with this teacher for the purpose of learning from that teacher. This person can offer encouragement, as well as

284

point out some of the joys and pitfalls that you will face in the year ahead.

6. Avoid isolation as a teacher. Become an active participant with the rest of your department faculty and with other teachers in the school.
7. Participate in a support group. Associate yourself with a group of other new teachers or just one other new teacher on a regular basis. There is comfort in knowing that others are facing some of the same problems you are. Your groups can serve to encourage and understand each other.
8. Engage in outside activities for personal enjoyment. Take time out for yourself and your family by participating in activities that are enjoyable. Exercising is one activity that can be particularly refreshing to the teacher.
9. Cultivate a good relationship with the school secretaries and maintenance personnel. These people can make your job much easier and more satisfying if you have a good relationship.

IS GRADUATE STUDY FOR YOU?

Graduation from an undergraduate professional preparation program does not, by any means, mark the end of the professional training necessary to become and remain an effective teacher. It was stated earlier in this chapter that much of what a teacher learns about teaching is learned in the school setting performing the teaching task. In addition, teachers need to constantly be in pursuit of opportunities which will enhance their teaching capabilities. Some teachers find these opportunities in such professional endeavors as conferences and inservice workshops which were discussed in a previous section of this chapter. Another excellent means of increasing teaching capabilities is through a formal graduate program in physical education.

Most new teachers are motivated to take additional classes for one reason or another. Some states require that teachers successfully complete a prescribed number of hours of classwork after graduation in order to receive regular or, in some cases, permanent certification. Most school districts have a salary schedule for their teachers whereby salary increments are partially based upon the number of hours completed beyond the bachelors degree. In some school systems tenure is partially based upon the number of hours of coursework completed beyond the bachelors degree. All of these are valid reasons for teachers continuing to take courses after graduation from a professional preparation program.

A formal graduate school program of studies leading to an advanced degree in physical education will probably appear in the plans of most new teachers within a very few years after graduation. The formal graduate program leading toward an advanced degree will not only satisify salary, certification, and tenure requirements for additional coursework, but it will also give the teacher higher stature in terms of degrees and may lead to new professional opportunities.

Caution should be exercised relative to how soon a teacher should enter graduate school. Everyone will not benefit equally from the experience and some are not ready to enter graduate school as soon as others. Graduate school is sometimes entered due to not being able to find satisfactory employment. This is not the best reason for one to pursue a graduate degree, although it sometimes proves to be beneficial. Often it is recommended that a teacher enter the professional field for a year or two before considering graduate school. This enables the teacher to adjust to the teaching field and test some of the theory and principles learned in undergraduate school. Many teachers feel that their graduate school program is more meaningful and helpful if they have first taught for a period of time. These experiences, accumulated while teaching, may allow them to become more of an active and participating member of the graduate school program.

DEVELOP AND MAINTAIN CONTACT WITH SIGNIFICANT OTHERS

Significant others is meant to represent those few individuals who may continue to have a significant impact upon your professional teaching career. These individuals might include a fellow teacher, your supervisory teacher during student teaching, your university student teaching supervisor, or a college or university professor in your major field of study. If you are teaching in close proximity to the university from which you received your professional preparation training, it will simply be a matter of maintaining contact with these individuals. However, if you have taken a teaching position in a new location you may need to establish new contacts. The three main purposes of maintaining contact with these significant others is that they can serve as a source of encouragement, teaching ideas, and evaluation.

Encouragement is needed by all teachers in small doses all the time, and in large doses at selected times. The encouragement that is most effective for teachers is received from someone of respected professional standing. Another teacher with whom you teach and have an established rapport may offer encouragement because the two of you share many of the same problems and concerns. In addition, the other significant individuals will be available when problems arise, or you simply need someone to turn to.

All teachers need to be constantly updating their teaching techniques. New teaching ideas are necessary to maintain effectiveness and to remain vibrant in the classroom. All of these significant others mentioned are excellent sources of new ideas and techniques. University and school supervisors of student teachers are good sources of new ideas from the research they are acquainted with, and also from student teachers with whom they come in contact.

Evaluation of class demeanor and teaching behavior is essential if a teacher is to remain effective. It is important that evaluation is received from someone for whom the teacher has respect as a professional. These individuals may help in evaluation by observing actual teaching, or by video taping a lesson and then discussing it. Another method of evaluation may involve the use of paper and pencil to record teacher and student behavior as it occurs in the class.

It should be added that maintaining this contact is not an imposition upon the other individuals. Although teachers may be seeking help as their primary concern, they will also be contributing to the professional development of others as well. For example, university professors need to maintain contact with teachers in the field to remain effective as they work in the professional preparation program. Many new ideas may be learned from these teachers which can then be passed along to the future physical educator who is pursuing an undergraduate professional preparation program.

TEACHING PHYSICAL EDUCATION AND COACHING

Stories are numerous of "throw out the ball" physical education teachers who then become dynamic coaches in the afternoon. They supposedly spend their day thinking about their coaching and planning strategy and practice schedules rather than teaching their classes. Knowing they have a strenuous practice to attend to in the afternoon, they loaf through their physical education classes. Without a doubt there are many of these teacher/coaches occupying positions in the schools. It is interesting to note that stories are never told of physical education teachers who so burn themselves out teaching physical education that they must loaf through their coaching assignment or that they spend their coaching time thinking about the next days physical education classes.

What is the reason for this occurrence? An informal poll within most physical education undergraduate programs would reveal that a substantial number of students were vitally interested in a coaching position and mildly interested in teaching physical education. Physical education is being used by these people as a vehicle to attain a coaching position. These individuals are pursuing an impossible dream in American schools. There are very few full time coaching positions in secondary schools. Many coaching positions are in combination with a teaching position and very often that teaching position is in physical education. This line of thinking can quickly be brought to closure by realizing that the individual who has a vital interest in coaching and little interest in teaching is soon going to be the person about whom the previously mentioned stories are told.

It is not necessary for this to occur. A rather simplistic, and yet accurate, assessment would reveal the person who cannot make a commitment to accept the responsibilities of both teaching and coaching should not accept the position. It is not ethical for teacher/coaches to sacrifice their physical education students so that they can receive their own fulfillment through coaching. The necessary commitment can and is made by many teachers. Earls (1981) reported that distinctive teachers (those vitally interested in their teaching, students, and self-improvement) have resisted the impact of coaching on teaching. In other words, they have retained their enthusiasm for teaching even though there were pressures and interests from their coaching responsibilities. In addition, all of us can probably remember at least one physical education teacher/coach who showed tremendous interest and energy in both the physical education class and on the athletic field.

Many teacher/coaches enter their professional careers with full intentions of being successful at both teaching and coaching. Within a short time some begin to lose their commitment to teaching and put all their energies into coaching. This may be due in part to a phenomenon spoken of as role conflict. *Role conflict* is concerned with problems that arise for the individual as a result of role incompatibilities (Grace, 1972). Teacher/coaches often view teaching and coaching as two distinct roles, and often they view coaching as their occupation (Massengale, 1981).

Locke and Massengale (1976) presented data which showed that "load conflicts" and "teacher/coach conflicts" cause widespread role conflicts for teacher/coaches. Load conflicts arise from incompatible expectations resulting from the combined work load of teaching and coaching. This difficulty in competently fulfilling the task expected in each role within specified time frames results in a conflict of priorities. When this occurs the teacher/coach retreats to the coaching role (Templin and Anthrop, 1981). Teacher/coach conflict relates to differences in role skills demanded in coaching and required in teaching. When inter-role conflict occurs the apparent adjustment is the selection of one role as the major role. Locke and Massengale (1978) comment; "Whenever there is an incompatibility in expected role behaviors, the choice simply goes to the major role, even at considerable cost to the successful fulfillment of the secondary role."

It seems rather obvious that most teacher/coaches who experience role conflict accept coaching as their major role. One answer to why this occurs may be seen by examining the expectations, conditions, and rewards of teaching physical education and coaching. Physical education teachers are asked to teach large numbers of students, whereas coaches normally deal with relatively small numbers of athletes. Teachers have students in the same class who range from very poor skilled to athletically gifted, whereas coaches work primarily with skilled athletes. Teachers have students who are present largely because of a requirement to be there, whereas coaches deal with athletes who are present of their own choice. Teachers work with classes that are only moderately motivated if at all, and coaches work with highly motivated athletes. This analysis of teaching and coaching conditions leaves little doubt as to which is the more pleasant situation in which to work.

There is also an imbalance often present of how the school administration and community view the role of teachers and coaches which probably contributes to the teacher/coaches' acceptance of a major role. Although the hiring practice of most schools promotes the idea that a person is being hired as a teacher first and a coach second, teacher/coaches soon perceive that this is not the true priority. They soon realize that teacher/coaches are seldom fired for teaching inadequacies, but their teaching expertise seldom substitutes for losing athletic contests (Massengale, 1981). Therefore, these teacher/coaches learn to place their coaching responsibilities as their number one priority. Add to this picture the fact that community interest is directed far more toward the outcomes of the athletic program than the teaching results and it can be understood why some teacher/coaches put their major time and energy into their coaching responsibilities.

To understand why some teacher/coaches do not give a good effort in teaching physical education is not the same as condoning it. Teachers know before they ever enter the teaching and coaching profession that employment as a coach in a secondary school will most often be in combination with a teaching position. It is at that time that the positive and negative factors should be carefully weighed in the mind of the individual. If, after weighing the consequences, a decision is made to pursue a career in teaching and coaching, a full commitment should be made. The commitment must be made to the complete job and not just to the coaching aspect.

Upon entrance into the profession the teacher/coach will face many difficulties. Although it may be difficult, the teacher/coach should stand behind their previous commitment and continue to meet the responsibilities of both teaching physical education and coaching.

SUMMARY

The undergraduate professional preparation program and student teaching are both important in the development of a teacher. However, it seems that the first year of teaching is also very influential upon the future behavior of teachers in the school setting.

The new teacher is usually enthusiastic about assuming a new career and is in possession of many new and exciting ideas. It is important for the new teacher to retain that enthusiasm. To do this he or she should align him or herself with an excellent teacher in the school from whom much can be learned. Also the teacher should become involved with a support group of other new teachers in the school, so they may help and encourage one another. The teacher should not attempt to bring about extensive changes in the routine of the school in the first year. Changes that are attempted should be relatively small and should be planned well to insure success.

It is wise for the new teacher to become acquainted and involved with the community. This will allow the teacher and parents to become more aware of one another and may prove to be good public relations for the school. The new teacher should also be active in professional endeavors such as attending conventions, clinics, and inservice workshops. In addition, the teacher may want to consider a formal graduate school program of studies within the first two or three years of teaching.

A phenomenon that has become critical to teachers in recent years is "burnout." Although teachers seldom face burnout early in their careers, they should take preventive measures. Procedures should be planned which help the teacher remain enthusiastic about teaching and which keep teaching exciting and rewarding.

Role conflict seems to be more prevalent among physical education teachers than other endeavors. The conflict occurs between teaching responsibilities and coaching duties. Those who accept jobs that involve both teaching and coaching should assume the responsibilities inherent in each aspect of the job. They must not allow their physical education teaching to suffer because of a greater commitment to coaching.

SELECTED READINGS AND REFERENCES

Austin, Dean, "The Teacher Burnout Issue," *JOPERD*, November/December, 1981, pp. 35-36.

Borg, W.R., "Moving Towards a Breakthrough in Teacher Education," *Education*, Vol. 95, 1975, pp. 302-323.

Crase, Darrell, "Socialization of Secondary School Teachers," *The Physical Educator*, March, 1979, pp. 9-13.

Earls, Neal, "How Teachers Avoid Burnout," *JOPERD*, November/December, 1981, pp. 41-43.

Farber, Barry and Julie Miller, "Teacher Burnout: A Psychoeducational Perspective," *The Education Digest*, September, 1982, pp. 23-25.

Grace, Gerald R., *Role Conflict and the Teacher*, Routledge & Kegan Paul, London, 1972.

Hoy, Wayne and Richard Rees, "The Bureaucratic Socialization of Student Teachers," *Journal of Teacher Education*, January/February, 1977, pp. 23-26.

Kohlmaier, Joe, "Organizing to Combat Burnout," *JOPERD*, November/December, 1981, pp. 39-40.

Locke, Lawrence and John D. Massengale, "Role Conflict in Teacher/Coaches," *Research Quarterly*, May, 1978, pp. 162-174.

Massengale, John D., "Researching Role Conflict," *JOPERD*, November/December, 1981, pp. 23 and 77.

Newbrough, Art, "Twelve Steps Towards Revitalization for Teachers," *Education*, Spring, 1983, pp. 270-273.

Penny, James. "Burnout," *The Science Teacher*, October, 1982, pp. 46-49.

Queen, J. Allen and John Gretes, "First-Year Teachers' Perceptions of Their Preservice Training," *Phi Delta Kappan*, November, 1982, pp. 215-216.

Templin, Thomas J. and Joseph L. Anthrop, "A Dialogue of Teacher/Coach Role Conflict," *The Physical Educator*, December, 1981, pp. 183-186.

Walter, Glenn, "A Veteran's Advice to Rookies," *Instructor*, August, 1982, p. 48.